Emotional Intelligence

FOR

DUMMIES®

Emotional Intelligence FOR DUMMIES®

by Steven J. Stein, PhD

Foreword by Peter Salovey, PhD

John Wiley & Sons Canada, Ltd.

Emotional Intelligence For Dummies®

Published by
John Wiley & Sons Canada, Ltd.
6045 Freemont Blvd.
Mississauga, ON L5R 4J3
www.wiley.com

For general information on John Wiley & Sons Canada, Ltd., including all books published by Wiley Publishing Inc., please call our distribution centre at 1-800-567-4797. For reseller information, including discounts and premium sales, please call our sales department at 416-646-7992. For press review copies, author interviews, or other publicity information, please contact our publicity department, Tel. 416-646-4582, Fax 416-236-4448.

Wiley also publishes its books in a variety of electronic formats. Some content that appears in print may not be available in electronic books.

Library and Archives Canada Cataloguing in Publication Data

Stein, Steven J., 1950–

      Emotional intelligence for dummies / Steven Stein.

Includes index.

ISBN 978-0-470-15732-9

      1. Emotional intelligence. I. Title.

BF576.S73 2009   152.4   C2009-902930-8

Printed in the United States

6 7 8 9 RRD 15 14 13

WILEY

About the Author

Steven J. Stein, PhD, is a clinical psychologist and CEO of Multi-Health Systems (MHS), a leading international test publishing company. He is a previous chair of the Psychology Foundation of Canada and has been president of the Ontario Psychological Association. Dr. Stein is a former assistant professor in the Department of Psychiatry at the University of Toronto and was an adjunct professor in the Department of Psychology at York University in Toronto.

Dr. Stein co-authored (with Dr. Howard Book) the international best-seller *The EQ Edge: Emotional Intelligence and Your Success* (Jossey-Bass) and is the author of *Make Your Workplace Great: The 7 Keys to an Emotionally Intelligent Organization* (Jossey-Bass).

A leading expert on psychological assessment and emotional intelligence, he has consulted to military and government agencies, including the Canadian Forces; U.S. Air Force, Army, and Navy; special units of the Pentagon; and the FBI Academy; as well as corporate organizations, including American Express, Air Canada, Canyon Ranch, Coca-Cola (Mexico), Canadian Imperial Bank of Canada (CIBC), and professional sports teams.

He has appeared on over 100 TV and radio shows throughout Canada and the United States. He has also been quoted in numerous newspapers, magazines, and blogs.

Dr. Stein has shared information on emotional intelligence with audiences throughout Canada, the United States, Mexico, Europe, Australia, and Asia. You can reach him for speaking engagements via e-mail at ceo@mhs.com.

Author's Acknowledgments

I must admit, I never thought I'd write a *For Dummies* book about emotional intelligence (EI). Although *Emotional Intelligence For Dummies* is my third book on the topic, it's my first that applies EI beyond the world of work to home, family, friends, and strangers.

When I got involved in this area of study almost 15 years ago, the most frequent question I was asked, especially by the media, was how long this fad would last. My answer was that as long as there was more than one person in the world, and she or he had to interact with someone else, emotional intelligence would be important.

I want to thank all the people at Wiley that encouraged me to write this book. First, my previous (and ongoing) editor at Wiley, Don Loney, for introducing me to the idea of a *For Dummies* book. Once I learned more about the nature of this series, I was convinced that this was a great way to spread the word about EI. Many thanks to my editor on this book, Robert Hickey, for patiently keeping me on track and gently educating me on how a *For Dummies* book needs to be written. And many thanks to my developmental editor, Colleen Totz Diamond, for all her suggestions and support, and making sure the words flowed. Thanks to my copy editor, Laura Miller, and project manager, Elizabeth McCurdy — and, of course, the publicity and marketing people who'll help make this book a success.

My appreciation also goes to all the wonderful and dedicated people at Multi-Health Systems. Because of their talents and the emotionally intelligent workplace created there, I have the time to embark on projects such as this book.

Of course, many thanks go to my wife Rodeen, for all her support and tolerating all the time I spent on this project, and to my children Alana and Lauren.

Publisher's Acknowledgments

We're proud of this book; please send us your comments through our online registration form located at *http://dummies.custhelp.com*. For other comments, please contact our Customer Care Department within the U.S. at 877-762-2974, outside the U.S. at 317-572-3993, or fax 317-572-4002.

Some of the people who helped bring this book to market include the following:

Acquisitions and Editorial

Editor: Robert Hickey

Developmental Editor: Colleen Totz Diamond

Project Manager: Elizabeth McCurdy

Project Editor: Lindsay Humphreys

Copy Editor: Laura Miller

Editorial Assistant: Katey Wolsley

Cartoons: Rich Tennant
(www.the5thwave.com)

Cover photo: Graham French/Masterfile

Composition Services

Vice-President Publishing Services:
Karen Bryan

Project Coordinator: Lynsey Stanford

Layout and Graphics: Heather Pope,
Christin Swinford, Julie Trippetti

Proofreaders: Laura Bowman, Caitie Copple

Indexer: Valerie Haynes Perry

John Wiley & Sons Canada, Ltd.

    Bill Zerter, Chief Operating Officer

    Jennifer Smith, Vice-President and Publisher, Professional & Trade Division

Publishing and Editorial for Consumer Dummies

    Diane Graves Steele, Vice President and Publisher, Consumer Dummies

    Kristin Ferguson-Wagstaffe, Product Development Director, Consumer Dummies

    Ensley Eikenburg, Associate Publisher, Travel

    Kelly Regan, Editorial Director, Travel

Composition Services

    Debbie Stailey, Director of Composition Services

Contents at a Glance

Table of Contents

Foreword

*W*hen you boil it down, *emotional intelligence* is the idea that emotions are useful; they are important sources of information. Emotions help us solve problems, and they guide our social interactions. And, importantly, some people harness the wisdom of emotions better than others.

So, who are these emotionally intelligent people? They are individuals you know, and you might be one yourself. If you are the kind of person who is skilled at reading emotions in another person's face or interpreting your feelings, if you are a person who can put your feelings into words, if you are a person who manages your emotions effectively and helps others to do the same, and if you are a person who uses your emotions to think clearly about something or as clues to what might be going on in social situations, well then, you are likely someone who is emotionally intelligent. And, if you are not so sure whether you are this kind of person, perhaps this book will help you to learn these skills.

In 1990, when John D. Mayer and I published the first scientific article describing a theory of emotional intelligence in the journal *Imagination, Cognition, and Personality*, we weren't sure anyone would find the idea that people differ in their abilities to identify emotions, understand these feelings, manage emotions, and use them to guide thinking and action all that interesting or persuasive. We were wrong. Today, in the spring of 2009, while writing this foreword, I typed the phrase **emotional intelligence** into the Google search engine, and it yielded more than three million hits. Interest in emotional intelligence has exploded, and we know a few things now that we didn't know two decades ago.

First, we know that you can measure emotional intelligence, and the author of this book, Steven Stein, is chief executive officer of the company that publishes assessment tools in this area of psychology, including a test we developed called the MSCEIT. Second, we know that high scores on the MSCEIT and other measures of emotional intelligence are related to psychological health, effectiveness at work, and fulfilling social relationships. And third, we know that people can learn how to improve these skills in many different ways. For example, our colleague Marc Brackett has developed and tested school curricula that help children learn emotional intelligence (and do better in school).

These conclusions make Dr. Stein's book especially timely. We know a lot more about emotional intelligence than we did 20 years ago, and he has synthesized this knowledge and presented it here for you in a very engaging and easily grasped way.

However, reading about emotional intelligence isn't enough. It won't make you more emotionally intelligent overnight. I strongly encourage you to engage in the exercises described by Dr. Stein in this book and look for other ways to hone your emotional skills — perhaps by reading great literature, becoming more committed to the arts, or simply spending more time observing other people and reflecting on your own abilities, motives, and behaviors. Once you become aware of the skills involved in being a more emotionally intelligent individual, "people watching" will never quite be the same.

There are no guarantees, of course, but I suspect _Emotional Intelligence For Dummies_ will motivate you to adopt a broader view of what it means to be smart, and you will find yourself further developing the emotional skills that allow you to lead a more satisfying life.

Peter Salovey, PhD
Chris Argyris Professor of Psychology
Yale University

Introduction

· ·

*E*motional intelligence — it sounds like an oxymoron, doesn't it? Just like jumbo shrimp. People tend to think of others as either emotional or intelligent, but not both. So, just what is emotional intelligence? And why are you hearing about it only now?

Emotional intelligence has a lot to do with being intelligent about your emotions. It involves the ability to recognize your own emotions as well as the emotions of other people. It includes understanding emotions. It also has to do with how you manage your emotions and how you manage other people's emotions.

Psychologists have known about many of the concepts behind emotional intelligence for years — decades, even. But the knowledge has been scattered, not really well organized or clearly formulated. When two psychologists — John (Jack) Mayer from the University of New Hampshire and Peter Salovey from Yale University — put together a theory that looks at both intelligence and emotions in 1989, the idea of emotional intelligence really started to take shape.

The first scientific paper on the topic was published in 1990. Since that time, millions of copies of books have been sold about it. A number of psychologists, including our own team at Multi-Health Systems (MHS), as well as groups at Yale University, Rutgers University, the Centre for Creative Leadership, and others, have carried out a great deal of research that looks at the impact of emotional intelligence at work, in families, with children, and basically anywhere that people interact with each other.

Organizations have used the information researchers have discovered about emotional intelligence to select and develop their employees and to produce better leaders; schools have used it to create more harmonious relationships among students; and it has been used with families to improve relationships. I hope an understanding of emotional intelligence can benefit you, too. It can help mean the difference between success and failure in many of the things you do.

About Emotional Intelligence For Dummies

What does it mean to be emotionally intelligent? Does it really matter? What can you do about your or your children's emotional intelligence? Or, for that matter, can you do anything to better manage the emotions of your relatives or friends? You can explore these questions, and many others, in *Emotional Intelligence For Dummies*.

The purpose of this book is to provide you with a clear understanding of what emotional intelligence is about. Emotional intelligence is still a new area of study, and you can already find a combination of folklore and science mixed together through the initial exuberance of the media on this topic. I cover some of the science that explains emotional intelligence, but I go carefully beyond the science by expanding on some of those scientific findings.

Here's some of the information that you can find in this book:

- ✔ The most common definitions of emotional intelligence
- ✔ Information about the most validated tests or measures of emotional intelligence
- ✔ Interesting ways to think about your own emotional intelligence, as well as the emotional intelligence of people around you
- ✔ Strategies to improve your and others' emotional intelligence
- ✔ The importance of emotional intelligence at home, at work or school, with friends, and when dealing with strangers

One of the differences between obtaining traditional knowledge and figuring out how to improve your emotional intelligence is the importance of active participation. Although you can find out about many subjects passively through lectures and reading, you need to be more active to get a grip on emotional intelligence. Reading this book can help you take the first step towards improving your EQ (Emotional Quotient). You also have to do some of the exercises and activities in this book to make a real difference in your ability to identify, understand, use, and manage your emotions.

Foolish Assumptions

I wrote this book making a few assumptions about you. I assume that you're a pretty well adjusted human being who wants to improve yourself and possibly some of the people around you. You've probably read books about or experienced self-development programs before. You may not have felt completely satisfied with some of these books, tapes, lectures, or Web sites.

You probably want to know what makes people tick. You may have come across people who surprised you with some of their behaviors. You may have wondered why some people who seem to be very smart in many ways have done some pretty foolish and self-defeating things; or you may want to know why some people are overly disrespectful of others. Getting the scoop on emotional intelligence may help you put together some pieces in this puzzle.

Conventions Used in This Book

I wrote this book (with the help of my editor, of course) in the *For Dummies* style, which makes the information that it contains easily accessible to almost anyone. I avoid using technical language or professional jargon as much as possible. When I do use technical terms, I define them for you.

I include a number of stories that can help make the discussions more real for you. Many of these stories are based on real incidents, or composites of situations and people I've known, but I've changed the names and circumstances to protect confidentiality.

If you really want to get the most out of this book, get a spiral bound notebook. Use that notebook to carry out the exercises and activities that I present throughout the book. Use your notebook often and reread what you've written from time to time to remind you of your progress and set forth your next set of goals.

What You Don't Have to Read

You don't have to read *Emotional Intelligence For Dummies* chapter by chapter, and you don't have to read all the sections in any particular chapter. However, I do recommend that you read Chapter 1, which gives you a basic idea about the meaning of emotional intelligence and how you can benefit from developing it. If your goal is to change someone else's behavior (not your own), then you should probably get that person to read the first chapter as well.

You can use the table of contents and the index to find the information that you need and to quickly get answers to your most pressing questions about emotional intelligence. Each part deals with a particular area in which you can apply emotional intelligence. So, if you're interested in work issues or parenting applications, for example, you can quickly skip to those areas.

How This Book Is Organized

Emotional Intelligence For Dummies is divided into five parts. Here's a description of what you can find in each part.

Part I: There's a New Kind of Intelligence in Town

Part I provides an introduction to the idea of emotional intelligence. It explores what emotional intelligence is (and what it isn't), and it begins to give you some insight into how an emotionally intelligent person operates. You can read about the benefits of developing your own emotional intelligence and that of those around you.

This part also looks at some of the ways emotional intelligence can apply to your life. I give you exercises and activities that can help improve your emotional intelligence. After you follow these activities, you may start to notice a difference in your relationships with other people.

Part II: The Essentials of Emotional Intelligence

In Part II, you can get to the essence of emotional intelligence and what it can mean for you.

I start with the science behind emotional intelligence. Although emotional intelligence is still a new area of study, the field has grown from one published scientific paper in 1990 to over 750 scientific papers in reviewed journals as of the time of this writing. Also, psychologists and graduate students have conducted hundreds of research presentations and have written articles for other research-oriented publications. The number of articles just keeps growing, which demonstrates that this is a legitimate area of study that's here to stay.

In this part, you can find out a bit about the parts of the brain that are involved in helping you manage your emotions. Then, I address some of the differences between emotional intelligence, personality, and cognitive intelligence.

You can read about the importance of emotional self-awareness — one of the key components of emotional intelligence. I include some exercises that can help you improve your self-awareness, and you can use what you figure out to better manage your emotions. These skills can help you be more in charge of how you feel.

Another essential component of emotional intelligence is empathy. You find out all about what empathy is, why it's important, and how you can improve it. Empathy is a skill that really differentiates the high performers when it comes to being emotionally intelligent. Finally, you can have more control over the emotions of other people with whom you deal. Your ability to influence others can help you better manage people you're close to, as well as complete strangers, even during times of stress.

Part III: Taking Emotional Intelligence to Work

You don't leave your emotional brain at home when you arrive at work. Emotions have a tremendous impact in the workplace. You may encounter difficult people and situations at work, and using your emotional intelligence can help you navigate through these experiences. I show you how to use your emotional intelligence when dealing with a bullying boss, obnoxious co-workers, and disrespectful subordinates.

I also explore the relationship between emotional intelligence and star performers at work. Understanding the importance of emotional intelligence and how you fit the job can help you figure out how you can go beyond personality and IQ in getting the right person in the right job. You can also find out how to deal more effectively with people at work.

This part deals with the relationship between emotional intelligence and leadership. Leaders — meaning anyone who has to get one or more people to follow her — need to be emotionally intelligent. You can learn how to develop the most important leadership skills related to emotional intelligence in this part.

I also talk about the emotionally intelligent workplace. How do you know whether you have one? How do you go about creating one? You can find answers to these questions and others in this part, as well.

Many parents have asked me about the importance of emotional intelligence in helping their kids get through college. A number of researchers and psychologists have done a great deal of research in this area, and you can read about some of it in this part.

Part IV: Using Emotional Intelligence at Home

How are your personal relationships? This part starts out by focusing on your closest or most intimate relationships, such as those with your spouse, intimate partner, or best friend. You confide in or bond with these people the most, out of all your relationships. Maintaining and nurturing these relationships often requires conscious effort. I provide you with steps and tools that you can use to build and enhance these relationships.

This part explains how you can be an emotionally intelligent parent, as well. How well do you manage your emotions when you deal with your children? This part shows you ways that you can improve your self-control, even when your child or teenager seems to get out of hand.

How do you raise an emotionally intelligent child? Everyone wants their children to succeed in life, and you know that, although IQ and ability are important, your child's emotional skills are every bit as important in his success. This part gives you some suggestions and examples that may be helpful when dealing with your children.

Part V: The Part of Tens

The Part of Tens is a feature of all *For Dummies* books. In *Emotional Intelligence For Dummies,* you can find quick lists that give you advice on how to improve your emotional intelligence, how to help difficult people you know with their emotional intelligence, and how to make the world a more emotionally intelligent place.

Icons Used in This Book

A unique and incredibly useful feature of all *For Dummies* books is the inclusion of helpful icons that point you in the direction of valuable information, tips, and tricks.

This icon points out helpful information that's likely to benefit your emotional intelligence.

The Remember icon marks a fact that's interesting and useful — something that you might want to remember for later use.

This icon highlights a danger, telling you to pay attention and proceed with caution.

The Activity icon indicates an exercise that you may want to carry out. Get a spiral bound notebook in which you can record your activities.

This icon indicates technical information, sometimes referred to as *psychobabble*. I try not to use too much of this language, but for purposes or accuracy, I sometimes need to. You can skip the sections marked with the Technical Stuff icon, although you may find them interesting.

Where to Go from Here

You can read this book in any way you choose. Although I recommend starting with the first part, each chapter stands on its own and can help you better understand, improve, and use your emotional intelligence. If you want to get started working on your own emotional intelligence, go right to Chapter 3. Then, move on to Chapters 5, 6, and 7. If you have concerns about someone in your life and you want to change her behavior, go to Chapter 8.

If you read this book through in its entirety and still want to go further in developing your emotional intelligence, you may want to contact a professional who's trained in this area. If you're looking for a professional trained in emotional intelligence assessment or coaching, contact us at eifordummies@ mhs.com.

Part I

There's a New Kind of Intelligence in Town

The 5th Wave   By Rich Tennant

"Well, that's just great! We're this close to landing 'Godzilla – The Mini-Series' and you lose your emotional distance over syndication rights!"

In this part . . .

In this part, I define emotional intelligence and give you some insight into how an emotionally intelligent person operates. You can see the benefits of developing emotional intelligence for both yourself and others around you.

I also show you some of the ways emotional intelligence can apply to your life. The activities that I provide can help you improve your relationships with other people.

Chapter 1

Feeling Smart

*W*hen most people think about what makes a smart person, they think of the school valedictorian — someone who's a whiz at math, flies through chemistry class, masters French and German, aces English literature, and tops the debating club. Being *book smart* means you can compute, retain, reformulate, and regurgitate all kinds of information.

Although being smart in these ways can help you get through school with flying colors, it may not be all it's cracked up to be. Smart people do get ahead in many ways, often finding academic success and opportunities for good jobs. You need to be book smart, for example, to get into most professional schools, such as medical, law, and engineering schools. But being book smart doesn't guarantee success and happiness in life.

Being emotionally intelligent, as described in this chapter and throughout this book, brings you much closer to achieving personal and even professional fulfillment.

Defining Emotional Intelligence

Psychologists have proposed several definitions of emotional intelligence (EI), but the original intent was to understand how some people who are so smart in some ways (have book smarts) can be so dumb in other ways (lack street smarts). A person can have book smarts, but not street smarts, because of a lack of emotional awareness and control, or *emotional intelligence*.

For example, you can probably think of a politician who was brilliant and ready to change the world. Then, out of nowhere (or so it seemed) came a sexual scandal or charges of taking bribes. The politician couldn't manage his or her sexual appetite or greed well enough (or long enough) to realize a successful political career.

In the opposite situation, say that a student in school has a great deal of difficulty mastering math, grammar, and literature. He finds getting a grade as high as a C a real challenge. But he has this huge network of friends, gets invited to every party, is the trendiest kid in class, keeps up with everything and everyone, and is known as a great kid by adults, as well. He makes all the right life decisions, in spite of academic challenges.

Not everyone struggles in this area, and the great news is that practice makes better — you always have the potential to improve. You can spot emotionally intelligent people pretty quickly. They're the people who

- Successfully manage difficult situations
- Express themselves clearly
- Gain respect from others
- Influence other people
- Entice other people to help them out
- Keep cool under pressure
- Recognize their emotional reactions to people or situations
- Know how to say the "right" thing to get the right result
- Manage themselves effectively when negotiating
- Manage other people effectively when negotiating
- Motivate themselves to get things done
- Know how to be positive, even during difficult situations

Although these behaviors don't fit within any formal definition of emotional intelligence, they represent typical behaviors for a person high in emotional intelligence. If the bar sounds high, don't fret — with practice, you can build on your existing skills to become more emotionally intelligent.

Getting a Handle on Your Emotions

More than most people think, folks judge you based on your actions, rather than on how much you know. We value the people who care about others more than those who can memorize the periodic table. The trick is being able to control your behavior, and you can't change how you behave if you're unaware of your emotions. For more information on how to become aware of your emotions, see Chapter 5.

Sometimes, the easiest way to explain emotional intelligence is to use an anecdote, which I do often in this book. Claudio, for example, is unaware of his emotions — and therefore is not in control of his behavior — when he ambles into his office, throws his papers on his desk, and slumps into his chair. The look on his face could read, "Beware of dog." His assistant, Jan, comes into his office, bringing him his usual cup of coffee.

"Here's your coffee, Claudio," she chirps.

Claudio just grunts and has a "get out of my hair" expression.

"Something wrong?" she asks.

"Not really. Could you please fix the Jackson file and get it ready?" he snorts.

Jan's shocked. He never treats her like that. She must have done something terribly wrong to be spoken to like that. She finds it hard to pay attention to her work for the rest of the morning. She can only think about what she must have done wrong.

Claudio is feeling in a bad mood. He can't quite put his finger on what's wrong, and that makes him angrier. He has already alienated several people at work and two people at the coffee shop. Something's eating away at him, and he can feel it in his stomach.

Claudio really uses the wrong way of dealing with bad feelings. By wallowing in them, you don't move ahead. In the 1950s and 1960s, many psychologists felt that you had to fully experience your bad or negative feelings in order to get over them. Most psychologists and psychiatrists now know that theory isn't true. The most prominent therapies today stress learning approaches — such as cognitive-behavior therapy as opposed to "catharsis" or releasing your anger.

Focusing on bad feelings tends to keep you in the same rut. Eventually, much of the pain of the bad feeling goes away, but in the long run, you can't move past the feeling without some understanding of why you're feeling the way you do.

For Claudio, his day starts out badly when his wife tells him, first thing in the morning, that their son failed an important exam at school. Not only is Claudio angry at his son for not passing, he's also angry at himself for not having been on top of his son's schoolwork. He was too busy at work to pay attention to what was going on. The bad news leads to an argument with his wife.

After trying to ignore his feelings, he leaves for work. Claudio has a close encounter with a red BMW that cuts him off when it enters the highway. He's enraged over the experience. Had it not been for the bad start to the morning, it probably wouldn't have bothered him so much.

By the time he gets to the office, everything's bothering him. The office waiting room's messy, nobody's available at the front reception desk, and he drops his keys on the way to his office. His mood is one big, angry blah.

Everyone in his path assumes that he's angry at them. Jan, for example, thinks of a number of things that she might have messed up and thus caused Claudio's anger. If Claudio was more emotionally intelligent, he'd have the following advantages:

- He'd know what each of his negative feelings was about:
  - Disappointment in his son
  - Anger for not paying enough attention to his son
  - Anger at arguing with his wife
  - Anger at the driver who cut him off
  - Anger at his office manager for not tidying up the reception area
  - Anger at his receptionist for not being at her desk
- By identifying these emotions, he could contain them and keep them proportional, taking the following actions:
  - Let Jan know that he was upset about something that had nothing to do with her (allowing her to focus on her work).
  - Manage each emotion separately and not roll them all together into one big, undirected, angry ball.
  - Use his first 20 to 30 minutes in the office more constructively by cooling off his emotions through various coping strategies (see Chapter 6).
  - Be more productive the rest of the day.
  - Resolve how he plans to deal with his son in a constructive way when he gets home (instead of just being angry at him).
  - Be better able, in general, to deal with small frustrations around the office.

Building your emotional muscle

Just like riding a bike, building your muscles in the gym, playing a musical instrument, or doing any other physical activity that requires synchronizing your brain and your body, you can hone your ability to manage your emotions and the emotions of others through practice.

Some people are naturals at emotional self-management and the management of other people's emotions. It's not too dissimilar from athletes, such as Tiger Woods, who are naturals in a certain sport. However, high levels of natural emotional-intelligence talent aren't widespread.

You may also identify limits to what you can accomplish through training. I know that as much as I practice my tennis, I'll never get to the level of Roger Federer or even Bobby Riggs (who you might remember lost to Billie Jean King). However, I'm good enough to stay on the court for the full two-hour doubles match with my friends, and we all improve the more often we play.

So, you can choose to go through life, day by day, without paying much attention to your emotions — or to anyone else's, for that matter. Being oblivious is an option, and many people seem to choose that route.

On the other hand, you can believe that improving your emotional intelligence is important stuff and make a commitment to improve your skills in this area. Ideally, then, take the time (something like three to four times a week, for a half hour or so) when you can devote your efforts to becoming more emotionally aware and in control. You're off to a great start just by reading this book. Complete the activities that appear throughout the book, and you'll be well on your way. Just remember, practice makes better.

People can improve their emotional intelligence, but not everyone can be a superstar in all areas. Some people take to the skills like a duck takes to the water, and for others, changing is a struggle. Two important factors for people who can effectively change are their motivation and their willingness to practice by using exercises such as the activities that appear throughout this book.

Understanding the Emotions of Others

Social intelligence reflects a person's ability to understand how other people feel and, to some extent, to manage the emotions and behavior of those people. If you live as a hermit, you probably don't care what other people feel and think. Perhaps even if you're a shepherd and spend most of your time with sheep, you don't find much use for emotional intelligence. (Although you might like to know how the sheep feel once in a while.)

Because most people in the world have to interact with others on a regular basis, social intelligence can help make those interactions more satisfying. By knowing how other people around you are feeling, you can

- ✔ Maintain good relationships
- ✔ Encourage a person to feel good about you
- ✔ Ask a favor from a person without alienating him
- ✔ Sell a person on an idea or a product
- ✔ Calm a person down
- ✔ Be a helpful person to others in need
- ✔ Have a network of friends and easily find others to do mutually satisfying activities with

Consider this story of two men, Danny and Wilfred, with contrasting levels of social intelligence. Danny's plane was delayed for over five hours. He takes a cab to his hotel in Boston, where he's attending a convention. Unfortunately, he didn't guarantee his room reservation, and the hotel's now completely full.

"What do you expect me to do?" he screams at the reservation clerk.

"I'm terribly sorry, sir, but I can call another hotel a few miles away and see if they have a vacancy," the young clerk replies.

"Absolutely not!" he shouts, attracting attention from across the lobby. "This is where I made my reservation, and this is where I'm staying."

Needless to say, Danny alienates the one person in his world who can make a difference for him at this point in time. The clerk, familiar with people like Danny, stands her ground. In his flurry of anger, Danny eventually has to find another hotel on his own.

Wilfred, who overhears the entire performance, is in the same situation. However, he tries a completely different tact.

"It must be really tough for you dealing with people like that all day," he calmly says to the clerk.

"Not really, and it doesn't happen all that often." She smiles.

"Well, I'm really sorry to bother you, but I was on the same plane that was delayed," Wilfred tells her. "Was there anything available? I'd even sleep in a closet somewhere if you could find one."

She laughs. "Well, let me see what I can do."

After about five minutes of computer clicking, she looks up and reports, "If you're willing to wait a few hours, I can get you a room. It's actually on the concierge floor and comes with breakfast and hors d'oeuvres. I can give it to you at the same price. You can check your luggage and wait in the bar, if you'd like."

"Wow, that sounds great. Thanks," he replies, very grateful.

When dealing with others, you often don't have to give very much in order to get the result you need. Paying attention to others and managing your own emotions can have tremendous payoffs.

Emotional intelligence isn't just about being nice to people. You also have to recognize another person's perspective and use your emotions appropriately. So, in some cases, emotional intelligence means that you must be tough with the other person, or show him or her that you're frustrated. Emotional intelligence is more about being able to read the other person and using your emotions *appropriately,* as described in the following sections.

Influencing a person's emotions

After you figure out how to read how someone's feeling, you're in a better position to influence the way he feels. You may want to influence someone's emotions to convince him about the virtue of an idea, concept, plan, or product. Sometimes, of course, you may convince someone for his own good. You may want to change the behavior of someone you love for his own benefit.

At other times, you might want to put a depressed or angry person in a better frame of mind so that you can deal with her more effectively. Or you may want to engage in some cooperative activity with that person.

You may also want to figure out how to read other people's feelings so that you can understand the other person. Being able to understand others comes with personal benefits. Think of it as a form of giving. For example, just by understanding the type of bad mood I'm in is enough for you to empathize with me and know I prefer to be left alone, that I don't appreciate being questioned, that I might enjoy a cup of hot tea, and so on. You may be helping someone simply by understanding him.

You need to be allied with someone you're trying to influence. If you both have the same goal, you can more easily work together to reach that goal. So, if you do anything to antagonize or aggravate someone, she becomes less likely to listen to you. If, on the other hand, you can show that you both have the same goal or endgame in mind, then she has at least one reason to go along with you. After all, you both have the same interest at heart.

Following the Golden Rule

Being nice to strangers can do more than score you points. At Oxford University, a math professor named Martin Nowak looked at this issue scientifically. He and his colleagues found that doing a good turn for a stranger today increases the chances that someone will do a good turn for you in the future.

The example they gave goes like this: If a man goes to a bar and buys a stranger a beer, it's generally expected that he gets a beer back in exchange, referred to as *reciprocity*. However, if a man goes to a bar and buys a round of beer for the house, with no expectation of being reciprocated, this random act of kindness is likely to be rewarded in the future. The theory holds that word will get around about the man's goodwill, so others will eventually treat him well.

The researchers mapped out various scenarios in computer models. Their model basically confirmed their theory, that being nice (even randomly with strangers) can pay off with future rewards.

How do you know when to be nice and when to be tough? You can't easily generalize, but being nice usually pays more dividends. Like your grandmother may have said, "You attract more bees with honey than with vinegar." Here are some situations in which you can be more effective by being tough:

- ✔ When someone is trying to take advantage of you, such as during a negotiation
- ✔ When you need to take a strong position on an issue so that you can convince people of your sincerity
- ✔ To stop an acquaintance from making inappropriate jokes by letting him know how serious you are about the issue

Be tough in moderation — don't overuse it.

Applying Emotional Intelligence at Work

One of the places that you can work on your emotional skills is in the workplace. Many years ago, before the concept of emotional intelligence was widely known, a senior executive at a large company told me that emotions have no place at work. You simply left half your brain at home and brought the other half with you to the office. Fortunately, most people's attitudes have changed since then.

The workplace, unfortunately, is a stressful place for many people worldwide, according to interviews that I've done and surveys that my organization (Multi-Health Systems) has carried out. We've helped pioneer the research that brought emotional intelligence to the workplace, and we found out much about how emotional intelligence can increase productivity, improve teamwork, and make you feel better about your work and your workplace along the way. You can improve your emotional intelligence skills by using some of the activities in this book at work.

The benefits of emotional intelligence at work

Based on a number of studies that Multi-Health Systems and others have carried out, increasing your emotional intelligence at work has many benefits, including the ability to:

- ✔ Better manage stress at work.
- ✔ Improve your relationships with co-workers.
- ✔ Deal more effectively with your supervisor.
- ✔ Be more productive.
- ✔ Be a better manager or/and leader.
- ✔ Better manage your work priorities.
- ✔ Be a better team player.

Because people who have high emotional intelligence are more in tune with the people and situations in the workplace, they generally get comparatively greater pay raises, according to a recent study by Stephan Cote and his colleagues at the Rotman Business School, University of Toronto.

The advantages of an emotionally intelligent workplace

After seeing many individuals in business settings improve in emotional intelligence, I was surprised to see that the organizations themselves didn't necessarily change for the better. That's when I came up with the concept of the emotionally intelligent organization. An *emotionally intelligent organization* is an organization that can successfully and efficiently cope with change and accomplish its goals, while being responsible and sensitive to its people, customers, suppliers, networks, and society.

If you look closely at some of today's most successful companies, you can find many have been selected as Best Companies to Work For in competitions. One example of a company that uses emotional intelligence organizationally is Google. They start out by hiring the best people, not just technically, but with many of the emotional intelligence skills I refer to throughout this book, such as independence, assertiveness, and interpersonal relationship skills. Google realizes that emotionally intelligent people can manage themselves and require less training and supervision to get the job done.

Emotionally intelligent people also encourage their managers to take risks. Google doesn't frown upon taking a risk on something, even if it doesn't work out. Of course, the company expects people to be motivated and well-meaning, and giving employees responsibility for and control over their work pays off big time in generating an engaged workforce. Google's profits are nothing to sneeze at, either.

To achieve emotional intelligence in the workplace, you must consider three factors (see Chapter 12 for more details):

✔ **The people:** When dealing with staff, employers must ensure they're

- **Hiring the right people:** Too often, organizations hire people for their technical skills alone. People who have emotional intelligence tend to be low maintenance, productive, and engaged.

- **Putting the right people in the right jobs:** Companies that match specific EI skills to the job get better performance.

- **Encouraging supportive co-workers or teams:** People with high EI have good interpersonal skills and are more supportive of teammates.

- **Fostering an environment where co-workers can socialize and develop friendships:** Research has shown that having a best friend at work makes you significantly more productive. You also have someone to sound off to when work problems arise.

- **Training managers and supervisors:** People often receive promotions to management positions because of their technical or sales skills. Being a good manager means knowing how to be a good coach to others.

- **Providing great leadership:** Good leadership skills are directly related to emotional intelligence skills, such as empathy, assertiveness, self-regard, and independence.

✔ **The work:** Critical to an emotionally satisfying job are

- **Having challenging work:** People who feel challenged at work, such as through setting and attaining specific goals, feel more motivated and engaged.

- **Not being overloaded or underworked:** Too much work leads to burnout, but too little work leads to boredom. Both emotions can make an employee underproductive.

- **Having the right tools to do the job:** Properly equipping people to do their jobs makes them feel better about their work and the organization.

- **Being fairly compensated:** It's not how much you pay someone that's important, it's whether they perceive their pay as fair. People are motivated by being paid fairly for their work.

- **Reducing low-value work:** Low-value or irrelevant work saps the drive from people who love the work their supposed to be doing.

- **Being satisfied with the work:** People who love their work do a better job.

✔ **The purpose:** Emotionally satisfied employees perceive a reason for their work, such as

- **Seeing how the work benefits the community, society, country, or world:** This view further engages people in their jobs and helps organizational leaders win the hearts and minds of their staff.

- **Knowing what the company stands for:** By being aligned with the organization's mission and values, employees have a better fit emotionally with their work.

Emotionally intelligent workplaces are productive, socially responsible, and profitable, and they attract the best talent. However, an emotionally intelligent workplace requires leaders who are committed to developing this environment.

Pursuing Successful Family Interactions

You may want to have a loving and meaningful relationship with your family. Developing emotional skills, such as empathy and emotional self-management, which are covered throughout this book, can help you develop these deeper relationships.

Every interaction gives you an opportunity to improve your emotional skills at home. When was the last time you could have been more considerate to your spouse? When could you have spent more time with one of your children?

Think of each interaction as a potential investment in the strength of your relationship. You can make deposits or debits. With each deposit (each positive interaction), you're building the bonds of trust and love in the relationship. With each debit (each negative interaction), you're weakening those bonds.

Each day, you have many interactions with your family members. By being more aware of how these interactions affect your long-term relationship, you can start to build better bonds within your family or improve the closeness of your family bonds.

Follow these basic steps, which demonstrate your ability to accept your family members, to show how important they are to you, and to care about their well-being, to strengthen the bonds that tie your family together:

1. **Become more aware of your own emotions during interactions that you have with family members.**

   What puts you in a bad mood or ticks you off? When do you get into a good mood and feel those warm fuzzies? You need to understand your reactions to situations and interactions at home to start to be able to manage them appropriately.

2. **Manage, or control, your reactions to situations and family members.**

   Be patient with your child. Don't get angry with your spouse. Getting a handle on your emotional responses can pay big dividends at home: your family's confidence, trust, and love.

3. **Listen and empathize with your family members.**

   Putting yourself in someone else's shoes allows you to think twice before thoughtlessly reacting to others. Why did your child make that request? What makes your spouse nag about that situation? Seeing the other person's side can enable you to get a grip on your emotions, think about where the other person is coming from, and then respond constructively — lowering the temperature of a heated issue.

Chapter 2

Assessing Your Emotional Intelligence

*F*or some people, the concept of emotional intelligence makes perfect sense. For others, it seems like an oxymoron — in the same vein as open secret, military intelligence, larger half, minor crisis, deafening silence — you get the idea. After all, how could someone be both emotional and intelligent? Aren't emotional people, well, too emotional? And intelligent people — aren't they logical and unemotional?

This chapter turns all those assumptions upside down. I show you how to measure emotional intelligence, what being emotionally intelligent feels like, and how to relate to an emotionally unintelligent person.

Measuring Emotional Intelligence

This basic question created the current field of emotional intelligence: "How can someone so smart do something so stupid?"

Consider Julius, who's smart as a whip. He always has the right answer in class, hands in the best papers, and stumps the teacher with his questions. No one's surprised that he's the school valedictorian. Everyone knows that he's the most likely to succeed.

Julius goes to Yale law school, graduates in the top third of his class, and is hired by a top-tiered law firm in New York. Julius is on a fast track.

But Julius doesn't have the perfect life. He winds up twice divorced and has two children who don't speak to him, and he very possibly may be disbarred for fraudulently using clients' money.

Scientists now understand that being very smart in one or two areas doesn't mean you're smart in all areas. You can be exceptionally intelligent academically but have low emotional intelligence.

Psychologists use several tests to measure emotional intelligence. The tests generally fall into three categories:

- ✔ **Self-report tests** compare your responses to a database of thousands of others and cover areas that include how you see yourself dealing with difficult situations, how you tend to interact with others, and how you might describe your mood at times. The most commonly used self-report test is the EQ-i, which is covered in Chapter 4.

  Beware of self-report tests of emotional intelligence you find on the Web. They probably don't meet the standards set by the American Psychological Association (APA) — in the same way that measuring your weight on a broken scale is likely to give you misleading results. The APA standards ensure the test is properly normed and validated.

- ✔ **360-degree assessments** include the perceptions of others. People who know you from different perspectives — your boss, your spouse, your subordinates — all report on how they see you behave in the same domains that you rate yourself. So, you may think that you're very assertive or socially interactive, but these people may see you differently. The most commonly used 360-degree assessment test is the EQ-360, which I cover in Chapter 4.

- ✔ **Performance assessments** are structured much like an IQ test. These tests measure emotional intelligence as an ability. People taking these assessments might be asked to recognize emotions in pictures of people, select responses to difficult life situations, or demonstrate an understanding of basic principles about emotions. The professional using the test compares a subject's scores on these items to the thousands of others who have completed them. The most commonly used performance assessment test is the MSCEIT. (See Chapter 4.)

All these tests relate to how you're likely to behave in the real world. They can predict how well you deal with stressful situations, who's more likely to be a good manager or leader, who can best influence others, and a number of other behaviors. Also, these tests help determine your strengths and weaknesses so that you can begin the journey to improvement.

Combining these three types of tests yields accurate results about how you see yourself, how others see you, and how you perform on emotional intelligence–related tasks. This information can help you begin your journey toward increasing your emotional intelligence.

EQ testing, when performed with reliable testing methods, can provide you with very useful information about yourself. I've found, having tested thousands of people, that many are a bit surprised by their results. For example, one person who believed she was very socially responsible and often concerned about others came out with an average score in that area. She was quite disappointed in her score. It turned out that she had very high standards for social responsibility and therefore was extremely hard on herself when she performed her assessment. In reality, she was more socially responsible than most people, but she believed that she could be much better than she was.

Here are some things to think about when looking at your own level of emotional intelligence. In your emotional intelligence notebook, record the responses to these items:

- ✔ I'm usually aware of how I'm feeling emotionally.
- ✔ I find it easy to express my feelings and beliefs to others.
- ✔ I really know what I'm good at and where I lack skills.
- ✔ I know exactly where I'm going in life.
- ✔ I depend on others when making important decisions.
- ✔ People feel I really listen to them.
- ✔ I have many friends and acquaintances.
- ✔ I spend a lot of time doing things to help others.
- ✔ I'm good at solving people's problems.
- ✔ I find it easy to change tasks.
- ✔ I live in the real world and tend not to daydream.
- ✔ I get through stressful situations without a lot of anxiety.
- ✔ I'm thoughtful, and I carefully plan my reaction to things.
- ✔ I tend to look at the bright side of things.
- ✔ I'm usually happy.

While you read through this book, you may note a number of examples of people who use higher or lower levels of emotional-intelligence skills. Think about how you might react in these same situations to help you gauge your EI. By taking an honest look at your own emotional skills, you put yourself in a better position to understand your situation and move forward in areas that can help you be more at ease with yourself and with others.

Feeling, Thinking, and Behaving Like an Emotionally Intelligent Person

Emotionally intelligent people have a certain way of thinking, feeling, and behaving. They're naturally confident. They bring out the best in others. When you're with someone who's highly emotionally intelligent, you feel like he or she is completely interested in you. He or she isn't distracted when talking with you; you get his or her full attention.

In times of crisis or difficulty, emotionally intelligent people make you feel more at ease. They don't panic, and they're focused on solutions. They offer a healthy perspective that helps you realize that things may be okay in the end.

In your next encounter with someone, pay more attention to the interaction. Do you focus on the other person, or do you get distracted? Give that person your undivided attention. Keep the focus of the conversation on the other person's issues. Ask questions that get at trying to understand where the other person is coming from and what he or she is feeling.

Feeling like an emotionally intelligent person

Emotionally intelligent people are in touch with their feelings and in tune with the world around them. If you're an emotionally intelligent person, you

- Know your mood most of the time.
- Possess a good understanding of why you feel the way you do.
- Know how others around you are feeling.
- Manage your feelings, especially by turning intense, or *hot,* negative emotions into less intense, or *warm,* emotions.
- Manage the emotions of people around you, making those people feel more at ease.

Emotionally intelligent people enjoy a full range of feelings. They're not robotic or unnatural in their experience of feelings. Their feelings are real and can be intense — especially positive, happy feelings. When they have intense negative feelings, they manage not to get overwhelmed. They get over negative feelings far more quickly than most people. Emotionally intelligent people tend to use all their senses — taste, touch, smell, vision, and hearing — to fully experience feelings.

Here's an exercise that can help you focus on the different senses while giving you a calm and relaxing feeling: Imagine yourself on a fluffy white cloud. You're lying on your back enjoying the view of other fluffy clouds above you. You're very comfortable. You feel the softness of the cloud around you. You smell the freshness of the gentle breeze that flows over your skin. You hear the quiet whispering sound of the wind while it passes. You taste the sweetness of the air. Your body is fully relaxed while you quietly watch the shapes of the passing clouds.

When you are focused, your attention is fully placed on what's important at the moment. Whether you're focused on a situation or on a person, you're at one in your focus.

Thinking like an emotionally intelligent person

In social situations, an emotionally intelligent person's thoughts are centered and focused on the other person. When an emotionally intelligent person talks to a friend about that friend's sick mother, he's thinking about his friend, what she's saying, how she feels about it, and how that might impact her life. An emotionally intelligent person doesn't think about how he would feel under the circumstances; he considers what he can do to help. An emotionally intelligent person thinks about what he might say to his friend to let her know that he understands and will support her in this time of difficulty.

Emotionally intelligent people look after themselves, but they're often thinking of the needs of others. They're very aware of their environment and the people around them. They're good at realistically looking at the big picture, picking out what's important, and responding appropriately.

In the preceding example, you might easily get caught up in the details about your friend's mother, the hospital, her treatment, your own feelings about hospitals and disease, and so on. However, by quickly evaluating the whole situation and identifying what's important here and now, you can see that focusing on and caring about your friend's current situation is the right choice.

An emotionally intelligent person generally approaches people with a WIIFY (what's in it for you?) attitude, rather than a WIIFM (what's in it for me?) perspective. When you think of others, you stay balanced and avoid becoming self-centered.

Emotionally intelligent people often ask questions such as, "How can I make this a better workplace? Community? Family? Situation? World? Country?"

Emotionally intelligent people are able to think logically about emotion. When they experience an unpleasant emotion after an event, they can ask productive questions about what caused the emotion.

For example, when Naomi hears that her boyfriend, Jim, was at a bar Friday evening with another woman, she feels an instant pit in her stomach. It's as though someone punched her.

Then, a feeling of extreme sadness takes over. This emotional change happens so quickly that she doesn't even have time to consciously grasp the situation. She wasn't overly confident about her relationship with Jim, so the news strikes her instantly with feelings of sadness.

After a short while, she starts asking herself some questions:

- How do I know who this person is?
- Could it have been a business meeting?
- What if it was a relative?
- Could he have female friends?
- Has he given any signals that our relationship is shaky?
- So what if he decides to see someone else?
- Would I like to be free to date other people again?
- Would it be the end of the world if we broke up?
- Can't I find a new relationship if I have to?

By asking herself these questions, Naomi moves away from her depressed feelings and experiences feelings of concern, instead. The next time she sees Jim, she brings up the subject in a nonthreatening way. Instead of being angry or accusatory, she's calm and inquisitive.

She's relieved to find out that Jim has a female first cousin he's close to and keeps in touch with. Part of his discussion with his cousin was about Naomi and him getting together with her and her boyfriend the following Saturday night.

What if Naomi had assumed the worst and greeted Jim with a fight? She may have damaged her relationship with Jim and caused her own self-esteem to suffer.

Behaving like an emotionally intelligent person

Nicole has a work deadline and a child to pick up from school, and her mother wants to see her this evening. Then, she has to come up with dinner for her family. She's much calmer than most people would be under those circumstances. Nicole manages her time, and her life, well.

Part of that management involves planning. Nicole has already broken her work requirements into the parts that she needs to complete and the pieces that she can delegate. She has a back-up plan in place in which another mother can pick up her child and have the children play together until dinner. Nicole calls her mother and has a very reassuring conversation with her, letting her mother know that she'll manage to see her later. Finally, she calls her husband and arranges for him to manage dinner.

Staying cool, calm, and collected while completing many tasks isn't the only way to demonstrate emotional intelligence. You also show emotional intelligence in how you carry out the tasks at hand while under pressure. Nicole broke her tasks into manageable parts, which helped her keep her cool.

When most people are frazzled, you generally want to stay away from them. But Nicole is so adept at working with people that they welcome being around her. Nicole's work team, instead of feeling stressed about the deadline, enjoys the challenge of the tasks. Nicole makes them feel good about having the opportunity to participate in such exciting tasks. She can make her mother feel relieved and comforted after less than ten minutes on the phone. She knows just how to get her husband enthused about having his favorite dinner — and using his time to prepare it.

Emotionally intelligent people manage themselves, and the people around them, well.

You probably can't tell how emotionally intelligent a person is just by the way he or she looks — unless you really know what to look for. You might recognize his or her level of emotional intelligence by watching him or her deal with a stressful situation — in traffic, at the supermarket, or anywhere else you see people lose their cool. Although you shouldn't judge people by their looks, you can figure out a lot about them by watching how they behave — especially under stress.

Recognizing an Emotionally Unintelligent Person

People who are low in emotional intelligence tend to have low emotional self-awareness. As a result, they often don't even realize that they're out of sync with the people around them. Emotionally unintelligent people have no idea how they come across to others or why they run into various difficulties in living.

Because of their behavior, people with low emotional intelligence tend to lose out on things. Their behavior is often self-defeating. Because of poor impulse control, inadequate social skills, and low empathy, these people are often their own worst enemy.

People who have low emotional intelligence are generally not very happy, aren't in touch with their life goals, and have poor problem-solving skills. These deficits have real-life implications. They may have difficulty maintaining relationships with people, holding down jobs, being promoted at work, having satisfying intimate relationships, or dealing with stressful situations.

The important point to understand is that intellectually smart people can be emotionally unintelligent.

You can't always easily recognize that a person is low in emotional intelligence. Some people may seem to have EI skills, but in fact, they can simply cover up their deficits — at least, superficially. People can easily lie about EI. A person can tell everyone that he's self-aware and in tune with others. But saying it doesn't make it true.

In general, emotionally unintelligent people

- ✔ Get angry or anxious without realizing why or what they're feeling
- ✔ Don't know how they impact others
- ✔ Fail to understand how others feel in various situations
- ✔ Don't effectively manage other people's feelings or behaviors
- ✔ Behave in a self-centered manner
- ✔ Lose control of their emotions, especially when under stress
- ✔ Don't know the connection between emotions, thoughts, and behavior
- ✔ Bring out the worst in others
- ✔ Don't easily meet new people or maintain relationships

- ✔ Overestimate their own skills or abilities

- ✔ Keep getting into trouble because of poor problem-solving skills

- ✔ Become overly passive or aggressive in communicating with others

- ✔ Wind up aimless or directionless in life

- ✔ Look at the dark side of things much of the time

- ✔ Don't feel happy in life

- ✔ Don't adapt well to change

- ✔ Find that people avoid them

If a person appears to be emotionally unintelligent, don't assume that he or she is hopeless. With the right kind of coaching or training, almost anyone can gain some benefit in areas of emotional intelligence.

Ralph really believes he's a good person. He tries hard to say and do the right things for his wife, Jenni, and their kids. But, somehow, he often manages to say the wrong thing at the wrong time. When his wife asks how her new dress looks, he replies, "Honey, I think you look fatter in that dress than in the red one."

In fact, Ralph's kids stop bringing home friends because he embarrasses them so much. He makes fun of their hair and their clothes, thinking he's just being funny.

Ralph can't read the emotions of others. He has no idea how his wife feels about being called fat in her new dress. He can't clue into the world of his kids and their friends.

One day, Jenni sits down with Ralph and has a heart-to-heart talk. She begins by explaining how they both really wanted the same things — a good relationship, happy family, and good kids. She gets Ralph to agree on their family goals. Then, she gently explains how his behavior sometimes makes it difficult for the kids to have normal relationships with others.

She drives the point home by getting Ralph to remember some of the more unpleasant experiences he had as a child, in which he was teased and bullied by others.

"Is this the experience you want for your children?" she asks.

The thought sends a shiver through Ralph's spine. Jenni and Ralph work out a system in which she calmly signals him if he gets out of line when others are around. He figures out how to retreat from his obnoxious comments and pay more attention to others.

In Chapter 8, I deal more with managing the people around you.

Chapter 3

Finding Happiness

In This Chapter

▶ Knowing happiness through emotional intelligence

▶ Experiencing authentic happiness

Most people think of happiness as pure hedonism or instant gratification. The feeling of pleasure you get after eating chocolate, soaking in a warm bath, winning a prize, or having a great glass of wine is short-term happiness. What you really want to strive for in life is long-term pleasure and satisfaction that comes with true happiness.

True happiness involves taking an honest view of yourself and the world around you. It leads to discovering what's really meaningful in your life and capitalizing on those virtues. True happiness is values-based yet influenced by your emotions. People who have high emotional intelligence are optimistic, in tune with their passions, and emotionally self-aware, making them happier than people who struggle in these areas.

This chapter helps you see the connection between emotional intelligence and happiness, and offers some tools to help you increase your awareness of what can give you real happiness and how to achieve it.

Defining Happiness

We all know people who see the world through rose-colored glasses. No matter what's going on around them, they see the silver lining. Everything is great. But are they truly happy? *Merriam-Webster's Online Dictionary* defines happiness as "a state of well-being and contentment" and "a pleasurable or satisfying experience." This definition is pretty open to whether happiness comes from the inside (your experience of the world) or the outside (the outside event itself).

I believe that you create real happiness from within. You might get some short-term happiness from a box of chocolates, but you probably have longer-lasting, more meaningful happiness from working on a project that you're excited about or building a relationship with someone you love.

Universal agreement exists, even in non-Westernized societies, that happiness and life satisfaction are important; people everywhere think about happiness often. Studies by happiness-expert psychologist Ed Diener, of the University of Illinois, and his colleagues, who surveyed people around the world, show that only 6 percent of people rate money as more important than happiness. In fact, 69 percent of the people in a worldwide survey rate happiness as the most important thing in their lives.

The following sections describe some benefits of being happy and some ways that you can use emotional intelligence to change your emotions.

Seeing life as an adventure

Life is an adventure. Sometimes, you need to experience something new and exciting to appreciate life. Many people who experience and work their way through difficult situations, such as poverty, figure out how to really appreciate what life has to offer. People who are born with silver spoons often take life's trappings for granted.

The first time I traveled to Europe, I presented a scientific paper at a conference in England. It was a pretty unique and exciting experience. I was appreciative that I was there, but I was really struck by the reaction of a colleague I met there.

He was so excited to be in Europe. It was also his first trip abroad. He was a young professor at a small college in the United States. He came from a working-class family and was the first one in his entire extended family to have attended university (let alone become a PhD college professor). Traveling to Europe, funded by his college, was the thrill of his lifetime.

His ancestors had come from Wales, and he asked me to join him in finding the castle that carried his family name. Every day was an adventure, and even the smallest experience provided a new discovery. I really enjoyed being with him, in part because he was so grateful that he had a job that would sponsor him on such a great experience.

We eventually found the castle that bore his name. It was in a pretty sorry state — mostly a ruin. And to add insult to injury, even after showing the ticket lady his passport and driver's license with his now-famous last name, we still had to pay full admission to get in. But my friend wasn't deterred. He was incredibly happy just being there and soaking up the experience.

If it wasn't for my new friend, I probably would have taken this trip for granted. Although my trip was also sponsored by my workplace, I selfishly felt it was just part of my job. By reframing the experience through his eyes, I figured out how to really appreciate this trip. Even though we had dumpy accommodations, the weather was rainy, and we got lost searching for the castle, every minute of the trip was a real high.

I've done a tremendous amount of travelling to various parts of the world since that time. I sometimes end up staying in five-star luxury hotels. Far too often in these places, people complain about the silliest little things. They may have a lot of money and travel in style, but they don't seem to be very happy people. Happiness has more to do with how you view and manage situations around you and less to do with material possessions.

Understanding the benefits of being happy

People who feel good see life as an interesting challenge, even when they encounter bumps along the road. Because they feel good, they attract people to them, enlarging their circle of friends. Having more friends gives them more resources when they are in need. When you're in a good mood, you're better positioned to take on challenges. Happy people are more confident, optimistic, likeable, and energetic, and they feel better about themselves.

People who feel good for a great deal of the day tend to feel good about their work and home, and they're happier overall about life. In fact, research shows that people who are happier in life are more successful in certain aspects of living. For example, happier people are more successful in marriage, friendships, income, work performance, and health.

Many people ask which came first, the happiness or the success. We know definitively that happiness *precedes* these success experiences. The ability to put yourself in a good mood leads to better enjoyment of work, marriage, home, and health. When you're happy, you simply have a better overall attitude about life. Practicing emotional intelligence provides the skills you need to be able to put yourself in a good mood, even when life isn't going your way.

Exercise and the road to happiness

You can do a number of things to make your mood more positive and therefore increase your happiness. People often influence their mood through some form of exercise.

Many studies have examined how exercise affects your mood. In one interesting study that included sets of twins, J. H. Stubbe and his colleagues in the Netherlands followed 8,000 people between the ages of 18 and 65, looking at the relationship between leisure-time exercise

participation and happiness. They found that people who took part in exercise reported higher levels of life satisfaction and happiness.

Setting up an exercise routine doesn't have to be complicated. You can go to the gym or exercise at home. You can walk around the neighborhood or use an elliptical trainer in the basement. Exercising at least three times per week can help you, not only physically, but also emotionally, giving you more energy and helping lift your mood.

Changing your emotions

You can improve your happiness by taking steps to change your emotions. Now, you don't want to change all your emotions. You simply want to decrease your negative emotions and maintain or augment your positive emotions.

One way to sustain positive emotions is to become more aware of what types of thoughts are associated with those emotions. Looking at your positive emotions as a consequence or outcome, try to figure out which thoughts give rise to these feelings. So, for example, if you feel good each time you think about a problem you're trying to solve or the dinner you're planning to cook, you can increase the amount of time you have these kinds of thoughts during the day.

You more likely want to change the negative emotions. Use the starting point, the consequence, as your opportunity to identify which of a wide range of emotions you're experiencing.

After you identify the emotion that you want less of, you can change the thoughts that lead up to that emotion. Psychologists call this type of emotional change *cognitive reappraisal,* which means you're developing a new way of looking at your world.

Chapter 5 covers the ABCDE method, which you may find to be a useful tool in helping you identify the causes of your emotions.

Giving anger the boot

Imagine that you're waiting for an elevator. It's been a long, hot day. The elevator finally arrives at your floor, the door slowly opens, and the elevator is quite crowded, although you see enough space to get in. You step into the elevator, bumping a few people, and you turn around to face the elevator doors.

You feel hot and sweaty while the doors slowly close. Suddenly, you feel a sharp jab in your back. You don't say anything at first because you excuse it as an accident. While the elevator slowly descends, you feel another sharp jab in your back. You now start getting upset, but you don't want to create a scene in the elevator.

While you get hotter and sweat more, you just want to be off this elevator. You start feeling angrier about this situation, and all of a sudden, you get one more jab in the back from that person. Now, you're ready to blow a fuse. You get ready to turn around and blast whoever that person is. The elevator stops, the doors open, and when you turn to give that person a piece of your mind, you realize he's blind and holding a cane.

Your anger suddenly transforms to guilt. It takes less than two seconds for the anger to completely disappear and the new emotion, guilt, to replace it.

What happened to the anger? Like magic, it disappeared. You have the ability to change your emotions — and to change them quickly. Sometimes, it takes a jolt from the outside, but you can do it from within, as well. By reevaluating situations, you can make significant emotional changes.

Addressing problems with optimism

Highly emotionally intelligent people are optimistic people. *Optimism* involves a strategic approach to challenging situations. It includes acknowledging challenges while, at the same time, believing that a solution exists. Optimism also involves actively working toward the possible successful outcomes.

Here are some tips to help you become more optimistic:

✔ Recognize and acknowledge when you're in a difficult situation.

✔ Recognize and acknowledge your top skills in dealing with difficult situations.

✔ Know where you can get help with any skills you lack.

✔ Actively address problems when they arise.

✔ Remember similar situations in which you've overcome problems.

✔ Keep your focus on applying solutions going forward, and don't get stuck in the past.

✔ Reframe negative circumstances as challenges to overcome.

When you build and practice your skills in optimism, you can more effectively deal with and overcome adversity. Optimistic skills are directly related to happiness.

A recent study by Hilary Tindale at the University of Pittsburgh followed more than 100,000 women aged 50 and over for eight years. The study, run through the Women's Health Initiative, found that women who were highly optimistic had a lower risk for early death, cancer, and heart disease than women who weren't very optimistic. These results held true, even after the study factored in other risk factors, such as smoking and lack of exercise.

Knowing your strengths and weaknesses

Emotionally intelligent people are self-aware. They know themselves well. They can read their own emotions and know how to manage them. They're also good at knowing their own strengths and weaknesses.

An important emotional skill that happy people possess is self-regard. By knowing your strengths and weaknesses, and accepting yourself for who you are, you can deal with challenging issues that you encounter. Building your confidence based on a realistic appraisal of your skills gives you the inner strength to approach situations that you encounter.

This activity can help you see how well you know yourself. When I want to get a general idea of how emotionally connected someone is, I start by asking some questions. In your notebook, write each question in the following list, then write your responses below each question:

- ✔ What are your five greatest strengths?
- ✔ What do you consider your greatest or signature strengths?
- ✔ How have your signature strengths helped you deal with adversity?
- ✔ How can you use your signature strengths in different or new situations?
- ✔ What are your weaknesses?
- ✔ What one thing do you want to change about yourself?
- ✔ How would you go about making that change?

Acknowledging your strengths and weaknesses, and building on them, helps build your confidence. Building your confidence makes you feel better about yourself and gives you a more positive attitude. Your positive attitude improves your ability to stay focused and solve problems.

Be sure to honestly and critically evaluate your skills so that you don't artificially inflate your self-esteem. By being critically honest about your strengths and limitations, you build true confidence in yourself.

Finding Authentic Happiness

The current thinking about happiness suggests that it's a long-term goal and that you can gradually reach a much happier life situation by following a number of exercises. Through specific activities, such as those described below, you can elevate your state of mind, which can affect various aspects of your life success.

Martin Seligman, a former President of the American Psychological Association and pioneer of the Positive Psychology movement, outlined a number of aspects of what he calls *authentic happiness*. According to Seligman, you can experience three types of happiness:

- **Pleasant life:** Pleasures, instant gratification, or hedonism

- **Good life:** Getting the things that you want or desire

- **Meaningful life:** Belonging to and serving in something larger and more worthwhile than just your own pleasures and desires

Authentic happiness combines all three lives and provides for the *full life* — a life that satisfies all three criteria of happiness.

Seligman tried a number of exercises with many people that were designed to increase happiness among the thousands of visitors to his Web sites. Two of the exercises demonstrated a long-term effect, increasing happiness over six months:

- **Three good things in life:** In this exercise, you write down at the end of each day three things that went well for you that day. You also record what caused the good thing to happen. Carry out this exercise for a week. As well as the cause of the thing that went well, write down an explanation of why you think the good thing happened.

- **Using signature strengths in a new way:** In this exercise, people select their "signature" strengths from a list of strengths. These strengths might include social skills, creativity, negotiating, leadership, caring for others, peacemaking, humility, optimism, enthusiasm, fairness, honesty, teamwork, self-control, and so on. Although merely identifying your top five strengths doesn't have much benefit, you can see a long-term benefit by trying to use one of the top five strengths in a new and different way for a week.

Finding long-term happiness

As a child, I loved music. I took private lessons on the saxophone and played throughout high school in concert bands and smaller groups. In college, I played in the school's marching band.

After I entered the world of work, I put away my saxophone because work-related time pressures took over. Only recently (after 30 years of neglect), I started to realize how much I missed playing music. I got my sax back into working condition, took refresher lessons, and joined a band.

The community band I play in commits time to playing in seniors' and veterans' residences and hospitals. I'm truly amazed at the joy our big band brings to seniors when they hear songs from their past such as "Summertime," "Harlem Nocturn," "Satin Doll," "Don't Get Around Much Anymore," and other tunes from the 1940s and '50s.

A live big-band concert brings back many happy memories to seniors, and I often listen to their stories of a different era, when Glen Miller, Benny Goodman, Tommy Dorsey, and other big bands came to town and entertained. Watching their smiles and the twinkle in their eyes while they relive a bygone era really warms the heart. I never expected that entertaining seniors would bring some extra joy to my life.

You can do many things to be more socially responsible through helping others, and as a result, increase the joy in your life:

- Get involved in community organizations.
- Participate in charitable activities and organizations.
- Donate money and time to charitable events.
- Be more sensitive to the needs of others in your world.

By caring more and involving yourself in helping others, you can find a different form of contentment. Giving to others, in the long run, brings you more happiness than being overly focused on your own materialistic gains does.

Part II

The Essentials of Emotional Intelligence

The 5th Wave   By Rich Tennant

"I heard it was good to use humor when you're having an argument."

In this part . . .

In this part, you can get to the essence of emotional intelligence and what it can mean for you. I give a whirlwind tour of the science behind emotional intelligence and a chapter-by-chapter breakdown of the components of emotional intelligence. You can see the importance of emotional self-awareness — one of the key components of emotional intelligence. I also offer some tools for cultivating empathy in your life, which is one of the hallmarks of emotional intelligence. You can find out how to get some control over the emotions of other people with whom you deal — people you're close to, as well as complete strangers.

Chapter 4

Investigating the Science Behind Emotional Intelligence

*I*n psychology (like other sciences), every once in a while someone discovers something new. This discovery then goes through a scientific process that uses the *experimental method,* which means that the discovery gets looked at again and again in carefully controlled studies, and other researchers *replicate* (repeat) the results.

In order for the psychological community to recognize emotional intelligence (EI) as a real phenomena, it had to go through the experimental method. Although the science of emotional intelligence represents a very recent area of research, the field has grown rapidly from one published scientific paper in 1990 to over 1,650 publications today.

In this chapter, I show you why emotional intelligence is important and how you can tell the difference between it and other psychological concepts, such as cognitive intelligence (IQ) and personality. I show you how to recognize the difference between emotional skills, personality, and cognitive intelligence so that you know what you can change and what you can't. The good news about emotional intelligence, unlike IQ and personality, is that you can change it through the right kind of training or coaching. In this chapter, I also show you how psychologists and human resource specialists can measure emotional intelligence.

Understanding the Difference between Emotional Intelligence and IQ

Most psychologists still haven't agreed on a definition of overall intelligence, although studies have proven that at least two forms of intelligence exist. Those two forms of intelligence are cognitive intelligence and emotional intelligence:

- **Cognitive intelligence:** Cognitive intelligence focuses on the ability to act purposefully, think rationally, and deal effectively with your environment. To measure cognitive intelligence, psychologists administer IQ tests, which rate your intelligence quotient (IQ).

  Simply put, *IQ* is a measure of an individual's intellectual, analytical, logical, and rational abilities. An IQ test measures your verbal, spatial, visual, and mathematical skills. It gauges how readily you understand new things; focus on tasks and exercises; retain and recall objective information; engage in a reasoning process; manipulate numbers; think abstractly, as well as analytically; and solve problems by the application of prior knowledge. If you have a high IQ — the average is 100 — you're well-equipped to pass all sorts of examinations with flying colors and (not incidentally) to score well on IQ tests.

- **Emotional intelligence:** Psychologists define emotional intelligence in various ways, depending on which expert you ask. Most definitions of emotional intelligence focus on your ability to be aware of, understand, and manage both your own as well as other people's emotions in order to adapt to life's demands and pressures. Let me define it for you as the ability to tune in to the world, to read situations, and to connect with others while taking charge of your own life. Psychologists measure emotional intelligence by using any of several EQ tests, which measure your emotional quotient (EQ). The two most accepted tests are the EQ-i and the MSCEIT, which I talk about in the section "Understanding How EQ Tests Work," later in this chapter.

Organizational consultants often use the term *emotional intelligence* (EI) interchangeably with the term *emotional quotient* (EQ). Just like IQ (intellectual quotient) is the measurement of cognitive intelligence, EQ (emotional quotient) is the measurement of emotional intelligence.

Most people know that you can find a world of difference between school smarts and street smarts — between braininess and general savvy. Cognitive intelligence has its place, but emotional intelligence, although more intangible, is much more interesting to many people because it provides us with a new and exciting way to look at ourselves that focuses less on our fixed intellectual assets.

Discovering emotional intelligence

The "discovery" of the concept of emotional intelligence came about serendipitously. Peter Salovey, a psychologist at Yale University and expert in emotions, was friends with his colleague John (Jack) Mayer, a psychologist at the University of New Hampshire. These two friends were also collaborators in research projects related to emotions, intelligence, and personality.

Both Peter and Jack had hopes for a young presidential candidate named Gary Hart. They saw him as young, fresh, and intelligent — a sure winner. Then, something unbelievable happened. During the primaries, a reporter confronted Gary Hart and suggested, based on some rumors, that he was having an extramarital affair. He famously responded by denying the allegation and then daring all the reporters around him that day to, "Follow me around. I don't care. I'm serious. If anybody wants to put a tail on me, go ahead. They'll be very bored."

Within 24 hours, the Miami Herald broke the story of his now-famous affair with Donna Rice. Peter and Jack, while painting Jack's house one afternoon, were trying to understand how someone so intelligent could do and say something so lacking in intelligence under the circumstances. Could it be that he was very intelligent in one area (political policy) and not so intelligent in another area (managing his emotions)?

They then came up with the idea that people must have some other kind of intelligence, an emotional intelligence, quite separate from the cognitive intelligence (or IQ) that everyone knows about. They reasoned that they could probably find some way to measure this intelligence in the same way that widely used intelligence tests measure IQ.

Peter and Jack further developed the concept and then wrote a scientific paper titled "Emotional Intelligence," which they published in a relatively obscure scientific journal.

Knowing How Your Emotions Affect You

Your emotions can affect your ability to understand or learn to deal with a new situation in a number of ways. How do you determine whether emotion simply influences intelligence, or whether it's a separate intelligence on its own?

For one thing, if emotion was part of general intelligence or cognitive intelligence, the two attributes would be associated with each other. People who have high cognitive intelligence would automatically have high emotional intelligence, as well as the reverse. In reality, your cognitive intelligence and emotional intelligence have very little in common, based on the available research.

Someone can be very intelligent (meaning book smart) and have very little emotional self-awareness, empathy, or social skill. Think of the stereotypical absent-minded professor. This person is very bright intellectually, but not always very aware of what's happening in the world around him. This person is often oblivious to people's needs, including people very close at hand. On the other hand, of course, someone can be a star in empathy, yet not be a rocket scientist in intellect. Therefore, cognitive intelligence and emotional intelligence are independent characteristics.

But, even though these two intelligences are separate, they work together. Someone without a strong level of emotional intelligence might let his feelings affect his reasoning, preventing him from being rational. Or, even if someone's presenting a well-reasoned argument, her words might not be well received if she's not managing her emotions properly.

Many people recognize Jodi's story. Jodi has to deal with a situation that's new and difficult for her. She has to give a speech in front of her local community council regarding a new development that she believes would adversely affect the environment.

She wants her presentation to be intelligent because the attendees will include many of the movers and shakers in her community, as well as many of her neighbors. She starts out by doing her homework. Here are some things that she does:

- Becomes informed and up to date about the neighborhood
- Finds out the neighborhood's history
- Reviews the nature of previous developments
- Understands the full scope of the proposed development
- Does general research on the impact of development on the environment
- Studies up on the proposed development's likely effects on the environment

The activities in the preceding list prepared Jodi for the knowledge portion of her presentation.

Now, Jodi is as knowledgeable as she can be about the subject matter. But she has never given one of these presentations before. Emotions can impact her performance on several levels.

While preparing her presentation, what if Jodi becomes so angry about the situation that her mind can't absorb all the information about her neighborhood and the effects of development? If she can't be calm — even enthusiastic — during her research, she might not do her best job preparing for the meeting.

If her mind is preoccupied with anger, for example, she may be busy thinking things such as, "Those no-good politicians just want to line their own pockets." And while she's busy having all these angry thoughts, she distracts herself from the task at hand, maybe not even noticing that she flips past an article about how certain developments change traffic flow, which can increase pollution and pose a danger in areas where children cross the streets.

After Jodi energetically and enthusiastically (note the helpful emotions) puts together her arguments, she has to actually present them to the overflow audience at the town hall. She might be armed with all the knowledge she needs, but is she emotionally ready?

Some people, when they see the crowd, become anxious or even fearful — they may fear making a mistake at such an important time, or they may worry about what their neighbors will think of them if things don't go well. Some surveys have even suggested that public speaking is the number one fear that many people have — higher than death and chronic illness.

On the other hand, when speaking, some people become so angry and determined to get their point of view across that when a councilor asks them a question, they might just gloss over it without listening properly and without taking it seriously. Their emotions might get in the way of their being able to do a good job, disabling them by making them appear defensive and unreasonable in the situation.

Anger is a hot emotion; it tends to burn out of control. Although your anger may alert you to a situation, it can't help you problem-solve your way out of a bad situation. In fact, it often gets in the way and escalates the negative consequences. To find out how to tone down "hot" emotions, see Chapter 5.

Making the Case for Emotional Intelligence

Think about the differences among people you know.

You probably know some people who are smart as a whip when it comes to solving math problems and others who struggle doing even the most basic of math questions. So, some people have a lot of a math ability of some kind, others have a bit, and the rest, well, they have trouble counting their loose change.

Now, think about emotions. You probably know some people who are always concerned or caring about other people. For example, you might know someone who truly shows interest in how you are whenever you run into her. This person seems to really care about how you're feeling, whether things are going well in your life, how your family is doing, and so on.

On the other hand, can you think of people you know who really couldn't care less about you or how you're doing? You can probably classify the people you know into categories of those who really care about you, those who care somewhat, and those who are rather oblivious to your plight. Like solving math problems or performing other cognitive intelligence tasks, psychologists can rate people in terms of the degree and the ways in which they really care about others they know.

Caring about others — or, more precisely, knowing how others feel (which is called *empathy*) — is one of the hallmarks of emotional intelligence. Chapter 7 covers empathy in detail.

An important distinction exists between sympathy and empathy. *Sympathy* refers to how you feel about someone else. It usually involves an I sentence, such as, "I feel sad about your husband's illness." Although sympathy is a valuable emotion, it differs from empathy, which tends to involve a "you" sentence. For example, you might say, "You must be feeling angry about what that woman said to you." Empathy demonstrates that you understand what another person is feeling.

Studying the brain

Charles Darwin, in his work on evolution and survival, documented the importance of emotions as a signaling system. The angry look on a wolf's face serves as a signal that the hunter ignores at his peril. The "flight or fight" response kicks in when reading the anger on the wolf's face. This ability to read these emotions, according to Darwin, led to humans' survival. The lower, more primitive areas of the brain mediate this response. These are the same parts that control your emotional responses today. These sections of the brain are called the *limbic system* and the *hippocampus*.

These emotional parts of the brain influence the way humans' higher, more advanced areas — called the *neocortex* — function. When you make complex decisions (such as when you interact with people, solve problems, and so on),

the lower parts of the brain are still active; they play a role in how effectively you carry out various tasks. Emotions affect your decisions and your reactions to events (even seemingly insignificant ones) and people.

Having good emotional intelligence involves optimum functioning of your higher and lower brain functions. The lower parts of the brain that helped humans survive as hunters by helping them keep vigilant to dangers and opportunities are just as important today in ensuring people react appropriately to everyday stressors and possibilities they encounter. By moderating your reaction to challenging people and situations — reading them correctly — you learn to moderate your "flight or fight" response into more socially acceptable responses. Being smart combines knowing what to do as well as how to do it best.

Understanding how EQ tests work

Organizational consultants, psychologists, and educators most commonly use the EQ-i, EQ-360, and MSCEIT to test for emotional intelligence. In the same way that psychologists have validated IQ tests, psychologists and other researchers in business and education have validated the EQ-i (along with other tests of emotional intelligence, such as the EQ-360 and MSCEIT). Test developers have standardized these tests by testing thousands of people throughout the world. A number of factors (or scales) in these tests reflect the different areas of emotional intelligence.

The EQ-i

The first published and most widely used self test of emotional intelligence in the world (now translated into 25 languages, with 11 more in process) is the Emotional Quotient Inventory (EQ-i) by Dr. Reuven Bar-On. Well over one million people worldwide have been tested with the EQ-i, and that number is growing. The EQ-i was developed looking at the general idea of an emotional and social intelligence quotient, or EQ.

The EQ-i has been normed, as mentioned above, with thousands of people in various parts of the world, ensuring that your results are meaningful for your particular location and culture. Also, there has been a great deal of validity and reliability carried out on this instrument, which is the very first test of emotional intelligence created.

Bar-On identified and defined 15 factors, grouped into five areas of emotional and social intelligence. The areas and their factors are as follows:

- **Intra-personal:** This area concerns your ability to know and manage yourself. It embraces the following:

    - **Self-Awareness:** The ability to recognize how you're feeling and why you're feeling that way, as well as the impact your behavior has on others.

    - **Assertiveness:** The ability to clearly express your thoughts and feelings, stand your ground, and defend a position.

    - **Independence:** The ability to be self-directed and self-controlled, to stand on your own two feet.

    - **Self-Regard:** The ability to recognize your strengths and weaknesses, and feel good about yourself despite your weaknesses.

    - **Self-Actualization:** The ability to realize your potential and feel comfortable with what you achieve at work and in your personal life.

✔ **Inter-personal:** This area concerns your "people skills" — your ability to interact and get along with others. It is composed of three scales:

- **Empathy:** The ability to understand what others might be feeling and thinking. It is the ability to view the world through another person's eyes.

- **Social Responsibility:** The ability to be a cooperative and contributing member of your social group.

- **Interpersonal Relationships:** The ability to forge and maintain relationships that are mutually beneficial and marked by give-and-take and a sense of emotional closeness.

✔ **Adaptability:** This area involves your ability to be flexible and realistic, and to solve a range of problems as they arise. Its three scales are as follows:

- **Reality Testing:** The ability to see things as they actually are, rather than the way you wish or fear they might be.

- **Flexibility:** The ability to adjust your feelings, thoughts, and actions to changing conditions.

- **Problem-Solving:** The ability to define problems and then move to generate and implement effective, appropriate solutions.

✔ **Stress Management:** This area concerns your ability to tolerate stress and control impulses. It has two scales:

- **Stress Tolerance:** The ability to remain calm and focused, to constructively withstand adverse events and conflicting emotions without caving in.

- **Impulse Control:** The ability to resist or delay a temptation to act.

✔ **General Mood:** This area also concerns your ability to be positive and in a good mood. It has two scales:

- **Optimism:** The ability to maintain a realistically positive attitude, particularly in the face of adversity.

- **Happiness:** The ability to feel satisfied with life, to enjoy yourself and others, and to experience zest and enthusiasm in a range of activities.

Definitions presented with permission of Multi-Health Systems. Slightly modified from Bar-On, R. (1997) Bar-On Emotional Quotient Inventory Manual, Multi-Health Systems: Toronto.

Figure 4-1 shows each of the five areas of emotional intelligence based on the Bar-On model. Four of the areas — Intra-personal, Inter-personal, Stress Management, and Adaptability — are facilitated by your General Mood, which can lead to even better output or performance. So if you are happier and more optimistic, for example, you can accelerate your skills in other areas — such as being a better "people person."

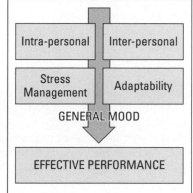

BAR-ON MODEL OF EMOTIONAL INTELLIGENCE

Intra-personal   Inter-personal

Stress Management   Adaptability

GENERAL MOOD

EFFECTIVE PERFORMANCE

Figure 4-1:
The Bar-On model of emotional intelligence.

Figure used with permission of Multi-Health Systems, www.mhs.com

Because of the complexity and detail of the results provided, only trained and certified counselors, human resource specialists, or licensed psychologists can administer the EQ-i. To find a qualified person near you, e-mail `eifor Dummies@MHS.com`.

The EQ-360

Psychologists can measure emotional intelligence by having others who know the person fairly well offer some input. The EQ-i has a companion instrument called the EQ-360. The EQ-360 takes the ratings that a person makes about herself and compares them to the ratings that others —her employees, friends or peers, boss, spouse, or any number of others who interact on a regular basis with the person — make about her. Like the EQ-i, the EQ-360 is administered by a qualified professional (career counselor, human resource specialist, or psychologist).

By looking at these behavioral ratings in conjunction with the self ratings, organizational professionals, business coaches, and psychologists can begin to see a clearer picture of your emotional intelligence. These professionals can measure

✔ Sensitivity to the feelings of others

✔ Expressiveness about feelings

  ✔ Kindness toward others

  ✔ Caring nature

  ✔ Perceived friendliness

  ✔ Stress-management skills

  ✔ Optimistic attitude

  ✔ Level of self-control

  ✔ Assertiveness

  ✔ Independence

By tabulating the ratings of the behaviors that lead to judgments of these areas and others, the organizational consultant or psychologist can begin to get a picture of someone's emotional intelligence. In addition to how the person rates himself, the professional can systematically compare this information with ratings given by others who know him. As part of the scoring process, this data is automatically compared to a database of thousands of other people who have rated people they know, giving a more accurate gauge of the person's emotional intelligence.

If you want to be tested with the EQ-360, send an e-mail to `taketheeq360@ mhs.com`, asking for a referral to a professional near you.

The MSCEIT

The MSCEIT (Mayer, Salovey, and Caruso Emotional Intelligence Test) is the most widely used ability (or performance) test of emotional intelligence. As an ability test, it works more like a traditional IQ test — but for emotions. Two of the authors, Dr. Salovey (Professor of Psychology and current Dean of the Graduate School of Arts and Sciences at Yale University) and Dr. Mayer (psychology professor at the University of New Hampshire), began the current interest in this field by looking at emotions as an intelligence.

The types of items in the MSCEIT are different from the items in other tests. MSCEIT includes asking you to recognize the emotion in pictures of people's faces and in designs, knowing which emotions can help you get through specific tasks or challenges, understanding how some emotions can blend with other emotions, and knowing how to use your emotions in specific challenging social situations.

The MSCEIT model, shown in Figure 4-2, includes four specific areas or branches:

✔ **Perceiving Emotions.** Perceiving, or identifying, emotions involves your ability to successfully read other people's emotions. It also includes your ability to express emotions accurately to others in order to be an effective communicator. Getting the emotions right in the first place helps you better use your emotions.

✔ **Facilitating Thought.** Facilitating thought, or using emotions, involves using your emotions to get you in the mood. The way we feel has a big influence on how we think. Also, emotions can help us focus our attention and guide us as we solve problems. In order to best use our emotions, however, we should really understand how they work.

✔ **Understanding Emotions.** Understanding emotions helps us use our emotions to predict our future. Knowing our emotions helps us navigate through life. It helps to understand why we feel sad, angry, or giddy. For example, feeling angry because of bad traffic in the morning, and then taking that anger out on your co-workers, is not going to help you at work. Understanding where your anger comes from makes it easier to deal with it. By understanding our emotions, we're in a better position to manage our emotions.

✔ **Managing Emotions.** Managing emotions is where you can really put your emotions to your advantage. By managing the way you feel, you can get along better with others, solve problems better, make better judgments, and manage your behavior better.

Figure 4-2:
The MSCEIT model for emotional intelligence.

For more information on the MSCEIT, visit the Web site www.msceit.com. If you're interested in taking the MSCEIT through a qualified administrator, e-mail takethemsceit@mhs.com.

Understanding how EQ tests work compared to personality tests

By using the same best practices from the development of IQ tests, EQ tests have been developed. These tests have been found to be reliable and valid measuring up to the same standard as widely used IQ tests.

If you were taking an ability-based EQ test, you might be presented with an item similar to this:

Two boys, Ali and Sam, are playing basketball in the schoolyard. They suddenly start fighting over who should get the next shot at the basket. You happen to be walking by and see them fighting. You decide to

> a) Ignore them and keep walking.
>
> b) Yell at them to stop fighting.
>
> c) Take the ball from them and tell them that if they don't behave, neither of them can have it.
>
> d) Interrupt their fighting and get them to each explain to you the rules of the game they're playing.
>
> e) Tell them that you'll report them if they don't stop fighting.

The format of the preceding question is similar to what you see on an IQ test. The main difference between IQ-test and EQ-test questions, however, is that the test questions on an IQ test clearly have a correct answer. For a math question, you can take a calculator and do the math, and you get a single *right* answer.

But while you progress through the items in some IQ tests, the questions get harder and harder. The answers to the hardest items may seem a bit more subjective — in other words, you can't just get a calculator or go to a dictionary to figure them out.

On an ability-based EQ test, the possible answers to the questions may appear subjective. You may even argue that you can see a valid reason to respond with each of the options. What makes one response more correct than another? The test authors generally decide the correctness of an answer in one of two ways:

✓ **Norm group:** Give the items to over 1,000 people who represent the population at large who will take the test in the future. Then, look at how the majority of people respond to the item. The majority response would most likely be the correct response — a social consensus of the right thing to do in the situation.

✓ **Expert review:** Present the items to a group of known experts in the field of emotions. These experts are scientists who understand the basic and advanced theories about emotions, have conducted research on emotions, and have contributed in some way to the scientific literature and to researchers' better understanding of emotions. These experts use their expertise to pick the best response to each of the items. If the vast majority of the experts agree on the best response, that response becomes the correct one.

Differentiating Personality from Emotional Skills

Most people are pretty consistent in their *personality* — the long-enduring traits that tend to define them. Some people wear their personalities on their sleeves, while others need to be comfortable in order to show their true colors. You probably already have a good sense of your personality.

Here's an activity that helps you to look at your personality in more specific terms. You can start to get at those traits or characteristics that describe your personality by looking at your attitudes and behaviors. For example, do you see yourself as extroverted or introverted? Are you often anxious and driven or more calm and laid back? Think about the characteristics that most define you as a person — to others and yourself — and write a few of them in your notebook. Reflect on this list and refer back to it from time to time. The following questions may help guide your thoughts:

✓ Are you outgoing and the life of the party, or do you prefer to stay home, reading or watching TV?

✓ Do you like being with a lot of people or just a few close friends?

✓ Are you generally calm or often fairly hyper, nervous, or anxious?

✓ Do you like telling other people what to do, or do you prefer following other people's instructions?

✓ Do you have a number of long-standing habits that you follow, or is every day a new experience and opportunity to try new ways of doing things?

> ✔ Are you rather curious about how things work, or do you just want to use something and then move on?
>
> ✔ Do you have a strong need to achieve (for example, make money, get the best job, be a professional, or be the most popular in your group), or are you just happy-go-lucky and laid back?
>
> ✔ Do you tend to worry about doing your best on tasks, or are you more relaxed and accept that mistakes happen?

One of the most popular personality theories among psychologists is known as the "Big Five" or Five Factor Model. This refers to five traits that have been found consistently across people and cultures. These traits are

> ✔ **Openness:** receptive to new experiences and new ideas
>
> ✔ **Conscientiousness:** self-disciplined and careful as opposed to being spontaneous
>
> ✔ **Extraversion:** tending to seek stimulation, the company of others, exhibiting high energy
>
> ✔ **Agreeableness**: cooperative and compassionate
>
> ✔ **Neuroticism:** easily upset or often experiencing negative emotions such as anxiety, anger, and depression

Tracking personality across the life span

If you answer the questions, in the preceding section, about yourself and maybe even about other people you know, you can start to get a handle on personality. Your *personality* is made up of the long-standing internal traits or characteristics that you carry around with you. Research suggests that these traits tend to be lifelong. So, if you were shy and introverted as a young child, you're probably still on the quiet side and prefer staying home to attending loud parties. And these preferences very likely won't change in the foreseeable future.

Jack and Jeanne Block, psychologists at the University of California at Berkley, have carried out one of the longest-running studies that examines the personalities of children while they grow into adulthood. In fact, the Blocks have followed a cohort of children for over 30 years, carefully watching and assessing their development at regular intervals.

As you might expect, they found differences among the children right from the beginning of the study. Hardly surprising — some children are relatively quiet and still, others are noisy and run like a motor, and many fall somewhere in between. Interestingly, although the study observed some small changes in people over time, the relative differences between people stayed fairly constant over 30 years.

If you think about someone you know who's honest and ethical, do you think that he would suddenly change and do a number of unethical things? Or think of the reverse situation. Do you think that someone who has a history of unethical or criminal behavior will suddenly become Citizen of the Year?

Intuitively and through your own experience, you probably agree that people rarely make significant changes to their basic characters.

If you've ever taken a personality test, you may know that counselors often divide people up into types, such as the introvert, the extrovert, the adventurer, the nurturer, and so on. Personality is often used to pigeonhole people into categories. Think of the Type A personality (hard-driving and prone to anger) versus Type B (relaxed and not overly ambitious).

The problem with these personality characteristics is that they don't support the ability to change or improve. Although you may find discovering your personality type interesting, knowing that personality type doesn't really give you a lot of direction for change. But you can change your emotional intelligence over time.

Changing your emotional intelligence

One of the benefits of knowing your emotional intelligence is that it helps you understand some of your strengths and weaknesses. You can further develop these strengths to increase your awareness and effectiveness, and you can even develop and improve on your weaknesses. Although you can't change your personality, by completing the activities in this book, you can increase your self-awareness and improve your EI skills.

When my colleagues and I developed emotional intelligence assessments, we tested hundreds of thousands of people across different socio-economic groups, countries and cultures, and levels of education. One of the many analyses we did looked at emotional intelligence across the age range shown in Figure 4-3.

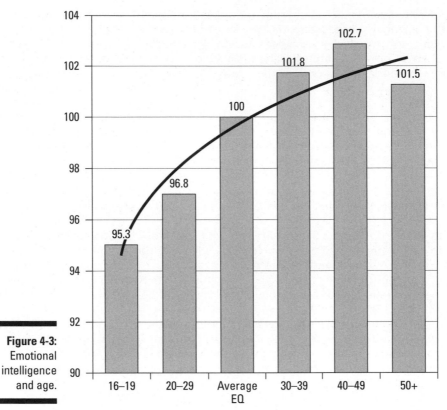

Figure 4-3:
Emotional
intelligence
and age.

As you can see in the graph in Figure 4-3, from about the age of 20, people's emotional intelligence increases until somewhere around age 55. At that point, these emotional skills start to decline a bit. So, over time (to a point), you can see a steady, gradual increase in these emotional skills. This pattern probably relates to the concept of *maturity* — or getting older, but wiser.

Emotional intelligence is perceived by some people as an aspect of wisdom. This mirrors the idea that you get "older but wiser." For example, your impulse control probably becomes more manageable while you age, which may affect your problem-solving ability and increase your reality testing. *Reality testing* is your ability to see things as they really are as opposed to the way you wish they were. Another emotional skill that grows as you age is your ability to see past your own circumstances; as they age, many people begin to focus less on themselves and more on others and the world around them.

Although you might increase your EQ over time while you age, through the lessons life teaches you, I'm sure you want to speed up the process. Organizations have done studies that focused on increasing emotional skills. These studies have shown that people can make significant gains in relatively short amounts of time.

The kind of understanding that you need if you want to make these changes, most often, goes beyond the understanding that you can get from reading books (even practical books such as this one). If you want to accelerate the changes that take place naturally over time, you'll require the right kinds of experience. You gain that experience by constantly interacting with the people and the world around you.

As you can see throughout this book, psychologists have found specific techniques useful in helping people improve their emotional skills. Often, these interventions require that you interact with one or more other people. By going through these repeated interactions, and practicing some trial and error, you can develop these skills.

I've seen people make significant life changes after they develop their emotional skills. And it's never too late to make changes in your life. Yes, even people in their 80s can change — they can become more self-aware, optimistic, and even empathic. Education, gender, social class — you don't need to look at any of these factors as barriers to developing your emotional intelligence.

Chapter 5

Becoming More Aware of Your Emotions

In This Chapter

▶ Discovering your emotions

▶ Getting to know your emotions

▶ Dealing with negative emotions

*I*n this chapter, you can get to the heart of what emotional intelligence is all about. I start out with a big assumption: that everyone has feelings. Unless you're Spock from *Star Trek* (and sometimes I have my doubts about him), somewhere within you, you have feelings. You laugh, you cry, you get angry, you get sad, you're perplexed, you're excited, you're surprised, or you're just plain bored. Day or night, rain or shine, if you stop and think about it, you're feeling something.

Well, you don't experience feelings if you have a disorder called *alexithymia* (pronounced *alex-i-thyme-ia*). The literal translation from Greek is "lack of feelings." Alexithymia is a rare psychiatric disorder, although a large body of research shows that it can exist in various degrees in the population — mostly in men, and not in huge numbers.

Generally, these people can't identify, understand, or describe their own emotions. They can't tell one feeling from another. They don't know whether they feel happiness, sadness, or some other emotion. And if you ask them to describe how they feel, they tend to look at you with a blank stare. They also have trouble imagining events that would help them identify feelings.

So (assuming you're not alexithymic), in this chapter, I explore ways in which you can be more aware of your emotions.

Defining Feelings

Much debate exists around the definitions of and differences between emotions, feelings, and moods — but even so, you may find the following simple definitions useful:

✔ **Feelings:** A *feeling* includes your subjective, or personal, experience of an emotion or sensation. "I feel sad," or "I feel pain," or in the words of a famous U.S. president, "I feel your pain." A feeling is the way that you personally experience something. I may think you look happy or indifferent, but you tell me that you feel sad. Who am I to argue? The expression "gut feeling" really drives home the idea that a feeling is subjective — you can't prove or demonstrate why you feel that way.

✔ **Moods:** A *mood* is your mental state (or a state of mind) at a particular time. Your mood sums up your thinking and feeling, and it usually lasts longer than a feeling. It can also refer to a group. You may be in an irritable mood, or the country may be depressed (not just the economy, but the mood of the people). You probably know to stay away from certain people when they're "in one of those moods."

✔ **Emotions:** An *emotion* is an objective way to look at feelings or what psychologists call "affect." Most psychologists agree on clear definitions of emotions. So, although you may feel "yucky" (a feeling), a psychologist tries to determine whether the emotion is sadness, depression, irritability, or anger.

You can easily remember the difference between emotions and feelings with this idea: Emotions are the objective state of feelings. Emotions are clear, well-defined, and experienced by all people. Psychologists have identified dozens of emotions that they can define. You can also have a blend of emotions. Think of mixing ingredients together in the kitchen — when you combine flour, milk, and eggs, and then heat the mixture, you create a crepe. Annoyance and irritability can combine to create rage if you don't check those emotions. Joy and anticipation can lead to optimism.

Feelings are the more subjective aspects of emotions. Some people are better at identifying their feelings than others are. You may find feelings less clear than emotions. For example, Julia overhears a co-worker telling someone that Ted just got the job promotion Julia had applied for. She had been so sure that she was next in line for the job. As soon as she hears the news, Julia has a queasy, upset feeling in her stomach. She says she feels bloated, probably from something she ate. Although she believes she's feeling queasy — at least, that's her subjective experience — an outside observer could probably figure out that she really feels a bit traumatized and depressed.

What about mood? Well, Julia could probably tell you that she's in a bad mood. But she might think that she's in a bad mood because she ate something that upset her stomach.

Without feeling, you don't really live. Your ability to feel joy, happiness, excitement, and even pain, hurt, and loss makes you human. In many ways, modern society takes away your ability to feel. You're overly focused on your thinking skills throughout school, work, and your social life. Going through life without feelings is like living in a black and white movie. You experience shades of gray — when life feels bad, your feelings get darker, and when things feel better, they get lighter.

Of course, you also don't want to go to the other extreme, where every nuance of your life is dramatized in living Technicolor on the big screen. I'm sure you know people who get overly emotional about the slightest thing — not being constantly complimented and admired, or not being noticed by others or properly acknowledged. Having too much emotion in life can be draining — not only for you, but also for those around you.

Strive to have a good balance of emotions. Knowing just how much emotion you need to get through a situation or event helps you keep in balance. Without enough emotion, you might not be motivated; with too much, you could be overly anxious. For example, if you know that you have a big exam coming up this week, you probably have strategies to prepare for it. Although some people like to stay up late at night and cram in as much information as possible before the exam (not highly recommended), others prefer to prepare in advance so that they can go to bed early the night before and be well-rested and alert at exam time.

Think about some of the emotions you experience throughout the course of a day. You may have had a few frustrations or annoyances that led you to feel anger, or some successes or accomplishments that led to feeling happy. If you reflect right now for a few moments, see what emotions you've experienced over the past 48 hours. Write them in your notebook. Consider the following questions:

- How many different emotions did you experience?
- Did you experience them gently or intensely?
- How much difficulty did you have identifying them?

Paying more attention to the emotions you feel is one way to make yourself more emotionally aware. Did you experience only a few different emotions over the past two days, or did you have a wide variety?

Identifying Your Emotions

The English language has many different words for emotional experiences. In this section, I present you with a list of emotional words. Some emotions are positive, some are *neutral* (neither positive nor negative), and others are negative. Emotionally intelligent people tend to have a rich vocabulary of words to describe their feelings. I don't mean the show-off "look at how smart I am" type of person. Rather, I'm referring to people who can give you a very accurate sense of where they're coming from. They're good at communicating their emotional state to others.

When expressing emotions, people with better emotional vocabularies tend to use more context that helps flush out what they mean.

Compare

> "I feel pretty yucky."

to

> "I feel discouraged after trying to get his attention three times already."

By having a good emotional vocabulary, not only can you make yourself more clear about your feelings, but you enable others around you to understand exactly what you mean. By understanding yourself better — and being better understood by others — you're more likely to have your needs met. You can find not knowing why you're feeling the way you do or being a mystery to others frustrating. You can have problems fixing something when you don't know how it's broken.

This activity helps you assign language to your emotions. First, review the following list of emotions:

aggressive	awed
aggravated	bashful
alienated	blissful
amused	bored
angry	cautious
annoyed	cheerful
anxious	confident
apathetic	confused
appalled	curious

delighted	interested
depressed	jealous
determined	joyous
disappointed	lonely
discouraged	loved
disgusted	love-struck
ecstatic	miserable
elated	negative
embarrassed	optimistic
enthusiastic	paranoid
envious	peaceful
excited	proud
exhausted	puzzled
fearful	regretful
frightened	relieved
frustrated	sad
glad	satisfied
guilty	shocked
happy	sorry
helpless	sure
hopeful	surprised
hostile	suspicious
humiliated	undecided
hurt	withdrawn
hysterical	

After you review the list, follow these steps:

1. **Record in your notebook each emotion that you've experienced over the course of your life.**

2. **In your notebook, write a + next to each emotion you think is positive, a – next to each emotion that's negative, and a 0 next to each emotion that's neutral.**

3. **Rate the intensity of your most vivid experience of the emotion.**

   Using a scale from 1 to 10, rate each emotion. Use the following anchors: 1 to represent minimal, 5 for average, and 10 for extreme.

4. **Add up the total number of emotions you've experienced and write that number in your notebook.**

5. **Add up the number of positive emotions, then add up the number of negative emotions. Write these numbers in your notebook.**

6. **Compare your balance of negative versus positive emotions.**

   Do you feel more positive or negative emotions? What is the average intensity of the positive emotions you recorded compared to the negative emotions? Do you think the intensity of your emotions has an effect on which ones you notice more (positive or negative)?

You can use this list of emotions to help you better understand and label your emotions. Sometimes we don't pay attention to the emotions we feel. By keeping a vocabulary of emotions nearby, at the end of the day, you can refer to it and get a better understanding of what you've been experiencing.

People who have a wide range of emotional experiences tend to lead richer lives. They experience life more dimensionally. Also, in order to accurately perceive, label, and empathize with someone, you must be able to describe and apply your knowledge of the various emotions that humans can experience.

To expand your vocabulary even further, try to find synonyms for those emotions that you report feeling the most. By using a greater variety of words, you can more precisely describe what you and others are feeling.

Digging Deeper into Your Emotions

Sometimes, just seeing the name of an emotion may not help you recognize what you're feeling. Or even knowing that you don't feel right about something may not help you really deal with the feeling. You can better understand why you feel the way you do at certain times, with certain people, or in certain situations by examining your behaviors, your body responses, and other people's behaviors.

Interpreting behaviors

You're probably familiar with situations in which someone's behavior doesn't seem to match what he or she is telling you. Someone might have told you how funny you are, but his demeanor and voice seem to tell another story. Or a child tells you that she didn't take any cookies out of the cookie jar, but her shifting eyes, fidgeting, and smirking, and the lilt in her voice, tell a different story.

Behaviors are often clues about what you're really feeling and thinking. You need to become sensitive and aware of how others behave to pick up on these cues. In the same way, your behaviors provide clues to others about your feelings. Paying attention to all the non-verbal cues of someone with whom you're interacting can help you begin to understand what he or she might really be feeling.

For this activity, try observing people from a distance:

✔ **Act as a bystander.** You don't need to get involved as an active player, but rather behave as an uninvolved bystander. Be creative in this exercise. Observe people in a public place, such as a hotel lobby, popular downtown outdoor lunch place, or shopping mall. (Just be discreet, and don't stare too long!) You can also do this activity while watching television or a movie, but seeing people live is much more realistic. Rather than acted out emotions, you get to see real emotions live, as they happen. Practice by yourself at first. After you feel you're getting pretty good at it and feel like you can interpret behaviors, you can do this activity with a partner and compare your observations when you finish.

✔ **Record your observations.** For each scenario you observe, complete the following information in your notebook (see the example in Figure 5-1):

   • Each time you observe an emotion being expressed, note whether the emotion is positive or negative, and rate the intensity on a scale of 1 to 10 (1 = low and 10 = high).

   • See whether you can identify the trigger that set off the emotion in the person.

   • Identify the cues that led you to identify the emotion (for example, body language, tone of voice, facial expression, and so on).

   • Include the context in which you observed the identified emotion.

Emotion Observed	Direction	Intensity	Trigger	Cue
female happy	(P) Y N	1 2 3 4 5 (6) 7 8 9 10	he said something to her and looked at her	she's smiling, wide expression on her face, moving towards him
female concerned	P (N)	1 2 (3) 4 5 6 7 8 9 10	he spoke softly, looked at his coffee cup	she wrinkled her brow, looked down

Figure 5-1: Observe others and record your observations.

Although you can sometimes suppress, deny, or hide your actual feelings about someone or something, those feelings manage to seep through, often through your behaviors. At times, you've probably behaved in certain ways without really knowing why. For example, do you avoid certain people or situations for no reason you can identify? Or have you ever overreacted to a statement that someone makes, which on the face of it, was an innocent comment? To gain insight into your emotions, look for habits or behaviors that you seem to perform routinely without knowing exactly why.

Examining self-destructive behaviors

Think of some of the most self-defeating habits, such as smoking, overeating, or drug abuse. Many people start smoking to make themselves feel cool, sophisticated, or one of the crowd. At first, the feeling you get when you hold or puff on a cigarette (even though the activity doesn't feel natural or pleasant) makes you continue to smoke. Your emotions or feelings about yourself (looking or feeling cool) get you into the habit of smoking. For some, insecurity or anxiety gets them started. Most often, people start smoking for these reasons during late adolescence.

Imagine if more people could identify these *trigger feelings* (emotions that set off a particular behavior) at the time they start smoking. Understanding that these feelings exist and knowing why they are happening can open the door for alternative behaviors or habits. Although, admittedly, a number of smokers have told me that even if they knew how they felt and had the choice to start smoking or not, they'd still pick smoking. So, although this awareness may help many start-up smokers to not smoke, or at least lead to a more informed choice, recognizing trigger feelings doesn't necessarily put an end to smoking.

After some time, smoking becomes more habitual. In the process, the trigger emotions become more controlling. Many smokers say that they get an urge to light up a cigarette at certain times. The urge is the emotional trigger. So, for example, starting to feel anxious before an exam or interview can be the trigger to light up. Smokers believe that the act of smoking can prevent an even greater feeling of anxiety to come. For a habitual smoker, trying to stop lighting up likely leads to even greater anxiety.

If you look at substance abusers or overeaters, you find much of the same pattern. These kinds of behaviors usually have emotional triggers. While in the early stages of these uncomfortable feelings, you tend to control the behavior that deals with the emotion. You feel anxious or sad, so you get something to eat. You then feel a bit better or (if you use certain drugs that give a high) a lot better. You repeat the pattern whenever you experience an unpleasant feeling, and you need more food, drugs, or whatever to deal with the emotion.

Some people deal with less extreme habits or behaviors that they sometimes find difficult to explain. They prefer certain areas of seating in a restaurant or movie theater, choose specific types of foods, avoid some people, interrupt certain people a lot, don't look someone in the eye during conversation, or argue with a certain type of person. For example, some people automatically react when they encounter males who have long hair, or people in military uniform or wearing certain religious garb. Do these examples of situations arouse certain types of feelings? Can you start to change those feelings, or transform them to lead to certain behaviors, if you're consciously aware of the feelings?

A person who's very different from you might initially arouse fear or caution, which may quickly turn into some other emotion or behavior. The behavior may lead you to avoid that person, experience some negative feeling, or make a negative comment. Some people who behave overly cautiously or don't want to appear fearful may react guardedly and very unnaturally to this person.

In many situations, your behaviors may point the way to your emotions and even deeper connections. Think of your behaviors as signals for certain feelings that you have. By looking at your behaviors differently, you may find clues that can help you better understand why you do what you do.

Being the master

In an earlier part of my career as a psychologist, I worked with adolescents who were having serious emotional and behavioral problems. Many of these youth were in trouble with the law. They often appeared defiant and oppositional. They would go to great lengths to show how "in charge" they were. So, although they presented this impression of being in charge of their behavior, in reality, they were often out of control of their lives — they were expelled from school, community activities, and peer groups. Not to mention, they'd been sent to court, mental health services, and sometimes inpatient services.

These kids habitually got themselves into trouble, while continually trying to give the impression that they were in charge of their destiny. I asked teens who'd gotten into these kinds of patterns (and worse) whether, if given the choice, they'd rather be a slave or the master. Without exception, they'd immediately respond, "The master." Then, I would ask, "So, why do you choose to be the slave?"

They'd often look in disbelief with a "What do you mean?" expression on their faces. I'd explain, "Your emotional urges have become the master, and you're nothing but a slave to your emotions." They were no longer in control of their lives. Because they couldn't control their emotions, they'd get into trouble and abuse drugs or alcohol.

Most adolescents don't like being slaves, or even being told what to do by others. Reframing the issue gets them thinking about the problem in a new light. After all, if they were the master, they should at least have some control over their emotions. I'd then challenge them to prove me wrong by showing me areas in their lives in which they were in control.

This challenge put me in a win-win situation. If they controlled their behaviors going forward (and I was wrong), they'd start to show improvement. If I was right (they misbehaved), they'd want to find out more about how not to be a slave.

When you try to get people to change habits, you need to start off by gauging their readiness to change. The first stage of change is referred to as the *pre-contemplation stage.* The person who needs to change says, "I'm just fine the way I am, thank you." At this stage, interventions such as invoking fear or providing education, or even therapy, don't likely change someone's behaviors for very long.

In order to motivate change at this stage, you may want to reframe the problem in a way that offers a combination of self-interest and opportunity for self-control. Show the person how she can change her behavior, but only if she wants to improve her life. For example, a friend of mine was having some serious dental work done. The dentist told him he needed to floss his teeth each night as part of his recovery plan. He told his dentist that he was far too busy for that. At that point, the dentist could have scared him, educated him, or used any of a number of techniques. Instead, he simply said, "Okay, just floss the teeth you want to keep." By giving the person the right framework in which he or she can take charge of the problem, you increase your likelihood of success.

Understanding body language

Studies show that your body language communicates up to 50 percent of what you want to say. If you don't believe people can read your body language, you might want to spend some time with some world-champion poker players. They seem to be very good at reading people's intentions. Still skeptical? Try a few rounds of poker with one of them.

Poker players call nonverbal reactions during the game *tells* — probably because these reactions tell a lot about you. You're probably familiar with subtle facial cues, such as raising an eyebrow, scratching a head, or biting a lip. Poker players often wear sunglasses and visor caps to hide some of these cues.

You can learn a lot about dealing with people from the observations of poker players. For example, if you see someone looking unhappy, he may be feeling vulnerable and weak. You may use that as a cue to support that person. Likewise, an overconfident look may signal that the person is overly sure of herself. Signs to look for that may imply weakness or vulnerability include a faster heart rate, dry throat, muscle twitches, trembling hands or voice, and dilated pupils. On the other hand, a confident person may also have a faster heart rate. Someone trying to lead you the wrong way or deceive you in how he feels may hold his body still and restrict his breathing.

Poker players also report that posture can be an important tell. A player may change posture in reaction to a hand. Slumping is believed to represent a weak hand and lack of confidence. Leaning forward is believed to be associated with bluffing, and sitting straight and attentive is supposed to represent having a strong hand. Think of someone's posture as you interact with him. What signals can you read from his leaning towards you, shifting away from you, or maintaining a stiff and awkward position?

You can better understand your own body language by observing the body language of other people. Paying attention to others can help you become more aware of how facial expressions and body posture change to reflect various emotions. That knowledge can help you improve your ability to recognize some of these behaviors in yourself. For more on this topic, check out *Body Language For Dummies* by Elizabeth Kuhnke (Wiley).

Identifying anger

Think of the last time that you saw someone who was angry. What clues did you have about this person's emotional disposition? You may have noticed some obvious signs, such as

- Yelling and screaming
- Pushing or kicking

✔ Bulging eyes

✔ Red face

✔ Bared teeth

✔ Pursed lips

✔ Sneering or snarling

✔ Clenched fists

✔ Leaning his or her face toward the other person, invading that person's space

✔ Staring or squinting eyes

Some of these signs may seem obvious or exaggerated, but the angry person can also express them in more subtle forms.

Recognizing fear or anxiety

You probably have some idea about what a person looks like when he or she is nervous or afraid:

✔ Sweaty face

✔ Pale complexion

✔ Dry mouth and throat

✔ Darting eyes

✔ High-pitched voice

✔ Tense muscles

✔ Fidgety body

✔ Increased heart rate

If people feel defensive, they often cross their arms or legs.

Sensing sadness

People feeling sad give you clues through their body language, including

✔ Drooping body

✔ Downcast eyes

✔ Teary eyes

- Downturned mouth
- Trembling bottom lip
- Speaking using a flat tone

These signs might be more subtle in some people than in others.

Seeing embarrassment

Another emotion revealed by body language is embarrassment. People who feel embarrassed may

- Become red or flushed in the face
- Look away from others
- Avoid any direct eye contact
- Have a false smile or grimace
- Try to avoid certain topics of conversation

Spotting surprise

When someone's surprised, you may notice that his or her

- Eyebrows go up
- Eyes widen
- Mouth opens
- Body makes a sudden backward motion or movement

Knowing happiness

Some of the signs of people who are happy include

- Smiles on their faces
- Smiles that include both the mouth and eyes
- Relaxed bodies
- Smiles that show teeth
- Open arms and legs
- Open hands
- Relaxed and prolonged eye contact

Reading your emotions through other people

Other people can often read how you feel about something before you're even aware of your feelings. Sometimes, no matter how hard you try to hide your feelings (or even disguise them as other feelings), someone else can see through to your true feelings. You're usually thinking of the thing itself — some bad news or good news, for example — and you don't focus on your reactions to the news. People around you can often easily read these reactions, especially if you're close to those people.

In the work world, human resource consultants, business coaches, or psychologists often assess leaders and executives by *360 degree assessments,* which are inventories or checklists in which the leaders rate themselves on a number of dimensions. (For more information on 360 degree assessments, see Chapter 4.) These dimensions can include items such as

✔ I'm patient.

✔ I listen to people around me.

✔ I rarely get ruffled or shaken.

Look at the emotions checklist you complete in the section "Identifying Your Emotions," earlier in this chapter. (If you haven't done that activity yet, do it now.) With that completed list in hand, follow these steps:

1. **Review the emotions that you marked as negative and select the one that you want to reduce in frequency or intensity.**

   Choose one of the emotions, such as anger or annoyance, that occurs most frequently in your day-to-day activities.

2. **Review your positive emotions and select one that you want to experience more frequently or intensely.**

   These emotions can include happiness and calmness.

3. **Identify how you typically display each of the emotions you select in Steps 1 and 2.**

   How does your face look? What about your body posture? Are you obvious, or do you tend to be more poker-faced? Imagine yourself experiencing the emotion. Imagine looking at yourself from the outside during the emotional experience.

4. **Gather input from someone close to you.**

You can turn to a spouse, friend, or anyone else you see on a fairly regular basis. Tell him that you're curious about some of your reactions to things:

a. Ask whether he has ever noticed times when you experienced the negative emotion that you picked in Step 1.

Start with a general question, such as, "How do I seem to you during those times?" If that question isn't specific enough, ask how he can tell when you're experiencing that negative emotion — what do you say, how do you look, and how does it make them feel?

b. Ask whether he has noticed times when you were experiencing the positive emotion that you chose in Step 2.

How did you act during those times? How did you display the emotion? How did your emotional state affect the other person? Although most people appreciate positive feelings from others, some people may find them annoying. Usually, people don't find the positive feeling annoying, but rather the way in which that feeling is expressed.

When you get feedback from others on your emotions, you can better gauge your emotions. Sometimes, you're so focused on what's happening around you that you don't stop and think about how that situation is actually affecting you. Enlisting the help of those you know, and who know you, can help you get an outside opinion that provides an additional dimension to your understanding.

Changing Negative Emotions

Sometimes, you want to change your emotions. Most likely, you want to change your emotions when they're on the negative side. Nobody really enjoys feeling depressed, angry, humiliated, jealous, or any of a number of negative emotions. Does this mean that you should always be feeling happy? Definitely not.

Some negative emotions, such as grief, are part of the normal human experience. Not only would you find it difficult to eliminate an emotion such as grief, eliminating that emotion wouldn't make sense. Grief is a part of the human experience that all people undergo at some point in their lives when they lose someone dear to them. It's your built-in way of dealing with loss, and it forms part of the healing experience. Ignore your grief at your own peril. People who try to ignore deep emotions such as grief usually pay an emotional price over time. Bad feelings (often triggered by memories) tend to resurface again and again if a person doesn't resolve them by working through the intense feelings of loss.

So, when might you want to change your emotions? Most likely, when those emotions are self-defeating and don't help you get on with your life. How do you know when emotions are self-defeating? One clue is that they're thwarting your goals. When the emotional experience interferes with your ability to deal with other people constructively, to accomplish things at work or school, or to contribute in any positive way to the world around you, you may have a problem.

Recognizing negative emotions

Negative emotions are strong feelings that interfere with your ability to do things in life you want to do. They get in the way when you're trying to think clearly and deal with the person or situation that's upsetting you. Emotions evolved as a signaling system. Your negative emotions are designed to signal and motivate you to action, so think of those negative emotions as a message that something's wrong.

The problem that people often face, however, is that the strength of the message makes it get in the way of useful action. People often wallow in the emotion itself, which becomes the focus of their attention, so people don't deal with the cause of the emotion. (I talk about getting to the cause of the emotion in the section "Using the ABCDE theory of emotions," later in this chapter.)

You can identify how unhelpful your negative emotions are by thinking of them along a temperature-like scale. Negative emotions are hot at the intense end of the scale and cool at the calm end of the scale. Hot feelings tend to spiral your mood and thoughts in a tornado-like fashion. Cool feelings, on the other hand, although still unpleasant, aren't as extreme.

You can be more effective if you experience cool feelings in response to adverse situations, such as a job loss or troubled marriage. Table 5-1 shows you the difference between hot emotions and their cool counterparts.

Table 5-1	Hot and Cold Feelings
Hot Feelings	*Cool Feelings*
Rage, fury, and anger	Annoyance and irritation
Despondency, despair, depression, and pessimism	Sadness
Severe guilt, intense remorse	Regret
Self-worthlessness, self-hate	Self-disappointment
Anxiety, fear, and panic	Concern

This activity helps you become more aware of your negative emotions and their range. For each emotion that follows, give a definition and list as many synonyms as you can. This example shows you what I mean:

> **Emotion:** Anger
>
> **Definition:** An emotional state that may range in intensity from mild annoyance to rage. Anger has physical effects, including raised heart rate, blood pressure, and tensing of the facial muscles.
>
> **Synonyms:** Irritation, annoyance, fury, ire, outrage, rage, wrath

List definitions and synonyms for the following emotions:

- Disgust
- Fear
- Sadness

Using the ABCDE theory of emotions

The ABCDE theory of emotions, actually called the Rational Emotive Behavior Theory, was originally devised by psychologist Dr. Albert Ellis in the 1950s. Basically, it divides most forms of emotional upset (in milder forms) or emotional disturbance (in its more extreme form) into the following specific parts:

- **Activating event (A).** The *activating event,* or *A,* is an outside event that most people blame for their problems:

  - He insulted me.

  - My boyfriend left me.

  - They didn't give me the job.

  - The teacher gave me a lousy grade.

- **Beliefs (B).** Most people wrongly believe that outside events cause them to be upset, angry, nonproductive, and so on. The activating events don't actually cause people to be upset, but rather their *beliefs* (the *B*), meaning the things that they tell themselves about these events, lead them to feel negative emotions. For example, you might think, "He insulted me, so I must be a bad person." It would not be the insult itself that upsets you (many people get insulted without feeling bad), but rather dwelling on the second part of your belief — that somehow you must be flawed.

✔ **Consequence (C).** The *consequence* (the *C*) can be any number of self-defeating emotions — such as depression, anxiety, self-pity, or procrastination. Most people begin the ABCDE process at C — the consequence — telling you they're upset, angry, or some other negative emotion.

After someone identifies that she is upset, mad, sad, or some other negative emotion, that person usually makes a mental leap to A, the activating event. What was the activating event — what caused the negative emotion? So you would typically say, "I'm mad because he insulted me." You believe that the insult caused you to be mad (insult (A) = mad (C)).

In fact, most people think the activating events in their lives cause their consequences, meaning their emotional upsets. But it's thoughts, not activating events, that cause emotional upsets.

✔ **Dispute (D).** *D* stands for the *dispute* you raise about the beliefs (B) related to the activating event (A).

The dispute phase involves questioning both rational and irrational thoughts or beliefs that you have about the activating event.

✔ **Effect (E).** The *E* stands for the *effect.* When you experience cooler emotions, your mind and body are relatively relaxed and open to ideas about how to rationally approach a situation.

Chapter 6

Managing Your Emotions

● ●

In This Chapter

▶ Exploring some coping mechanisms

▶ Getting the best out of a bad situation

▶ Controlling your emotions

● ●

*E*veryone has bad days — days when nothing seems to go right. From the moment you get out of bed, you feel that it's not going to be a good day. You might start off with a low-grade headache. You may hear some bad news from your radio alarm. Your partner might greet your awakening with some unnecessary or unwelcome comment or information.

When a day begins in this way, are you doomed for the rest of the day? Why even bother to get out of bed? Maybe you can hide somewhere for the next 24 hours — say, in front of a TV screen or computer. Although these options might sound possible at first, you really can't run away from the day. For all sorts of reasons, you have to face the rest of the day — or, at least, some portion of it. In this chapter, I show you some ways to try to navigate your way to a better destination — mentally, that is.

Okay, I Feel Sad, Mad, or Bad — Now What?

In Chapter 5, you see how to identify feelings that cause you problems. Generally speaking, you can break down these feelings into groups:

✔ **Sad:** Depressed

✔ **Mad:** Angry, jealous

✔ **Bad:** Anxious, fearful

Now, suppose that these negative feelings are severe enough to get in the way of your everyday level of functioning. The following sections provide some tools to help you regain your focus.

If your negative feelings are severe enough to require professional attention, call a help line, psychologist, psychiatrist, social worker, or any other professional who may be accessible.

Using cognitive restructuring

One widely used approach to dealing with negative feelings is referred to as *cognitive restructuring.* This is a form of cognitive-behavior therapy originated by psychologist Dr. Albert Ellis and psychiatrist Dr. Aaron Beck, who worked independently of each other. You can find some variations in how psychologists and other mental health professionals apply cognitive restructuring in practice, but the general principles are pretty standard. Basically, the main idea of this approach can be summed up as "you are what you think."

The basic premise of the technique is that you figure out how to dispute or refute cognitive distortions. *Cognitive distortions* are the sets of thoughts that you tell yourself about a situation or person, such as a troubling situation. You want to replace the irrational or distorted cognitions with healthier, more accurate or beneficial thoughts.

According to this theory, your unrealistic or unhealthy beliefs directly cause your negative or dysfunctional emotions and the behaviors that result. People have resolved the following unhealthy feelings by using cognitive restructuring:

- ✔ Stress
- ✔ Social anxiety
- ✔ Impulsiveness
- ✔ Procrastination
- ✔ Low self-regard

Follow these steps to go through the process of cognitive restructuring:

1. **Think of a situation or time in which you experienced negative feelings, such as stress, anxiety, depression, or anger.**

   Try to remember as much as you can about what happened, how you felt, what you thought, and your behaviors.

2. **Write the following column headings across two pages of your notebook:**

   - Activating Event

   - Feelings About Event

   - Initial Thoughts

   - Supporting Thoughts

   - Non-Supporting Thoughts

   - Balanced Thoughts

   - Mood

   - Action Plan

3. **In the Activating Event column, write the situation (or activating event) that you believe caused the bad mood.**

   For example, suppose that Alice receives negative feedback from her boss at work on a report that she prepared for him. Her boss tells her that the report was poorly done. He expected so much more from her. So, in the first column, Alice writes down a brief description of the situation or event with her boss.

4. **In the Feelings About Event column, record your feeling about the event.**

   Remember, stick to feelings or emotions, not thoughts. Usually, you can describe an emotion in a single word; anything longer probably constitutes your thoughts or interpretations.

   In Alice's case, she feels dejected, sad, and humiliated.

5. **In the Initial Thoughts column, write your automatic or initial thoughts about the situation.**

   Alice's thoughts included

   - My work was awful.

   - I must be really bad at my job.

   - My boss is a jerk.

   - I feel worthless.

   - I must be a bad person.

   - Maybe I should quit my job.

6. **Use the Supporting Thoughts and Non-Supporting Thoughts columns to dispute the negative thoughts.**

In the Supporting Thoughts column, you write evidence that supports the thoughts. In the Non-Supporting Thoughts column, you record evidence that doesn't support the thoughts.

Alice's supporting thoughts include

- This was not my best work, and I can see where he would have found flaws.

- Maybe I could have spent a bit more time putting it together.

- I was distracted when working on this project.

Evidence that doesn't support Alice's thoughts might be

- The work may have some flaws, but it's not awful.

- This one project isn't a measure of how good I am, overall, at my job.

- I've done better work in the past, so I am capable of good work.

- I know it's not my best work, but it's not awful. And even if it was bad, does that make me a bad or awful person?

- One bad assignment doesn't mean I can't do my job or that I should quit.

- How does the quality of my work, especially on one project, define me as a person?

- Not everyone gets everything right all the time.

7. **In the Balanced Thoughts column, fill in conclusions you reach after analyzing the situation.**

   Balanced thoughts are thoughts that, after you look at the supporting and non-supporting thoughts, get you to a more fair and balanced place. You may even want to discuss everything up to this point with someone you trust or whose opinion you value. Having another person weigh in on the facts of the case and your thoughts about it can help you come to a more balanced conclusion.

8. **After you review all your thoughts and feelings, write in the Balanced Thoughts column your more balanced take of the situation.**

   Alice might write

   - I really didn't apply myself well in this case, and I seemed to lose focus. But I know that if I'm determined, I can do a much better job.

   - My performance at work — or anywhere else, for that matter — doesn't define me as a person.

   - In the past, I've received praise for my work on projects similar to this one.

9. **In the Mood column, record any change you experience in your feelings about the situation.**

   Based on your findings, what can you now do about the situation? If you can change the situation by doing something different, you can start planning that action. In some cases, you may not be able to change the situation, but you might change your thoughts and feelings about it. By thinking about the situation in a more realistic and constructive way, you will begin to feel differently about the situation.

10. **Use the Action Plan column to create a plan for how you want to move forward with this situation.**

    In Alice's case, she could list what she wants to say to her boss. Perhaps she'd apologize and acknowledge that her report could have been better. She might write down some follow-up actions, such as taking back the report and reworking it, as needed. Don't forget to assign due dates to each task.

Cognitive restructuring is a useful tool to help you think about the problem in a different way and actually change your mood or emotions. Use your notebook and the structure provided in this section to help you work your way through difficult emotional situations.

For more about this topic, check out *Cognitive Behavioural Therapy For Dummies*, by Rob Wilson and Rhena Branch (Wiley).

Methods of distraction

At times, you may feel so bad that all you want to do is escape. And, at times, escape can be a helpful strategy. Getting away from a bad situation, as long as you're not shirking responsibilities, can help you rest and refocus — especially in stressful situations. The simplest method, of course, is to simply remove yourself from the situation. Depending on the size of the bad situation, you could do something as easy as silently counting to ten or leaving the room, or as complicated as taking a vacation.

Taking yourself out of the situation can give you some time to coolly and thoughtfully reflect on what's happening. It also may prevent you from escalating your bad feelings and perhaps saying something you might regret later. Think of this kind of break as recharging your batteries.

You have many options that involve distracting you from your current situation. Some of these options are helpful, and others may be harmful. Here are some helpful methods for coping:

✔ Take a deep breath

✔ Go for a walk

✔ Count to ten slowly

✔ Look for alternative strategies

✔ Make lists

✔ Let your emotions surface

✔ Exercise

✔ Talk to someone close to you

✔ Meditate, practice yoga, or listen to soothing tapes

Some structured ways of relaxing involve temporarily distracting yourself from your negative feelings and the world around you. The following sections cover these forms of relaxation or awareness, including deep muscle relaxation, breathing exercises, meditation, and mindfulness.

Relaxation, meditation, and similar activities

You can use a number of physical and mental activities to become calmer and more relaxed. Using these techniques not only impacts your mental condition, but also changes your body's physiological state for the better. The most effective way to use these techniques is to make them part of your everyday routine. Instead of waiting for a crisis to occur, then searching for a quick fix, integrate one of these techniques into your lifestyle.

Most of these activities can be done in ten minutes or less. Considering the amount of time you may currently spend having coffee, reading the newspaper, surfing the Web, or watching TV, ten minutes is a small price to pay to create a calmer world.

Activities that involve motion help you physically by releasing endorphins, especially when you use a physical exercise routine. People who exercise regularly not only reduce stress but also tend to be more cheerful. Also, having a sense of control over your body increases your confidence.

Progressive relaxation

Originated by the psychologist Edmund Jacobson and further refined by Robert Benson and Joseph Wolpe, progressive relaxation can be effective in reducing high blood pressure, irritable bowel syndrome, and general anxiety.

You don't find relaxation exercises very effective during sudden or acute anxiety attacks. For these kinds of episodes, you might want to check out belly breathing and acupressure, covered in the following sections.

To begin, you need a quiet, carpeted area, free from distractions. Follow these steps:

1. **Take off your shoes, loosen your clothing, lie down on your back, and close your eyes.**

2. **Clench your fists tightly for ten seconds and focus on the tension in your hands.**

3. **Relax your grip.**

   Notice the sensation of heaviness and warmth.

4. **Flex your biceps for ten seconds, again focusing on the tension.**

5. **Relax the area and note the difference in the sensation.**

6. **Follow the same flex, hold, and relax procedure with your forearms.**

7. **Wrinkle your facial muscles, then relax.**

8. **Work your way down, flexing and relaxing, through your shoulders, chest, stomach, lower back, buttocks, thighs, calves, and feet.**

   While you carry out the tensing exercises, tell yourself that you're becoming more relaxed.

9. **After you finish a complete cycle, lie still for a while and enjoy the calm.**

10. **When you're ready, get up slowly.**

    You might feel a bit light-headed getting up. This is normal after this procedure. Move carefully for the first few minutes.

Don't attempt these exercises if you suffer from any muscle ailments. If necessary, you can modify the exercise to adapt to your condition, but check with a healthcare professional first.

Diaphragmatic or belly breathing

At first, belly breathing might sound unusual and maybe even peculiar. Usually, when you breathe, you fill your lungs with air by lifting your ribcage while inhaling and lowering your ribcage when exhaling. Breathing this way can actually magnify your hot emotional states. It can also raise your heart rate, adding to the feeling of anxiety.

When you belly breathe, you hold your ribcage steady. You actually breathe through your diaphragm, which is located lower, down in the stomach area. Wind-instrument musicians commonly breath from the diaphragm. When I first started to play the saxophone as a child, I practiced breathing through my diaphragm. Now, when I'm practicing or performing, this type of breathing comes naturally.

Follow these steps to belly breathe:

1. **Find a quiet area that's relatively free from distractions.**

2. **Loosen your shirt or blouse and take off your shoes.**

3. **Lie on your back and close your eyes.**

4. **Place one hand on your chest and the other one on your belly.**

5. **Start breathing normally.**

   Pay attention to what happens to your body. Notice how your hands move with your breathing.

6. **Breathe through your nose and let your belly expand and power your inhalation.**

   Keep your chest and ribcage as still as possible.

7. **Exhale slowly through your partially opened mouth.**

When you practice, you can soon let your expanding belly do the inhaling for you and allow your contracting belly to direct your breath out.

Repeat this cycle for five minutes. Afterwards, you should feel refreshed and relaxed.

One of the advantages of belly breathing is that you can use it during moments of stress. You can belly breathe while you're sitting, standing, or even walking. If you can't close your eyes, you can focus on an object nearby and continue the breathing.

Acupressure

Acupressure works along the same principles as acupuncture and Shiatsu massage. To practice acupressure on yourself, follow these steps:

1. **Using your thumb and forefinger, squeeze the fleshy area between the thumb and forefinger of your other hand.**

   You should feel a slightly uncomfortable, but not painful, sensation.

2. **Keep applying the pressure for about five seconds.**

3. **Repeat, using your other hand.**

4. **Repeat the entire cycle (both hands) two more times.**

   Any sense of tension should recede.

Purposeful distraction

You can practice purposeful distraction in a number of ways:

- ✔ **Write down a list of things that you can do when you feel overtaken by stress.** Sometimes, just writing out a list can give you a sense of control. It helps build confidence because you're planning ahead.

- ✔ **Replace thoughts.** Whenever you start having worrying thoughts, practice replacing them with pleasant and peaceful images, such as a seashore, clouds floating in the sky, or a forest filled with the sounds of birds.

- ✔ **Identify thoughts or actions that worsen your anxiety.** For example, when you're stuck in traffic, continuing to look at the clock every 30 seconds makes you more tense. Change your car display from the clock to something else, such as the temperature, if you have that option. You can also switch from talk radio to a classical-music or soft-jazz station.

Give yourself worry breaks by following these steps:

1. **On a piece of paper, write down the issue that causes you to worry.**

2. **Next to the issue, write down a time and date that you plan to revisit the issue.**

   For example, today at 7:10 p.m.

3. **Put the paper in an envelope and seal that envelope.**

   After you write down the worry and a time to focus on it, try to stop thinking about it until then. Just tell yourself that you've taken care of it for now.

4. **When the designated time arrives, open the envelope and give yourself exactly three minutes to think about the issue and how to deal with it.**

5. **If, at the end of three minutes, you're still not satisfied, write down a new time to think about this issue and put the piece of paper back in an envelope until then.**

6. **Repeat the process until the worry no longer bothers you.**

How mindfulness works

When you practice mindfulness, your purpose in life becomes being awake and aware of the moment, first and foremost. Mindfulness is one of the more popular versions of meditation that psychologists, coaches, and trainers use. Dr. Jon Kabat-Zinn developed this technique, which centers around being aware of the present moment. Using this method, you leave behind any judging, thinking, or reflecting that may be part of your usual pattern. You think of the moment as a breath of air and focus on one breath after the other, moment by moment.

Follow these steps to practice an exercise in mindfulness:

1. **Sit in a comfortable chair or lie down in a comfortable position.**

   Try to maintain a posture of dignity and wakefulness. This is a position in which you feel very secure and sure of yourself while being awake and aware.

2. **Think of this moment.**

   Forget about anything in the past or the future that you may have been thinking about and focus on now.

3. **Hold this moment in awareness.**

   Try, for as long as you can, to keep your focus on the moment.

4. **Attend to your senses.**

   Pay attention to what you smell, touch, hear, and taste, as well as your breathing.

5. **Focus on your breathing.**

   Pay attention to your breathing without trying to change it. Feel the breath coming in and out. Breathe gently in and out. Follow the air as it moves into your belly and then out again.

6. **(Optional) You can close your eyes, if you want, but continue focusing on your breath.**

   Keep feeling it going in and out. Rest in your awareness by relaxing and keeping your focus.

7. **Try to ignore your thoughts.**

   Your thoughts naturally try to comment on your experience. But drop down below, to a deeper, gentler level of awareness and experience your breath.

8. **Anytime you notice that your mind is no longer focused on your breath, let your awareness recognize what's on your mind.**

9. **Return to focusing on your breath, thus focusing on the present.**

Mindfulness is a skill that you need to practice if you want to get the most out of it. After you master remaining in the here and now, you can expand your awareness to your different senses. Instead of getting involved in sounds, thoughts, emotions, and so on, however, you just observe them passing through you. In your restful, calm state, you simply attend to the passing experiences. You don't judge or deal with any of your thoughts while they pass through your mind. You observe them, like a person outside of yourself, and then focus back to awareness of your breath.

Working Your Way Out of a Bad Situation

Although you can try to protect yourself by preparing yourself for the bad things that hit you in life, surprises do happen. In fact, life is full of surprises. And some of those surprises are bad ones.

You can have a wide range of bad experiences, from the really big ones (such as serious illnesses and loss) to the smaller ones (such as someone taking your coffee cup at work). A person's first reaction to bad news or a bad situation is always an emotional one. If the emotions run hot, then you may have more trouble problem-solving your way out of the bad experience.

Short-term approaches

You can't always predict where your next surprise will come from. But you can start to inoculate yourself to deal with unexpected events. Start by looking at your current way of dealing with unexpected events. How do you react, for example, when someone you know has let you down? Do you spring into anger mode? Or do you get depressed and blame yourself?

People aren't always reliable. At least, they don't always behave the way you want them to. Everyone has expectations of other people, and everyone has experienced people not living up to those expectations. So, part of your strategy should involve accepting that piece of reality.

When someone lets you down, you can react, in the short term, by accepting it. Acknowledge to yourself that something unpleasant has happened, and then start to look at any alternatives you may have for dealing with the behavior itself and your feelings about it.

You have to accept your feelings, as well as the other person's behavior. If you initially feel anger or depression, prepare yourself so that you can change anger to frustration or annoyance, or depression to sadness or disappointment. The sooner you can manage your feelings, the sooner you can deal with your thoughts and move on to the next steps of your life.

Consider Jeanette's situation. Jeanette's waiting outside a theater, looking up and down the street. She was supposed to meet George 15 minutes ago, and she still sees no sign of him. She tries calling his cell phone, but he doesn't answer.

The movie's starting, and she doesn't know what to do. It's unlike him to stand her up. Something must be wrong. She decides to call him one more time.

"Hello," he finally answers.

"George, where are you? I'm waiting outside the theater for you," Jeanette pleads.

"Oh, no. I forgot. Sorry, Jeanette," he sheepishly answers. "Something's come up, and I can't make it."

"Something's come up? And you're telling me now?" she responds. "What could be so important?"

"Things got crazy at work, and I didn't realize it would go this late. Sorry, I'll make it up to you. What about Friday night?"

"Forget it. Talk to you later. Bye." Jeanette hangs up.

She's perplexed. How could George do this to her? What's the matter with him? Doesn't he even care?

Jeanette has a choice at this point. She can stew in her anger and think of all kinds of things she can do to get revenge. Or she can accept that George might be unreliable and move on to consider the kind of relationship she really wants to have.

Setbacks such as the one Jeanette experienced can give you opportunities to reflect — time to stop, step back, and look at the big picture.

Long-term solutions

Taking a long view means you look at the way you see yourself here and now, as well as look ahead at where you want to be in two, five, or ten years down the road. Every once in a while, stop and think about your world and how you fit in — what you like, what you want to change — because you want most of your energy and effort in life to be going towards your long-term goals and happiness.

By using your emotions, you can make a *gut check*. How do you feel — in your gut — about your current place in the world? Follow these steps to get in touch with your gut:

1. **In your notebook, write a list of things that you're currently happy with in your life.**

   Spend a few minutes reflecting on your accomplishments.

2. **Write a list of those things that you want to change in your life.**

   This list can include your job, some of your friends, or how you spend your leisure time. Use your feelings to guide you along.

3. **Write where you want to be in the areas that you want to change.**

   This list might include such things as new friends or new hobbies.

Taking a long view can help you better prepare for some of life's roadblocks. Having alternatives that you can pursue when your world changes or when you're ready to change your world can really enhance your life down the road. It makes it a bit easier to deal with some of life's major changes.

Changing Your Emotions for the Better

Practicing some of the techniques covered in this chapter can help you better manage your emotions. You want to be in charge of your emotions, instead of being enslaved by them. You don't have to (and shouldn't) minimize or restrict your feelings, but rather control the dosages and timing of your emotions.

Some people still believe that you can't change your emotions. They think that things happen; you get mad, sad, or even glad; and you can't do anything about it. If you believe that emotions have a life of their own or that you can't influence them, consider the following example.

Ilana just finished getting feedback about her work from her supervisor, Rob. Although Rob was pleasant and offered a number of suggestions for Ilana to improve her performance, he also gave her some specific comments about a report she had recently written.

He started his conversation by telling her the report was superficial and would need substantial changes before being approved. At that point her head started to spin. She was in quite a shock. She had spent weeks putting her heart and soul into that report only now to have it criticized. She heard little else of the conversation after that.

After Rob left the room, her emotions turned to anger. She was absolutely furious at Rob for belittling her work. In her anger she fired off an e-mail to her boyfriend: "That loser Rob did it to me again. I can't understand how he got to be a supervisor here. He's such an idiot. I don't even think he read my report, he just gets off on putting me down. See you for dinner, Love Ilana."

Unfortunately her boyfriend's name also happens to be Robert. So when she typed the first few letters of his name in the "To" field she quickly accepted her e-mail application's autocomplete suggestion and pressed the Send button.

A second afterward she realized she forgot to check to which Rob she sent the e-mail. Her emotion quickly changed to fear. After she saw that she'd e-mailed her boss, she went into shock and terror.

Notice how her raw anger changed quickly into fear, followed by terror. In a very brief period of time it's possible to experience a number of different emotions. See the sidebar "Giving Anger the Boot" in Chapter 3 for another example of this.

Emotions can change, and they can change quickly.

Recognizing the importance of practice

Think of emotional coping and distraction techniques in the same way that you think of getting in shape at the gym or playing a sport. All these activities take practice. You can't just walk onto the tennis court, having not played for months, and expect to play a great game.

Whichever emotional change method you use — relaxation, mindfulness, cognitive restructuring — be sure to practice it. For example, practice meditation every day. Many people meditate twice a day.

If you choose to practice mindfulness, try to use it several times a day. One of the advantages of mindfulness is that you can practice it anywhere. For example, if you're waiting at the dentist's office, seated in your office chair, or waiting in the grocery store checkout line, you can practice following your breath, or concentrating on being present in the here and now.

Developing a positive psychology

Managing your emotions includes developing a positive psychology of life. *Positive psychology* has become a major movement in the field of psychology. It centers around awareness, understanding, and focusing on human strengths.

For many years, psychology has spent enormous energy and resources on the abnormal or problem aspects of people. Now, a lot of research and practice focus on the benefits of finding and developing your strengths.

This perspective can help you look at yourself differently. Instead of focusing on your weaknesses and areas where you know you're vulnerable, spend more time understanding your strengths and figuring out how to leverage them in your work and at home.

Lynn, for example, always worries about her academic skills. She knows she's not a strong student, and she feels that her difficulty with academic skills holds her back at work. She takes advantage of every training opportunity that's available to her at work. She goes to courses on grammar, basic accounting skills, speaking effectively, project planning, and more.

Although Lynn enjoys the training opportunities, she eventually realizes that she can progress only so far in these areas. She's fine with the basics, but the intermediate and advanced skills are over her head.

One day, almost as a joke, she decides to take a course in empathy training. She knows from feedback of others that she's a natural at listening to people and helping them through problem situations. But she's never heard of an empathy course before, and she's not even quite sure what empathy entails.

Right from the start, she's like a fish in water. Everything the instructor says makes so much sense to her. She excels in the course and goes on to take more advanced courses in related areas.

Lynn eventually realizes that she's been pursuing the wrong career path for years. She moves into customer service and discovers that she's a real fit.

Try to figure out what your strengths are. Seeing a counselor who's qualified in testing can often help you find out more about yourself. Taking tests such as the Emotional Quotient Inventory (EQ-i) (refer to Chapter 4) and a vocational interest test can help you identify your strengths.

Having a positive psychology means that you start to focus on some of your strengths. You might be good in the arts, sciences, creative endeavors, dealing with people, technical things, or something else. Starting out positively, believing that you possess hidden talents, and cultivating those talents can help you become more focused in your search. This increases the likelihood of your finding the career that matches your passions, skill sets, and talents, all making for a happier you.

People who feel that they're on the right path in their lives are generally more emotionally balanced. They feel more in tune with themselves and others around them.

Chapter 7

Understanding Empathy

You can view empathy as one of the hallmarks of emotional intelligence. It has a special role to play in just about every theory of emotional intelligence. Psychologists have done a great deal of research that looks at many aspects of empathy — how to define it, how it works, how to use it, how to improve it, how to explain it to others, and so on.

Empathy is so important, in part, because it can effectively and efficiently connect you with other people. It's also pretty versatile. On the one hand, empathy enables you to bond with your partner, children, close friends, and any other people you care about. On the other hand, empathy can help you out when you're in a tight spot with a difficult person.

Here's the good news: People can develop empathy. So, if you think you have mediocre or even poor skills in this area, you now know that you can improve. Even if you think you're pretty good at empathy, there's more good news — you can get even better!

After you obtain a good understanding of what empathy is (and what it isn't), you can improve your empathy skills. Like the other emotional intelligence skills I talk about in this book, developing empathy just takes some practice.

Knowing the Difference between Empathy and Sympathy

If you're like most people, you may not be clear on what exactly empathy means. In fact, most people tend to confuse one good emotion, empathy, with another useful emotion — sympathy.

Beginning with you, not I

Sympathy shows that you care about someone else's situation. An example of a sympathy statement is when Betty says, "Jill, I'm really sorry about your husband's accident."

Basically, Jill is expressing her feelings about Jill's husband's situation. This sentiment is very noble, considerate, and kind on Betty's part. It demonstrates that Betty cares about the tragic situation. A sympathy statement begins with an *I* declaration — it's about how I feel about you.

Empathy is a different emotion. *Empathy* expresses the notion that I understand how *you* feel right now. For example, John says, "Julius, you must be angry about what that driver just said to you."

In this example, John is saying that Julius must be feeling a certain way based on the circumstances. A good empathy statement acknowledges how the other person is feeling at the moment. John's statement has nothing to do with how John's feeling, but everything to do with John understanding how Julius is feeling. Empathy is like walking in another person's moccasins. One of the signature aspects of an empathy statement is that it usually involves a *you* statement, such as "you must be feeling. . . . "

The use of *I* versus *you* can help you distinguish empathy from sympathy. Empathy isn't better than sympathy; it's just different.

Knowing why the difference is important

You use sympathy when you want to express your feelings to someone else. Sympathy is very appropriate at certain times, such as when someone has just experienced a tragic situation — for example, the loss of a loved one, a serious accident or injury, or any other misfortune.

Expressing your sympathy to someone by saying you care about their situation is the decent thing to do. In times of pain, people feel comforted by the caring of other people. Experiencing someone's care and concern is a natural and important part of healing from loss or pain. Letting someone know how you feel is usually an end in and of itself.

Empathy, on the other hand, is often an opener. It enables you to get closer to the other person and helps you gain his trust. It shows not only that you care about his troubles, but that you really *know* what he is going through.

When you empathize with someone, you're enhancing the relationship and making it closer. You strengthen the ties or bonds of the relationship and feel you know that person better. Empathy is often the beginning of an interaction. It implies that you not only know what the other person is experiencing, but you're concerned about her ongoing plight. It also shows that you're not self-centered.

Most people today are too busy and self-absorbed to pay much attention to those around them. They hardly ever have the time or energy to deal with other people's issues. Expressing empathy shows that you stand out, that you're really interested in the plight of others. Of course, you have to be careful that you don't use empathy as a tool for manipulation, to falsely gain someone's trust, or use them in some way (see the sidebar, "Taking advantage of the power of empathy").

Taking advantage of the power of empathy

Here's a story of someone who uses empathy for her own ends. Karen was known as someone who took advantage of others. Sometimes it was obvious by the way she would get others to do things for her. She would start off by paying a lot of attention to the other person.

"Oh Ted, you must be exhausted after working so hard today," Karen began.

"Yes, I'm completely wiped," Ted replied.

"I'm sure you need a rest, let me get you a cold drink," she quickly volunteered.

"Gee, thanks Karen."

"Oh, Ted, while you're waiting, do you think you could move that table to the other side of the room for me? And when you're done I'd really appreciate it if you could hang those three pictures on the wall. They shouldn't be too heavy. Thanks for offering to help. That's so nice of you," Karen gushed as she fled the room to get the cold water (and escape the hard work she'd enlisted Ted to do).

Sympathy is a commonly expressed emotion. Most people display sympathy toward others who experience pain or misfortune. Empathy is less frequently experienced. You may know one or two people who are naturals at being empathic.

Journalists often described the late princess of Wales, Diana (sometimes referred to as the princess of hearts), as being a natural at empathy. Many stories appeared after her death from ordinary people who felt deeply touched by short encounters with her. Associates reported that her involvement in numerous worthy causes, such as AIDS research, were truly heartfelt. Her death was probably the most widely mourned, worldwide, in a generation.

Although people loved Diana for helping others, I believe her empathy was what made her especially endearing to the public. Many great and caring people have passed away over the past 10 or 20 years — world leaders, entertainers, charity workers, religious leaders, and others. But none have garnered as much world attention as Princess Diana.

Someone who's often mentioned as an extremely empathic person is former President Bill Clinton. I have spoken to several journalists who have spent time with him in interviews and at events. They have independently mentioned to me that when you're talking with Bill Clinton you feel like you're the only person in the room. He has a way of giving you his undivided attention.

How have his empathic skills served him? Well, apart from helping him get elected president of the United States twice, it probably was the most significant factor in getting him through the Monica Lewinsky affair relatively unscathed.

Using empathy to disarm others

Empathy has a way of disarming others. When you encounter a difficult situation with a service person, instead of getting angry, try empathy.

Jonathan has waited in line for over an hour to get into an exclusive nightclub with his date. The couple in front of him is starting to lose it. When the doorman tells them they have to wait another ten minutes, the guy decides to take it out on the doorman.

"This is stupid. Why can't you just let us in? We've been here an hour now. What difference does it make to you?" he says.

"Sorry, but I have to control the number of people getting inside. You don't have to wait much longer," the doorman replies.

"Screw you," the guy's partner says. "You're a jerk. What do you think you are, a cop?"

Needless to say, it was a long ten minutes until the doorman could finally admit them.

Jonathan, exasperated by this time, decides to take a different tact. "You must hate dealing with jerks like that," he tells the doorman.

"Comes with the job," the doorman replies.

"Still, guys like that must make you feel pretty awful. You have to be pretty cool not to let him tick you off," Jonathan continues.

"Yah, sure," the doorman chuckles. "Go on in."

Jonathan's natural inclination was to be upset and let his anger out. But he kept his cool and thought that honey would work better than lemons, in this case. Sure enough, it paid off.

Reading Other People's Emotions

Of course, empathy isn't simple — otherwise, you'd see a lot more of it in use. The first part of empathy involves knowing how to read someone else's emotions. Reading other people's emotions is a skill that you can develop.

Look at the four faces shown in Figure 7-1. Try to determine the emotion being expressed in each of the drawings. How strong would you say the emotion is in each face? Write this information in your notebook for each face:

- ✔ Emotion expressed
- ✔ Direction of emotion (whether it's positive, neutral, or negative)
- ✔ Intensity of emotion (on a scale from 0 to 10)
- ✔ Empathic statement that you can make based on this emotion

You can try to hone your emotion-reading skills by watching TV without the sound. Without hearing what people are saying, try to follow their facial expressions. Notice how you can see their emotional changes through both facial and body cues. Practicing this technique shows you how to pay more attention to the nonverbal signs of emotions.

You can start reading emotions by looking at another person's face. Is the mouth open or closed? Do you see more of a smile or a frown? Do the eyes match the emotion displayed by the mouth? One of the best ways to determine how honest someone's emotions are is to compare the eyes and the mouth. Someone's mouth may be smiling, but his or her eyes may look unhappy or appear blank.

Also, notice whether someone looks you directly in the eyes consistently, shifts his or her eyes back and forth, or simply avoids any eye contact altogether. Avoiding your eyes can be a sign of anxiety or shyness, or it may signal fear or dishonesty. When someone stares right back at you, that stance can be a challenge for power, to see who blinks first. It can also be a sign of mistrust — the person feels that he or she has to keep an eye on you.

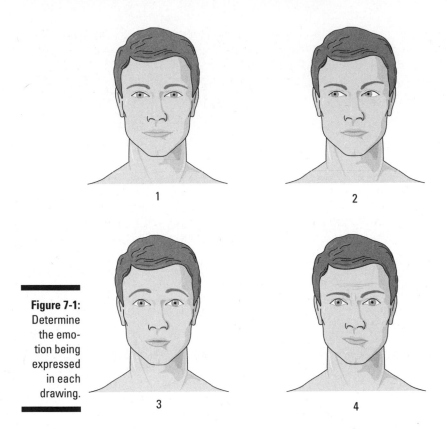

Figure 7-1: Determine the emotion being expressed in each drawing.

Eyes can tell you a lot about how a person feels. Look for wide-open and sparkling eyes for expressions of happiness. Downcast or dull-looking eyes reflect sadness. Although you can control your mouth to a large degree, you can't so easily control your eyes. William Shakespeare described your eyes as a window to your soul; they're also a signpost to your feelings.

Looking at a person's body language can also give you clues about his or her emotions. If a person folds his arms across his chest, he may be putting up a barrier, keeping others away. It can also signal hostility towards others. By looking at facial cues, you can get a better idea of where the person is coming from.

Slumped posture can indicate disinterest or boredom. An erect, tense posture can signal vigilance, attentiveness, or interest. Open arms or palms facing up can signal interest, and so can leaning forward, especially when the person also makes eye contact.

By paying more attention to people's body language and facial expressions, you can become more aware of what they may be feeling. Reading body language isn't an exact science, but it can provide you with clues or hypotheses that you can test out when you get more information. (Refer to Chapter 5 for more about body language.)

Walking in the other person's moccasins

Empathy is often referred to as "walking in the other person's moccasins." Your ability to know where another person is coming from, how he feels and thinks, helps make you feel like you really understand that person. You can often completely disarm a person by fully understanding him as another human being. By disarming someone you get to deal with his real feelings as opposed to the shell he wears for protection. Knowing how someone really feels allows you to offer him the help he might need.

Empathy, in many ways, is a form of selflessness. You step out of your own world — your problems, worries, joys, and responsibilities — to totally immerse yourself in another person's world.

Imagine that you're Norma. Norma's best friend, June, is going through a difficult time in her life. Her children have left home, and her ex-husband continues to cause her problems. She's never felt so alone in her life. She's at a real loss about what to do with herself. Until now, she was so busy raising her children that she had little time for interests of her own. Now, she feels empty.

Norma convinces June to go out for coffee together. Sitting at their table, June begins talking about her trials and tribulations.

"June, you sound like you're really feeling alone," Norma responds.

"Yes," June says, "I don't think I've ever felt this way before."

"It's not just the empty feeling," Norma continues, "but how hard it is for you to adjust to it."

Norma manages to reflect back what June tells her. She doesn't offer advice or interpret. Rather, she gets inside June's mindset and shows that she really understands how June is feeling and thinking.

Starting with what they say

So how do you go about empathizing with someone? Most importantly, you need to listen to the other person. Secondly, observe the other person.

When it comes to listening, you need to really focus on and pay attention to what the other person is saying. Sometimes, what someone says and what she means aren't exactly the same thing. You need to get to the bottom of what the other person *really* means. This process may take some practice. And you can usually connect more easily with people you already know.

When the other person is speaking to you, listen for any emotion in her tone of voice. For example, a friends says, "What Stan says about our relationship doesn't really bother me anymore." The tone and delivery might be contradictory. The person says "it really doesn't matter" with her words, but her tone of voice may be giving you the message that *it really does matter.* So, listen with your third ear. Your first two ears hear the words, but your third ear listens to the *music* — the tone, melody, and rhythm — that leads to the underlying meaning of the words.

If you read the person correctly, you may find yourself reflecting back something like, "You must feel very disappointed when he spreads those rumors."

When you correctly reflect the underlying experience of the other person, your relationship gets closer. A bond begins to develop. So, practice listening not just to the words, but to the music of the other person's voice.

Understanding what their faces tell you

When you interact with someone, pay attention to his facial cues. Here are some areas of the face you can observe and things you can learn about a person from them:

- ✔ **Eyes:** Someone's eyes can tell you a lot about where she is coming from. If the person is strong and steady, and believes in what she is telling you, her eyes look at you without backing away.

  Someone who doesn't look right at you is likely anxious or hiding something. She might look periodically at you but continue darting her eyes away. This behavior might signal some anxiety or avoidance.

✔ **Mouth:** Notice whether the person has more of a smile or a frown. The mouth can help you gauge the other person's feelings, especially when the eyes and mouth are telling the same story. Wide open, sparkling eyes along with a smiling mouth that has teeth showing display happiness. Narrow, beady eyes, pencil-thin lips, a scowl, or a grimace can display anger or discomfort.

✔ **Forehead:** Is the person's forehead smooth or wrinkled? A wrinkled forehead may be a sign of thinking or being perplexed. A sweating forehead can be a sign of anxiety.

✔ **Eyebrows:** The position of the eyebrows may also provide you with some clues to the person's feelings. Lowered eyebrows can signal deception or displeasure. They can be an unintended attempt to hide the eyes. Raised eyebrows, on the other hand, can signal surprise or questioning. For example, they can signal someone asking, "Are you sure?" Pushing together the eyebrows and raising the forehead can signal relief. Moving the eyebrows up and down quickly can be part of a greeting or welcoming gesture.

To become more empathetic, you must check with the other person to determine his feelings. If you try this exercise with someone close to you, hopefully that person can be honest. But remember that some people may not be truly aware of where they're coming from when they give certain opinions or try to express how they feel. By explaining why you came to your conclusion about how the other person was feeling ("Oh, it's just that you were looking down when you made that statement"), you may help the person take another look at what he was feeling.

When you practice reading someone's facial expressions, use a questioning tone. You can try phrases such as

✔ Are you worried?

✔ Are you happy about that?

✔ Is there something bothering you?

✔ Did I just upset you?

✔ Are you annoyed about that?

✔ Are you enjoying this?

Decoding body language

Reading another person's body language can help you become more empathic. People who are high in empathy are good at quickly reading another person and getting a sense of where she is, emotionally. Understanding how a person really feels is the first step to being empathic.

Here are some tips to look for in decoding someone's body language:

- ✔ An open body (facing forward, head up, extended arms, or arms at side) can indicate comfort and domination.
- ✔ A closed body (facing away, arms closed) can show inferiority.
- ✔ Leaning forward indicates interest.
- ✔ Leaning forward with a tense body can indicate anger.
- ✔ A drooping body, slumped shoulders, or poor posture can indicate sadness.
- ✔ A body posture that faces away from you can indicate embarrassment, shyness, or anxiety.
- ✔ Sitting or standing with arms open is accepting.
- ✔ Having arms folded is a defensive style.

I discuss body language in more detail in Chapter 5.

Showing People You Understand Their Feelings

The second part of empathy, after you correctly read someone's feelings, is to show the other person that you understand his or her feelings. Of course, you want to use empathy at a time and level that's appropriate. For example, you may not want to try to empathize too much with a person you just met in the supermarket.

If you're practicing your empathy skills with someone close to you, let him or her know that you're trying to be more understanding and ask whether he or she minds if you practice. When you're ready to test your skills with other people, try not to get too intense at first. You might want to start with the little inconveniences and annoyances in day-to-day living. For example, you might try to empathize with someone when he or she feels frustration dealing with a rude, pushy person in a crowded store.

Checking in

When you start to practice your empathy skills with someone else, you might want to start by checking in. After you do your best to determine what emotion the other person is feeling, you're ready to see how close you are.

By *checking in,* you check with the other person to see whether you found the right — or at least, the closest — emotion to what they're feeling. You can check in by using a question or a statement. Some examples of statements are

- You look like you're feeling a bit sad.
- You seem to be in a happy mood.
- You look a bit anxious right now.
- You're showing a lot of confidence.
- You seem like you're in pain.
- You look like you're a bit fearful.

Or you can use questions:

- Are you worried about something?
- Are you happy with your accomplishment?
- Do you feel angry right now?
- Is something making you ashamed?
- How pleased are you with your report?

Getting confirmation

After you check in (as discussed in the preceding section), you need to get some kind of confirmation from the other person. What good is all your work at trying to decipher an emotion and checking in if you don't find out whether you're right?

If you ask the right question or make the right empathic statement, the other person should confirm your observation of him or her, or perhaps lead you closer to a more accurate feeling. Sometimes, however, people can be noncommittal. North Americans don't socialize all that well when it comes to sharing feelings.

Also, don't be disappointed if you're wrong. You can't easily read everyone's emotions. You either have this skill naturally, or you have to work to acquire it.

So, when in doubt, check. If you don't get much of a response back, ask the other person directly whether you're reading him or her right. Consider the example of Tisha and Abe.

Tisha's concerned about Abe's mood over the past week. It was unlike him to be so uncommunicative. Usually, she can read his moods fairly easily, but he seems more distant than usual.

"Abe," she says, getting his attention, "You really seem to be troubled today."

Abe manages to glance at her, but he gives no response.

"Sorry, Abe, but I'm just trying to get a better understanding of how you're feeling. Just let me know if you're bothered by something," Tisha persists.

She continues to look at Abe until he finally looks toward her.

"Okay, I think I did really badly on my exam yesterday. It counts for 40 percent of my grade," he answers. His emotions now become transparent, and Tisha knows what the problem was all about.

As good as you may be at identifying someone's emotions, you can often get even better by checking in. You can save a lot of time and trouble by not going down the wrong track. Getting a confirmation helps you towards a better understanding, allowing you to focus on solutions, when needed.

Exploring Situations in Which Empathy Can Really Help You

On some occasions, empathy can really help you get a better handle on where someone is coming from — it can help you understand, and hopefully influence, their behavior. You can break down your use of empathy into three types of situations:

- ✔ Dealing with intimate relationships, such as with a spouse or child
- ✔ Dealing with friends and other relatives
- ✔ Dealing with strangers, especially in tense situations

In intimate relationships, empathy can work as a bond that helps keep the relationship close. With friends, it can also be an important part of keeping friendships strong. Empathy can even help you to deal with strangers, especially in tense situations.

Strengthening intimate relationships

You may expect that empathy is important in an intimate relationship. In an intimate relationship, you need to know the other person's feelings. In reality, intimate partners, or parents and children, often take each other for granted. You can too easily guess what the other person is feeling and make decisions accordingly.

The high number of interactions between partners and immediate family make it less likely that you check in with each other. With those people, you need to know when it's important to be empathic. Some couples and families make a habit of having regular times each week to talk over issues that come up. They don't have these talks in the bedroom or the kitchen, but rather somewhere with no history of frequent, emotional, or contentious interactions having taken place — in the house or at a local coffee shop, away from home.

Using empathy to deal with charged issues in these relationships can reduce the frequency of misinterpretation, disagreement, and accusations. Empathy allows you to understand how your significant other or family member is feeling. You can use empathy to avoid arguments by first understanding where each person is coming from.

After you understand clearly what frustrates, annoys, or just plain bothers your partner or family member, then you can begin to find constructive solutions or compromises. Likewise, after your partner or family member better understands your feelings about a situation, she can more easily deal with your issues calmly and logically.

To use empathy with your intimate partner or immediate family member, follow these steps:

1. **Plan a time when you'll have no interruptions.**

2. **Pick a neutral place that's quiet where you can talk.**

   Go somewhere other than the bedroom or kitchen — places where you already have frequent interaction (you may even leave home for a local coffee shop).

3. **The first person states an issue that concerns him, or which he finds positive.**

   The other person just listens.

4. **The other person reflects back, using an empathic statement, and tries to capture the emotion behind what the first person has stated.**

5. **The first person acknowledges whether the other person received the correct emotion.**

6. **If she didn't get the emotion right, the first person restates the issue, and the second person tries again.**

   This process continues until the listener acknowledges the emotion.

7. **Reverse roles, repeating Steps 3 through 6 with the other person stating her issue.**

You don't need to give your partner any suggestions, or any other response to the issue. This exercise just ensures that the two of you can deliver and receive messages, as intended.

Understanding friends and relatives

Sometimes, empathy can enhance your relationship with your friends and extended family members. You want to celebrate success with these people and console them during times of distress. With both friends and relatives, empathy can help you bond more closely.

In these cases, you don't need to bond at the most intimate level. You just want to use empathy as a check-up to ensure that you're on the same wavelength as your friend or relative.

Here are suggestions for using empathy with friends and relatives:

- ✔ Try to be spontaneous.
- ✔ Use empathy when your friend or relative is experiencing a clear feeling, positive or negative.
- ✔ You can use empathy with cool emotions, not just with hot emotions (refer to Chapter 5).
- ✔ Make your probes and responses flow as part of the conversation.
- ✔ Keep probes short — you don't need to have a long, drawn-out conversation.

✔ Look for acknowledgement from the friend or relative after you deliver your empathic statement.

✔ It you miss the mark, simply apologize and move on. Take note of how you may have misread the cues and use that information the next time you want to "check in" or be empathic.

Dealing with tense situations that involve strangers

When you have to deal with strangers in tense situations, empathy can really help you turn down the temperature or calm the situation. You can find no better way to diffuse a difficult situation than delivering an empathic statement effectively.

Empathy can help you diffuse a situation before it gets out of hand. When you start to sense that someone you're dealing with — a clerk, restaurant hostess, checkout person, fellow customer, and so on — is starting to lose it emotionally, you can step in. Don't turn the situation into a big scene, but rather use a statement of calm, showing that you understand what the other person is experiencing. You don't have to agree with the other person or give in to her, but rather you simply show that you understand where she is coming from.

An empathic statement can disarm an angry or upset person in times of stressful circumstances or interpersonal distress from dealing with others. Here's an example.

William's a regular at his son's junior league hockey games. Although he loves coming to see his son and the team play, he's often dismayed by the behavior of some of the other parents. On one occasion in particular, one parent's quite irate at the coach for not playing his son enough during the first period.

"Listen, you moron — Jason is one of the best scorers on the team! Get him on the ice!" the father screams at the coach.

The coach, somewhat surprised, ignores the comment.

When the father starts escalating his insults, William thinks maybe he should step in.

"Excuse me. I'm Adam's father. You're right, Jason's a great player. You've gotta be really mad about him sitting on the bench right now," William says, deliberately taking the other father's attention away from the coach.

"You bet I am. He's a top scorer. How can the coach keep him on the bench?" Bill replies.

"Yeah, I can see what you mean. That's frustrating. Do you want to get some coffee? Maybe he just wants to give each of the kids some ice time. It's not like this is a big game," continues William.

William intervenes in a way that prevents an escalation. He could have stood by and watched things get out of hand. Jason might have been suspended from the team because of his father's behavior. Also, physical fights have become a serious problem at kids' hockey games — mostly because of the parents. You can see William's emotional intelligence in both his decision to intervene and his way of both distracting and calming down the other father.

Here are some things to keep in mind when you use empathy with strangers. These can be in situations in which you are uncomfortable or uptight in meeting new people:

- ✔ Use empathy as a way to get to know someone whom you just met.
- ✔ Use empathic statements as ice breakers with strangers.
- ✔ Stick with cool feelings unless you have an overly emotional situation.

When dealing with a stranger in a tense situation:

- ✔ Be sincere when you use empathy.
- ✔ Don't use empathy as a way to one-up the other person or make him or her feel bad.
- ✔ Stay calm and cool yourself.
- ✔ Observe the other person's response.
- ✔ Use empathy in a way that de-escalates the situation.
- ✔ Keep your focus on the other person.

Empathy is a powerful tool. It can help you build closer, more rewarding bonds with people you know and open the door when dealing with strangers, helping to de-escalate contentious situations. You need to be genuine when you use empathy. People can usually tell when you fake it. By practicing this skill, you have the potential to make positive changes in many of your relationships.

Chapter 8

Managing Other People's Emotions

In This Chapter

▶ Controlling your reactions to others

▶ Influencing other people's emotions

▶ Dealing with obnoxious people

▶ Maintaining relationships with difficult friends and relatives

*Y*ou can't easily change the behavior of other people. You can try all kinds of things that often amount to nagging, pushing, or cajoling — usually to no avail. You may tend to tell the other person why you want him to change his behavior. However, by focusing more on the other person, and less on your own needs, wants, and desires, you can get closer to the desired change in the other person.

This chapter looks at why you can more effectively influence the behavior of others by managing your own emotions first. Then, I share some specific techniques that you can use to manage people you know, as well as the strangers you encounter. You can fit these techniques into your own personal style. Keep in mind the things you've tried in the past that worked and use what you've already figured out to help shape these suggestions.

Use these suggestions for common, everyday encounters with normal-functioning people. If the person you're dealing with has a serious mental health problem of some kind, consult a legally qualified psychiatrist, psychologist, or social worker.

Changing How You React to Others

The first step in managing the emotions of others is to understand your own emotions. Understanding where you're coming from — your needs, wants, and desires — can help you deal with others because then you can get a clearer focus on the task at hand.

You can often get lost in your own world and the way in which you see things, and that perspective sometimes gets in the way of dealing with other people. Think of the people around you, identifying those whom you want to change in some way. For example:

- I want my spouse to lose weight.
- I want my parents to stop nagging me.
- I want my best friend to care more about what I think.
- I want my girlfriend to be more open about her feelings.
- I want my friends to be more accepting.
- I want my mother to listen more to others.
- I want my sister to spend more time with me.

Think about some of the ways that you may have tried to accomplish these changes in the past. Start by looking at what you've tried before — what seemed to work and what didn't work.

Being aware of your gut reaction

You probably have people around you whom you want to change in some way. You may want to change the people close to you the most. You can usually tell how successful you can be at changing someone you know. You can more likely succeed with small requests, as compared to large requests. If you listen to your gut feeling before you make the request, you can have a pretty good sense of how successful you'll be.

Sometimes, your gut tells you for whom you want a person to make the change, as well. You may want the other person to change for your own reasons (for example, you want him to look or dress a certain way). You may want changes that are actually in the other person's best interest (for example, you want her to stop smoking or overeating). Or you may want changes in the best interest of others (for example, you want him to stop making noise that disturbs others).

You may have someone in your circle of people who's close to you and whom you've been trying to get to change in some way. To create a plan to help encourage them to change, follow these steps:

1. **In your notebook, write what you want this person to change and why.**

   What do you want her to change? Imagine her doing the behavior you don't like. What does that feel like for you? What about the behavior makes you feel that way?

2. **Write down how you and the other person might feel if the person changes her behavior.**

   Imagine what change in the other person's behavior would look like — what would she do differently? How do you think she'd feel differently as a result of the change? How would you feel differently?

3. **Focus on your feelings, writing down how the feeling would change your behavior.**

   What about this change in someone else's behavior would make you feel differently? Identify which of the following statements applies to you:

   - I don't have to nag her anymore.
   - I feel superior for making her change.
   - She shouldn't behave that way.
   - She's better off.

   If you select any of the first three statements in the preceding list, then you might need to look at your motives for change. The change you're looking for in someone else may be for your own benefit and not necessarily in the other person's best interest.

4. **In your notebook, list the reasons for change that benefit you and the reasons that benefit the other person.**

   Knowing these reasons can help you make your case for change because these can be your goals. We are more motivated to change when we have clear and desirable goals and outcomes.

Working through alternative responses

People find changing difficult for many reasons. Here are some examples:

- The behavior is now a habit, and habits are hard to break.
- The person sees benefits to staying the same.

> ✔ Changing involves work.
>
> ✔ He sees too few benefits for change.
>
> ✔ He may be fearful of change.
>
> ✔ He's trying to get even with you for something.

Decide whether the obstacles in the preceding list apply to your case. Also, try to come up with additional obstacles to change. Challenge these obstacles. For example, if the person believes he has too few benefits for change to make it worthwhile, draw up a list of all the benefits you can think of for change.

If he's afraid of change, think of ways to overcome those fears. How can you help make the change easier by dealing with or avoiding some of the fears?

Think of something that you want to change about yourself — your diet, hair style or color, behavior towards someone, spending habits, amount of time on the computer, and so on. To overcome your obstacles to change, follow these steps:

1. **In your notebook, write down the one change you want to make.**

2. **Write some of the obstacles to change.**

   What's been keeping you from making the change?

3. **Take each obstacle and write down an alternative to the obstacle.**

   For example, if you say that you don't have time to make the change, come up with some possible ways that you can change your schedule to make time.

4. **Present the best alternative responses to each of your reasons for not changing.**

   Get a sense of how convincing each of these reasons is for you. In many cases, you might be using similar reasons to convince others to change. Now, you can experience whether your reasons for change are compelling.

Managing Other People's Emotions

Instead of telling someone to do something, which doesn't usually go over very well, try to understand what's holding that person back from doing it herself. After you get a better idea of what's keeping her back, you can more effectively approach the situation.

You need *empathy* — the ability to walk in the other person's moccasins — to get at the other person's roadblocks. (Chapter 7 covers empathy in detail.) Before you can manage someone else's emotions, you need to understand them:

- ✔ Where is she coming from?
- ✔ How is she really feeling about this situation?
- ✔ Will she be angry if I bring up this subject, or is she looking for someone to talk to?
- ✔ Is this a good time for her to think about change?

Your chances of successfully changing the other person increase if you get a better handle on what likely motivates the other person. And even if you don't succeed right away, you're less likely to cause friction or to get into a painful argument. Remember, a person probably won't change because of your self-interest — she needs a reason for change that's in her interest. Figure out how she can benefit from the change you want.

Start with small changes. After you achieve some success in convincing someone to make small changes, you can gain confidence and credibility to move up the chain to the bigger requests.

Don't be manipulative, but rather work in the other person's real best interest. If you appear to be manipulative or insincere in your approach, you risk losing the other person's trust.

Suppose that your spouse doesn't like taking out the garbage for pickup. You've tried every type of nagging to get her to move, but the television or newspaper is much more attractive. Perhaps she doesn't move because she's comfortable and doesn't want to be interrupted.

You can start off by having a conversation in which you both agree that your household needs to get the garbage out of the house. Then, explore a good time when she could get involved.

You might build on her pride of the house that she helped select, build, decorate, and maintain. She can only enhance this sense of pride by keeping the house tidy.

You may find long-term habits hard to break. But by appealing to the emotional side of what keeps the negative habit going, you may have more success. Remember, the person may feel fear of a negative emotion if she acts, or she may not be able to see a positive emotion that she'd feel after acting. You need to artfully determine which of these drivers is stronger and build on it.

Identifying where other people are coming from

In order to understand where the other person is coming from, you may have to do some digging. Although you may be tempted to guess, or try to piece together some motivating factor for certain behaviors, you can always more effectively get at the answer by getting data. By taking the time to try to really understand the other person — to empathize with him — you can learn more about the driving forces behind his behavior.

You can most effectively get the information you need by asking. By using your observation skills and the right questions or probing statements, you may be able to tap into the emotions behind the behaviors. Here are some examples:

- ✔ You seem really happy when you're watching TV.
- ✔ What does it feel like when you're smoking?
- ✔ Does it bother you when you sleep in?
- ✔ Are you angry about something I did?

Start with the emotion that seems the most obvious. If someone continues doing a certain behavior, she probably experiences a positive emotion attached to that behavior (the relaxation or mind numbing you might get when watching TV, for example). However, she may also feel a negative emotion if the behavior is also self-defeating (for example, guilt or anger about the amount of time wasted watching TV).

By using your observational and empathy skills, you can perceive signs of the other person's emotion. If you can't perceive or recognize the emotion, you may want to try imagining yourself in the same situation. If you imagine what you might be feeling or thinking after performing a certain action (wasting time or eating more than you should, for example), you might start to gain an appreciation of the other person's state.

Of course, you may be a very different person and experience feelings not at all like the ones that the other person feels, but at least you can start thinking about the problem differently — which provides another way to begin empathizing with the other person. People who don't empathize well with others are usually too eager to blame other people for their faults or nag them into changing their behavior.

After you come up with a few reasons that might lead you to do the same behavior, start to think about what might be driving the other person. Is it consistent with what you *originally* thought drove the behavior?

Establishing a realistic alternative behavior

After you assess your own reaction to being in the same situation and determine what it feels like for you (as the preceding section outlines), you can start thinking about realistic alternative behaviors that the other person could perform. *Realistic alternative behaviors* are actions that you think the other person might be willing to do.

Select a behavior that you want the other person to change. Follow these steps:

1. **In your notebook, describe the behavior that you want the other person to change.**

2. **Record the alternative behaviors that you would replace it with.**

   Try to visualize alternative behaviors that the person could perform, in place of the behavior that you want to see changed. Practice visualizing alternatives until you come up with an alternative that would be more acceptable to you and the other person than the status quo.

3. **Using your empathy skills, think about how the other person would feel about your solution. Then, write your answers to the following questions in your notebook:**

   • How much change would you find acceptable? Try to be specific — for example, you may want the person to perform the alternative behavior once per week.

   • How likely is the other person to agree to your request for change?

   • If she probably won't agree, what do you think are some of the obstacles?

   • How might you modify your request or deal with some of the obstacles? Remember, the other person usually has to see that she can get something out of changing. The fact that you want her to change isn't always enough. Think of how she can benefit from the change.

In addition, you can follow these steps to deal with your feelings about the unwanted behavior:

1. **Imagine the person doing the behavior that you want him to change.**

   Pay attention to your feelings while you observe the unwanted behavior.

2. **Try to relax your feelings.**

   While focusing on your feelings, imagine yourself calming down. Now, in a calmer state, consider why the person may be behaving the way he does. Imagine what would motivate him to change the behavior.

3. List at least five possible motivators.

4. Select the one you think is most likely influencing their behavior.

Think about how you'd present this motivator to the other person.

5. Imagine the person carrying out your preferred behavior.

If you've achieved the behavior change you want, you should now be more relaxed about the situation once it occurs. Your feelings should continue to be more relaxed as you gradually accept the new behavior.

You can't get a guarantee that the other person will completely change long-standing habits or behaviors. However, if you prepare your case by looking at the situation through the other person's eyes, you have a better chance of at least getting some change.

Getting a person to want to change

After you examine the situation and how the other person sees it (as discussed in the preceding sections), you're ready to present your case. Set up a quiet time in a neutral place to talk to the other person. Let her know that you have some ideas about how she can change a situation that you're unhappy with. Let her know that you could then cut down on some behavior you do that might annoy her, such as your nagging (or whatever behavior you use that annoys the other person).

Here are some tips for having that important conversation:

✔ Let her know how the behavior bothers you.

✔ Acknowledge you understand that your feelings are your problem, but you really want to talk about what's bothering you.

If the person cares about you, she should be willing to at least discuss your concern.

✔ Let the other person know that you've been thinking of some ways in which you might both be able to change.

Suggest that if you feel better about the situation, you'll do some negative or annoying behavior, such as nagging, less.

✔ Suggest a possible motivator for behavior change (based on what you discover in the preceding section).

✔ See whether you two can come to some compromise or agree to work towards a compromise.

Even though you won't necessarily succeed in convincing the person to change during this conversation, remember to

- ✔ Not appear defensive.
- ✔ Show no blame.
- ✔ Take ownership of your part of the problem.
- ✔ Appear willing to compromise.

Applying these principles might bring you closer to getting some change from people you're close to. When you carry out your request for change in the spirit of goodwill, compromise, and each person's best interest, you increase your chances of success.

Encountering Obnoxious People

Sometimes you encounter difficult or, to put it bluntly, obnoxious people. You can find dealing with difficult people a challenge. In some cases, you might argue, dealing with such people isn't even worth your time. However, you may occasionally have no other choice.

Unfortunately, the world has become a much more violent place than it was even ten years ago. For example, road rage incidents that lead to serious injury or death happen frequently.

Imagine someone cuts off another person's car on a highway. The aggrieved person chases down the offending car, honking and screaming, and tailgates so close that the other person retaliates. He slams on the brakes, causing a collision. The two drivers jump out of their cars, and one ends up dead because of blows to the head. Many real cases are variations on this scenario.

You may find it difficult to know when to speak up for your rights and when to lie low for your own safety. What's the appropriate response?

You might think that while the education level and quality of life for people all over the world have increased, civility would be positively affected. Instead, aggression and bullying have only increased over time — so you're more likely to encounter an obnoxious, bullying, self-centered person in your daily travels than you might have even ten years ago.

But you don't need to give up your rights and give in to the bullies. You can still make yourself heard and get your point across — in a peaceful, non-confrontational way.

To a certain degree, the setting in which you confront the behavior affects how you deal with obnoxious people. Confronting someone at home can be a far different experience than confronting a stranger at the grocery store. Both the setting and your goal in dealing with the person can help you determine the strategy that you adopt in confronting the behavior.

Determining your best outcome with a difficult person

Set a goal for your interaction with the obnoxious person you have to deal with. Knowing who the person is and where the behavior occurs are factors that can affect your *goal,* or desired outcome.

Here are some desired goals that you may have:

- ✔ Change the undesirable behavior and maintain a relationship.
- ✔ Let the person know how you feel about her behavior and maintain the relationship.
- ✔ Let the person know how you feel about her behavior and expect only minimal or no further relationship.
- ✔ Ignore the person and leave the situation so that it doesn't escalate.

You may decide to maintain a close or cordial relationship with the other person, perhaps depending on your level of involvement with the person (family member or co-worker versus acquaintance or stranger). Just as with people you are related to, you can also keep a business-like relationship with acquaintances that you see often.

For people you encounter often, you probably want to maintain a cordial relationship. To maintain this kind of relationship, you often have to manage your emotions and, to some extent, the other person's emotions.

When dealing with strangers, you want to keep your cool, and managing their emotions may help you stay in control, as well. Your goal here can be to keep your dignity and walk away. You don't want to get dragged into an altercation with someone.

Diffusing conflict with strangers

Think of the last time that a complete stranger insulted you. You can choose a variety of ways to respond in these situations. Generally, you want to put keeping your cool at the top of your list. Unless you're a world-champion boxer or black belt in karate, you probably don't want to get into an altercation.

But you don't have to cave in to the other person. If you did something wrong, you can apologize. Let the person know you understand how he feels. You can keep your dignity intact by simply getting through a difficult situation quickly and moving on. You probably have better things to do with your life than spend time arguing on the street with some stranger.

Bob's driving around the mall parking lot for close to 20 minutes looking for a parking spot. Each time he sees an open parking space, someone manages to park in it before he can get his car even close.

Finally, he sees a spot opening up an aisle away. He races his car around the aisle and positions himself to drive in while the other driver backs out. He notices another car behind the backing-out car. Because Bob is waiting by the exiting car's front, he can drive into the spot as soon as the car backs out. The other waiting car is stuck behind the exiting car.

The driver of the other waiting car shouts out his window, "Hey, moron, I was here first."

Bob just looks at him while he slowly gets out of his now-parked car.

"Didn't you hear me? I was waiting for that spot," the other driver continues.

"Sorry, you must have been waiting a long time," Bob states. "After 20 minutes of driving around, I almost gave up myself. It's a real pain not getting a spot. Do you want me to help you find one?"

Not knowing how to react, the other driver just looks at Bob and says, "Forget it."

Bob nicely handled a situation that could have easily become an altercation. By keeping his cool, ignoring the insult, showing he understood the other driver's frustration, and even offering to help, Bob kept the interaction civil.

Developing techniques for dealing with difficult people

Although you can't always prepare for dealing with random strangers, you can prepare for difficult people with whom you already have a relationship. You have some history with these people, and typically you can read them fairly well — although you probably have to deal with some people who are pretty unpredictable or hard to read, as well.

You probably recognize your *hot buttons* — things that another person can say or do to set you off emotionally. You're most likely also aware of the other person's hot buttons — things that you say and do that can set off the other person.

You need to not only be aware of the hot buttons, but be able to control them, as well. To prepare yourself for dealing with hot buttons, follow these steps:

1. **In your notebook, write down some of the things people do that make you lose it emotionally.**

2. **Write down some of the things you say or do that set off other people's hot buttons.**

3. **Think about how you can control your own hot buttons. Then write these down in your notebook.**

   What can you say to yourself that can keep you — not your emotions — in control?

4. **Write a strategy for how to prepare for staying calm when something normally sets you off.**

   You don't want to have to decide in the spur of the moment how to handle the situation.

   For example, you can decide in advance that you won't allow certain comments (be they insults, teases, name-callings, belittlements, or whatever) to set you off. You can deflect them. You can depersonalize them.

   Imagine someone pushing one of your hot buttons. Then imagine your desired reaction: keeping your cool. I have used imaging exercises such as this, also known as positive mental rehearsal, with elite athletes preparing for performance. By mentally rehearsing the difficult situation, you get practice in coping with the challenges that arise. The mental practice prepares you for what happens in real life.

Practice the following ways to react when people press your buttons:

- ✔ Oh, that's a silly comment. I won't let it bother me.

- ✔ That comment says more about her than about me.

- ✔ I can keep my cool; I won't let him set me off.

- ✔ Just smile and say, "Thank you."

- ✔ I'll count backwards — ten, nine, eight. . . .

Being able to manage your own emotions is usually your first step in dealing with hot button comments. Thinking about ways to manage the other person's emotions is a good second step. Both of these steps take some practice for most people. When you have some free time, you can start to think about how you can manage these challenging situations. Too often, people just deal with these emotion-triggering situations when the time comes. And, too often, those people end up regretting what they say or do in the heat of the moment.

Set goals (as I talk about in the preceding section). Know your most likely successful walk-away scenario for the situation. You want to be cool, in some cases, stating your case or at least making it clear that you understand where the other person is coming from.

Dealing with Difficult Friends and Relatives

When you deal with close friends and relatives, you likely continue having an ongoing relationship with them. Of course, the closer the relative or friend, the more likely and frequent are these continued relations. People do sometimes completely cut off contact with relatives and friends, and you may find yourself in a situation in which no contact at all is your only sane choice.

However, in the following sections, I deal with cases in which you expect to stay in some kind of contact with these friends and relatives. Because you've likely known this person for a long time, you probably already have a good idea how likely she is to change. I assume that your relative or friend has ingrained habits or behaviors that you can't easily change.

Start with the endgame

Assuming that you still have to deal with this person for a long time to come, what can you hope for in the relationship? Here are some examples:

✔ See each other only at holidays and family gatherings (once or twice a year)

✔ Get together somewhat regularly (once every month or so)

✔ Interact regularly (at least every week or more)

The less often you need to interact, the more easily you can deal with the situation. Regardless of how often you see this person, mentally prepare for these interactions by first thinking about how you will stay in control when you greet this person. Picture yourself greeting her and asking some opening questions ("How have you been? What have you been doing since I saw you last?" and so on).

Also, think about how you want the interaction to end. Suppose you're spending a weekend with your mother. Each encounter up to this point has ended with you feeling very tense and emotionally drained, and barely speaking to your mother at the end of the interaction. At the end of this weekend, you want to leave on an even keel emotionally and in a calm and cordial mood with your mother.

Consider Jan's story. Jan has found it very difficult over the last few years to organize family time together with her aging father and her children. Grandpa Tom's a spry 78 years old. He still lives to a large degree in the past and has no use for modern contraptions such as computers, cell phones, or BlackBerries. He talks about events that happened 50 years ago like they happened yesterday.

His children and grandchildren have heard the same stories dozens of times, and at every family dinner gathering, he likes to monopolize the conversation with accounts of his exploits in the good ol' days. His daughter Jan is having a hard time dealing with his behavior, and it's making family time together difficult. Her children are becoming less willing to be part of the family get-togethers.

Jan has tried to talk to her father several times, but he just brushes her off, saying that he needs to educate the grandchildren. Unfortunately, few of the younger family members manage to stay at the dinner table past the main course.

Finally, Jan comes up with a new approach. She tells her father that the grandchildren not only want to hear his stories, but want his advice on their activities, as well. So, he can tell one story, and then listen to each of his grandchildren's stories. He can give his advice and comments after each story.

This plan keeps Grandpa involved, but puts the focus elsewhere. By getting him to share the limelight, dinner's more enjoyable for all. The endgame here didn't involve silencing or embarrassing Grandpa, but simply getting him to be part of the family occasion in a constructive way.

Getting to the relationship you want

If you want a less acrimonious relationship, a relationship that has a calmer and more civil discourse as an outcome, with your difficult relative or friend, you can take these steps to better manage your relationship the next time you meet:

- Don't take the other person's comments personally.
- Find out how to manage your emotions and stay calm. (Reading this book is a great start!)
- Refrain from saying things that you'll regret later.
- Take the heat. Accept being wrong on insignificant points (you may feel insulted, but so what?).
- Don't try to make points or win the arguments.
- Be gracious and polite (even when it hurts).
- Try to discuss topics on which you agree.
- When the other person brings up negative talk, stick to the positive.
- Bide your time — the encounter will end eventually, and think how much better you'll feel after you say goodbye to this person.
- Try to end your visit on a good note, verbally and emotionally.

You may never get to the point where you have the wonderful relationship of storybooks and 1950s sitcoms. However, you can experience less of the pain and guilt that comes with having a bad relationship with someone you're close to. Setting a realistic goal for the relationship can really help you frame your expectations in a more constructive way. Your expectations shape your encounters. If you start out with unrealistic expectations, you only get frustrated and angry when the interaction doesn't meet those expectations.

By following the straightforward rules that I outline in this chapter, you can have more control in these difficult relationships and be better able to manage them. By managing your emotions, you can avoid triggers that derail your efforts. So, by managing your emotions, you can better manage the relationship. By managing the relationship, you have a lot less stress in your life.

Part III
Taking Emotional Intelligence to Work

...and finally, do you feel well connected to the other members of your department?

In this part . . .

Emotions have a tremendous impact in the workplace. In this part, I show you how to use your emotional intelligence to navigate areas at work, such as the bullying boss, obnoxious co-workers, and disrespectful subordinates. I also explore the important ways emotional intelligence affects your job fit.

This part also deals with the relationship between emotional intelligence and leadership. You can find out how to develop the most important leadership skills related to emotional intelligence. I show you the secrets of an emotionally intelligent workplace — and how to know whether you have one. If you don't have an emotionally intelligent workplace, I help you create one.

Emotional intelligence in the workplace often begins by developing good emotional habits in college. Researchers have been hard at work in this area, and you get the scoop on their findings in this part.

Chapter 9

Dealing with Difficult Workplace Situations

*I*t's Monday morning. The alarm clock rings. You bang your head trying to reach it; your arm, swinging across the bed, knocks the clock off the table onto the floor. You make it into the shower, but you don't have any hot water. Your dog bites your leg on the way down the stairs. Your favorite breakfast cereal's box is empty. You get stuck in bumper-to-bumper rush-hour traffic. You finally have a patch of free road, and a red BMW cuts you off, almost forcing you into the lane of oncoming traffic.

Finally, you get to work, and one of your least favorite co-workers greets you with, "How was your weekend?"

You probably don't react by smiling and replying, "Great! How was yours?"

Contrary to what some managers believe, people don't leave the emotional part of their brains at home or park it outside the office with their cars. In this chapter, I examine why you need to both be aware of and manage your emotions, as well as the emotions of people around you at work. Not only can good emotional management help you navigate through difficult situations, it can also help you get ahead in your career. Knowing how to use your emotions — when to be appropriately glad, mad, sad, concerned, annoyed, and so on — can help you get more of what you want, or help you go where you want to go, at work.

Having Feelings at Work?

Do people leave their emotions at home and put on their work brains as soon as they arrive at work? Can they simply forget everything that's happened to them over the past few hours when they walk into the office? Not likely. Everyone brings their whole brains to work, and that brain includes all the good and all the bad that they experience before arriving.

If you let your emotions get the best of you at work, you become distressed and emotionally unaware. You get so stressed and focused on the stress that you lose sight of why you feel the way you do. So, while you're busy being grumpy in the morning, oblivious to the people around you, your co-workers or subordinates might be wondering what's going on with you. People around you start asking themselves questions such as, "What's with her anyway?" or "I knew he didn't like me, I can never do things right around him." You give others the impression that you're distant, uninterested, aloof, introverted — or a host of other characteristics that don't help your career.

Getting in touch with your feelings at work

Don't think that emotionally intelligent people don't get upset or angry in the workplace — they do. Emotional intelligence empowers you to get a hold of your emotions, instead of letting them get a hold of you. In Chapter 5, I talk about how to identify your emotions. Being in touch with your feelings enables you to become more aware of where you are — whether you're sad, angry, or frustrated. You can then more effectively change your unpleasant feelings, as described in Chapter 6. Knowing that you're angry and upset allows you to stop and think about the following questions:

- What upset me?
- What was upsetting about it?
- Why am I still upset?
- Can feeling upset help me in some way?
- Can feeling upset hinder me?
- Can I start to calm down in some way?
- How do I want to appear to my co-workers?
- Can I communicate effectively with them if I'm upset?

Stopping and thinking about these questions and their answers while you have your first cup of coffee before you encounter any human beings at work might help you get on the right foot to start your day. The following section provides a more comprehensive look at how this kind of reflection can help, as well as suggestions for how you can regain your composure.

Getting control of your emotions

When you get upset at work, stop and think — step out of the emotional abyss that you may be experiencing — whether you have to deal with an unreasonable boss, a gossipy co-worker, a rude customer, annoying e-mails, a missed promotion, or any other aggravation at work.

When those destructive feelings start to get in the way of work, remember to consider the questions listed above, and give the following exercises a try:

✔ **What was upsetting?** Consider, in the scheme of things, the size of the upsetting event. Often, people blow small and medium situations to a disproportionate size — making mountains out of molehills. Even if the event is a big thing, worrying can't solve it. Focus on how you can make things better — or, at least, not worse.

To do: Try a time-travel exercise. Think about five years from now. How much will this situation really mean in your life five years out?

✔ **What about the event upset you?** Think about the event or situation. What about it upset you? Would the same event or situation upset other people you know? Was it really the event or situation that upset you, or your interpretation of it? What if you took the same event and tried to interpret it differently? Pay attention to how you feel about the event or situation after you try alternate interpretations.

To do: Think about the upsetting event. Start to change some of the variables:

- If a different person was involved, would it upset you as much?

- If the event happened at a different time, would it be as upsetting?

- If you had certain people or resources around, would that change your emotional reaction?

- What if you had someone to confide in?

✔ **Why am I still upset?** If you tend to hold onto grudges or negative feelings about people, you may want to explore some strategies for getting over negative feelings that last too long.

To do: Imagine the bad feeling. In your mind, try changing the feeling to something more neutral. For example, if you feel anger, try to change it to mild frustration.

✔ **Will being upset help me in some way?** Having too much of a negative emotion rarely helps anyone. Psychodynamic therapists used to believe that letting out all those bad emotions, such as anger, would help you, through catharsis, become a calmer, more complete person. In fact, expressing too much anger can do damage to you, both psychologically and physically. You're more likely to successfully deal with these intense emotions if you can turn extreme emotional upset into minor frustrations and annoyances. After all, how can being extremely upset help you get through a bad situation?

To do: Letting off steam may feel good, temporarily, but it doesn't really help you deal with your anger. Imagine someone really upset at you. When you think about her angry words and actions, are you inclined to change, or are you more likely to defend yourself?

Most people become more defensive. However, by reinterpreting the situation, you may be more effective in diffusing your anger. For example, suppose the reason she insulted you is because she feels inadequate about herself. Realizing that her insults had little to do with you or your behavior may help you think differently about the situation.

✔ **Can feeling upset hinder me?** In fact, being extremely upset can make a bad situation even worse. Besides the physical problems of being overly upset, such as the increase in your blood pressure, throwing a lamp at someone, putting your fist through a wall, or screaming at people can't really improve any situation. Anybody who experiences your extreme negative emotions probably thinks even worse of you than he might have before.

To do: Think of a person who's very angry at you. How flattering does he appear? Do you want a closer relationship with this person?

✔ **Can I start to calm down in some way?** You can get yourself out of these negative emotions. The simplest way is to declare a *time out* — pull yourself out of the situation, both mentally and physically.

You may need some practice in this technique. Basically, you want to have alternate thoughts ready that you can call up at these difficult times. Come up with some rather pleasant, or at least neutral, images that you can use — a beach scene, climbing a mountain, a musical interlude, or a scene from your favorite movie. When your emotions overwhelm you, force yourself to call a time out and switch gears into one of these scenes for a couple of minutes or so. Then, you can return to the problem at hand, feeling a bit calmer.

To do: When you feel out of control, you can count. Try counting backwards from ten. By the time you reach three, you should be rational enough to start thinking clearly again. Then, you can do the imagination exercise (refer to Chapter 8).

✔ **How do I want to appear to my co-workers?** Do you like working with someone who's moody? How about angry, always complaining, or unpredictable? So, why would anyone want to be around you if you behave this way? People like to be around likeable people. People tend to find interacting with optimistic, happy people more rewarding than being with sullen, negative people. Also, people like to be around others who take an interest in them. Showing others that you care about their welfare increases the probability that they care about yours. And you never know when you'll need the support of others.

To do: Think about a leader you worked for or a teacher at school you really admired. What was it about her behavior under stress that you appreciated?

✔ **Can I communicate effectively with them when I'm upset?** When you're out of control, you're probably so focused on your own problems and issues that you have little room left to communicate effectively with others.

To do: After you calm yourself down (try belly breathing, or any of the other techniques described in Chapter 6), focus on the other person and where he's coming from. You may find it difficult to take your mind off your own upset feelings, but try to break away and think of the other person before you respond.

Exploring Situations That Bring Out Your Worst at Work

People often get upset over things that happen to them at work. The event could be silly, such as someone leaving her coffee cup on your desk, or it could be more serious, such as someone taking credit for your work. Either way, be prepared to deal with these situations.

Generally, when something goes wrong, you start off with an emotion. Something happens. You then feel queasy, upset, frustrated, or maybe even angry. First, get control of your feeling. Get a clear sense of your emotion — whether it's big or small. You must know your emotion before you can manage it.

Getting emotional about work

Being unaware of your emotions can have unfortunate consequences at work, as the following story demonstrates. Mary's boss, Bob, just left Mary's office. Mary's now feeling something unpleasant in the pit of her stomach. It's like butterflies, only with a burning sensation. Although her stomach is achy, it's not quite painful. Her head feels tight, and she has trouble focusing. Her mind just keeps flipping from one thing to another. She has no idea what's the matter, and she wants to just close her eyes and rest.

Jill, Mary's best friend at work, comes into Mary's office.

"You look awful," Jill tells Mary.

"Well, I feel worse than I look," says Mary. "I don't know what's wrong."

"How are you feeling, exactly?" asks Jill.

"My stomach feels like it's having a butterfly attack, I feel jittery, and I just can't concentrate," she replies.

"When did you start feeling like that?"

"Well I was fine all morning. Then Bob came in and started criticizing the report I gave him. I did it exactly the way he requested, but now he says he wants it all reworked. He wants all the tables redone and the figures moved, and he wants it by 4 o'clock. I took notes about what he said, but the moment he left my office, I started feeling queasy," says Mary.

"Is there any other time you felt that way?" Jill asks.

"Well, come to think of it, I felt this way last week, when Bob asked me to stay late to work on a project he was supposed to finish," Mary replies.

"Mary, do you think Bob's behavior might be getting to you? It seems he's around each time you start feeling this way," Jill suggests.

Mary looks at her, a bit surprised, nodding her head in agreement.

Mary's been too upset to even be aware of what her emotions are telling her. Fortunately, having a best friend at work helps Mary illuminate the nature of the feeling. Being in tune with what you feel helps you recognize the feeling when it occurs again.

Sometimes, you may feel too upset to even notice the pattern of the bad feeling's origin. In this example, Jill thinks the situation is pretty obvious. But Mary, who seems overcome by the feelings, doesn't see what seems like an obvious connection.

Tackling hassles

The moment you recognize that you're feeling aggravated at work, you can begin to identify why you're feeling that way. More likely than not, something small is bothering you. Studies at work have shown that you're more affected by the little hassles and frustrations, over the long term, than by a major positive event, such as a biannual company party. If you perceive many hassles over the day or week, these hassles erode your feelings about your work or the organization. Going to the company party likely doesn't turn around those negative feelings about the ongoing hassles.

Some people can be oblivious to these hassles — especially if you're in the perfect job or doing the kind of work that you really love. For example, if you love animals and work in a pet store, you may ignore the hassles of cleaning up litter, being barked at by angry dogs, cleaning out dirty aquariums, and other menial tasks.

However, for most people (who tend to like their work but may not love it), hassles can increase stress levels and paint an unfavorable picture of the workplace. Very few jobs come without hassles, and although people all have a certain level that they willingly accept, after the threshold is breached, employees begin to lose their goodwill.

What can you do about hassles? Follow these steps:

1. **Identify the hassles you experience at work, both big and small.**

2. **Determine how each hassle prevents or impedes you from getting your job done.**

3. **Brainstorm solutions about to how you can remove or reduce each hassle. Record these in your notebook.**

   Come up with a few ideas for each hassle.

4. **Meet with your supervisor to discuss the hassles that you're facing and your suggested solutions.**

   Let your supervisor know that you want to be as efficient as you can during your workday — you want to get the most bang for your buck at the end of the day.

Good managers are sensitive to the hassles that people who report to them experience, and those managers can effectively remove roadblocks so that their employees can get the real work done.

Vanessa's story offers a good example of an employee whose manager helped eliminate an obstacle that was causing unproductive emotions. Vanessa loves her job, but she's constantly frustrated by the snail's pace of her computer. As a customer service representative, she handles between 10 and 20 customer calls a day. Most of these calls require a series of lookups into a complex database for details into each customer's purchase history and resolution. Often, she has to ask the customer to let her call him back after she retrieves the record. On the return call, another question might arise that requires a further callback.

During her performance review, Vanessa tells Dave, her manager, about the complexity of some of the customer inquiries. He's perplexed by the amount of time it takes to resolve some of these issues. While Vanessa gives him examples of actual situations that occurred recently, Dave notices the frustration in Vanessa's voice each time she refers to having to call a customer back.

Dave then says, "It seems like this situation has been really frustrating for you. Do you have any suggestions about how to fix it?"

"Actually, I've thought of a few possibilities," replies Vanessa. "A good option would be the capability to get the entire file onscreen immediately. Then, I could resolve the situation in one phone call. But the company would have to significantly upgrade the hardware. As another possibility, the reps on the phone could collect the information and then pass it on to someone else in the office to resolve. Each of us in customer service would be able to handle more calls."

"Okay, it sounds like you've really been thinking about this," Dave says. "I think the company could look into upgrading the hardware."

By spending a relatively small amount of money on upgrading the computer equipment, the company realizes large gains in its ability to serve its customers. This computer upgrade also has many other benefits. In addition to reducing customer frustration, this change cuts the company's long-distance phone rates, reduces the number of callbacks, cuts the time taken to resolve problems, makes Vanessa feel better about her job, and serves more customers in less time.

In this example, Vanessa used her initiative to come up with potential solutions to the problem before meeting with her boss. Fortunately, Dave had enough emotional intelligence to let Vanessa identify and provide possible solutions to the hassles that prevented her from working at her best.

Dave realized that having employees at their best on the job is motivational for everyone. By listening to her and acting on her suggestions, Dave made Vanessa feel more empowered in her position. Also, this interaction strengthened the manager-employee relationship.

Coping with fears

For some people, the obstacle they face at work isn't a workplace situation; it's their own fears. You might have experienced this obstacle: You're asked to do something that makes you anxious or frightened, and those emotions start to take over. Soon, your work suffers because you can think about only your worries. However, identifying and investigating your emotions can help you take control of the situation and enable you to move forward.

Janice, for example, lets her fear of public speaking sabotage her performance at work. She has to present her division's sales results to her team in less than a week. Janice is terrified of presenting in front of others. So, she's been putting off getting her report together.

Janice's fear is causing her to procrastinate at work. Of course, she sees it as just being too busy with other things. She continually drops her report as a priority. Panic sets in the day before her scheduled presentation.

If Janice had good self-awareness skills, she'd realize that her fear of presenting keeps her from working on the report. After she identifies this fear, she can begin to deal with it.

Janice can deal with her emotion in a couple of ways after she recognizes it:

✔ **Ask questions about the fear.** What exactly is she afraid of? Does she worry about making a mistake in front of the team? Looking silly? Not doing a perfect job? Asking the right questions can get to the bottom of the fear.

After she gets answers to her questions, she can start looking realistically at the fear and challenging it directly. For example, what might happen if the presentation isn't perfect? Who says you have to give a perfect presentation every time?

You can tame the emotion by understanding it and disputing the worst negative consequences of the situation. Although Janice may find it unfortunate or inconvenient if the presentation doesn't go as planned, that presentation is still acceptable. Nobody says the presentation must be perfect — except, of course, in Janice's mind.

✔ **Use visualization or imagery.** Janice could imagine herself giving the presentation to her team. Ideally, she should imagine herself making some mistakes or not knowing the answers to some questions. Then, she can come up with some remedies to these situations.

For example, she imagines that one of her junior colleagues asks her a very difficult question that she can't answer. At first, she might imagine herself turning red, being extremely embarrassed, at a loss for words, and panicky. But on further reflection, she could picture herself pause, take a breath, and respond that she doesn't have that information handy but could get it later and report it to whoever wants to know. Then, she could imagine herself smiling and calmly carrying on.

Exploring Situations That Bring Out Your Best at Work

You may notice that you're happier at work at certain times, and at other times, you're annoyed or frustrated. Pay attention to these feelings or moods. By identifying them, you can start to determine a pattern so that you can increase the amount of time you're happy and reduce the occurrence of negative emotions.

Stay on top of your feelings at work by keeping a feelings diary, as shown in Figure 9-1. Get a small notebook (different from the one you are using for the activities in this book) and use one page for each day. Just follow these steps:

TIME	FEELING	EVENT	P/N
9:00	Excited	Arrived at work, chatted with Bill	+
10:00	Calm	Caught up with e-mails	+
11:00	Anxious	Realized I'm behind with work	–
12:00	Tense	Tried to finish task before lunch	–

Positive times of the day: 9:00, 10:00 ...

Negative times of the day: 11:00, 12:30 ...

People with "+" response: Bill ...

People with "–" response:

Tasks that are "+": Dealing with other people at work

Tasks that are "–": Dealing with unhappy customers

How I can increase "+" during the day:
    Spend more time with people
    Set up meetings at down times of the day

Figure 9-1:
Keep a
diary of your
feelings at
work.

How I can decrease "–" during the day:
    Prepare myself when dealing with customers (put myself in the mood)
    Practice dealing with difficult customers
    Try to deal with unhappy customers at a specific time of day

1. **On each line, down the left margin, write the times of the day, in one-hour increments.**

   For example, if your workday starts at 9 a.m., write 9, 10, 11, and so on.

2. **During the day, at the top of each hour, record your current feeling next to the time.**

   For example, you might write happy, sad, frustrated, or indifferent.

3. **Next to your feeling, record the most recent event that occurred.**

   Write down an event such as sent an e-mail to Bill, talked to Sam, or on the phone with Fran.

4. **Once a week, sit down with your notebook and go down the feelings column, marking each feeling as positive (+), negative (–), or neutral (0).**

5. **Work your way down the negative feelings, one at a time. Note the situations that led to the negative feelings. Start to look for patterns.**

   Does dealing with certain people always trigger a negative response? What about doing certain kinds of things at work? See if you can come up with two or three things that seem to cause the most negativity for you.

6. **Go through all the positive items that you've checked.**

   Look for patterns in the situations. Are there certain people or kinds of work that make you feel good over the course of a day? Do you notice that you feel more confident, happy, or generally positive at certain times of the day or when you're doing tasks that you excel in?

7. **Come up with ways that you can increase the number and quality of the good situations and decrease the frequency of the negative ones.**

   For example, if you find that you're happiest when dealing with other people — customers or co-workers — look for ways to improve both the amount of time you spend interacting with people and the quality of your interactions. What can you do to get more out of your interactions with people? Can you find networking opportunities that can help you further your career? Can you increase sales with your people skills? You may want to explore how your social skills can lead to greater work happiness and success. Then, formulate a plan to build your social skills to their full potential.

8. **For the negative patterns, investigate whether they're related to a particular hassle or anxiety.**

   For more about how to tackle these negative situations, see the section "Exploring Situations That Bring Out Your Worst at Work," earlier in this chapter.

9. **Try to use the patterns to identify any areas of weakness that you may need to address.**

   If your negative emotions occur around tasks that involve accounting, for example, do you need to improve these skills? Or perhaps you feel that you (or your supervisor) should delegate these tasks to someone else more suited to them. Your negative emotions at work should provide a signal for you that something may need to be changed. By analyzing the situation, you can then determine the nature of that change. Sometimes, you need to make only minor alterations. Other times, you may need radical surgery, meaning major change to your work.

To see how keeping a diary at work can help you develop your strengths, consider Bruce's story. Bruce keeps a feelings diary at work, and he's figured out that his happiest times at work are after successful customer interactions. This information gives him clues about his strengths: He's good at interacting with people, and he has a flair for customer service. Next, he asks himself what he can do to build on his strengths — how can he improve his customer skills even more?

Take a good look at your strengths. Try to determine whether you're maximizing your strong areas. You may be able to use your strengths at work in ways that you haven't considered yet. You may have a flair for public relations, sales, training, or any number of areas that require good interpersonal skills. If your strengths are more technology oriented (your best times at work are when you use the computer), you might want to move towards research, programming, database management, or any number of more technically oriented jobs. Do you enjoy helping others with their computer questions? Training or technical support may be logical directions.

Having more control over workflow, yet getting the same amount of work done (or, as often happens, accomplishing even more work), benefits everyone. If you have the mood that's most productive for your work, you feel like you're in control of your job, instead of the job controlling you. Feeling that sense of control improves your attitude towards the job, the workplace, and the organization as a whole. If you know that your supervisors and top management are really interested in helping you do your best work, then you're more motivated to perform.

Managing the Emotions of Others at Work

You may not believe it, but many managers I encounter proudly proclaim that their workplaces are no places for emotions. Although this philosophy may have seemed true 20 years ago, attitudes in the workplace have changed significantly since then. Progressive managers realize that they deal with whole people — not just assembly line cogs, each with a specific task.

For years, managers tried to influence their employees by telling them what to do. (Many still do!) This approach often works. However, it also often yields resentment.

Most people today want to know why their managers ask them to do things. I don't mean drawn out, lengthy explanations — but good, rational, and (may I add) emotional justifications. When a manager makes a request acknowledging that employees like to be considered part of a team, with a stake in a project's outcome, she gets better results from her employees.

An emotionally intelligent manager keeps the following tips in mind when he makes requests:

✔ Don't give orders.

✔ Give some background or rationale for the request.

✔ Approach your employee like you're a fellow team player, not a boss.

✔ Show the mutual benefits to the request.

✔ Let the person have some control over whether to accept the request and how to perform it.

✔ Ensure that the person feels good about the interaction.

Here's an example of an effective request. Sandy's facing a tight deadline and needs some extra work from one of her staff.

She says, "George, I hate to give this to you at this late date, but one of our large customers, Helix, needs a justification for the bigger unit we quoted them. I wouldn't ordinarily ask you to do this now, but it'll really mean a lot for our monthly performance if we get this sale. We need it by Thursday at 2:00. Can I count on your support for this?"

In this example, Sandy gives George a reason for the request, so he knows Sandy isn't just throwing things his way to aggravate him. (Believe me, I've seen this done in organizations, and you probably have, too.) Additionally, Sandy wants George to see they're both on the same side. Getting this order doesn't just benefit the company — it benefits everyone. George needs to feel part of a team — when the team does well, they all share in the success.

Finally, George needs to feel that he has some control in the situation, so Sandy asks for his support. George could, of course, say that he's too busy. He probably won't give that response, however. Sandy knows that if George willingly takes on the task (as opposed to Sandy ordering him to do it), he'll put more of his heart and soul into the work.

Hawthorne: Birthplace of the emotionally intelligent workplace?

Back in 1927, a group of industrial psychologists studied workers at the Western Electric Hawthorne Plant in Cicero, Illinois. In this series of studies, psychologists were trying to show (probably for the first time) that if you paid attention to workers' needs, you may get more productivity.

In one of the experiments, the researchers did nothing more than increase the lighting of the assembly area. Instantly, the workers became more productive than they had been the week before. Unfortunately, after a week or so, they settled back into their old levels of productivity. Each new change that the psychologists implemented — dimming lights, adding more rest breaks, offering fewer rest breaks, playing soft music — lead to spurts of increased productivity.

These interventions were all short lived. This study showed the researchers that simply paying attention to someone can cause changes in his behavior. Watching someone work, under these circumstances, may make him work harder, at first. However, these effects wear off over time. After you get used to being watched and the novelty wears off, you go back to your old behaviors — your original rate of working.

The Hawthorne findings became controversial over time because some psychologists later claimed the researchers got the results not because of the attention that the researchers provided to the workers, but rather because of the rest periods that occurred between changes in conditions (increased lighting, rest, then decreased lighting, for example). Others claimed that the changes occurred because the workers caught on to the purpose of the experiment.

Although the Hawthorne studies remain controversial to this day, one finding stands out: If you pay attention to people at work, you can change their behavior. Smart companies and managers have figured out how to put this principle to work.

Chapter 10

Succeeding Through Emotional Intelligence

*O*ne time, I was about to speak to a large group of human-resource specialists in London, England. Before I began, an older gentleman approached me and asked, "What exactly is it you're going to speak about?"

"Emotions at work," I happily replied.

"Well, you can go right back to America," he stated flatly. "We British don't have emotions at work. We leave them at home. Some of us don't have them at home, either."

Fortunately, times have changed since the mid-1990s, and both workplaces and schools throughout England have widely accepted and implemented emotional intelligence. In the U.K., management consultants and psychologists have carried out a great deal of pioneering research on the importance of emotional intelligence on workplace productivity, sales performance, and management.

Some psychologists and management consultants working in this area in the early years of emotional intelligence being studied at work, including myself, realized that jobs in which you have to deal with other people, such as sales and customer service, require emotional intelligence. But, in those early years, most of us didn't yet appreciate the role of emotional intelligence in technical jobs, such as engineering, law, and programming. This chapter explores how being emotionally intelligent can help you succeed in a variety of business areas, including sales, customer service, technology, graphic design, and management. I also provide examples that show how you can leverage your emotional intelligence skills to get ahead in your job.

Finding the Right Job

Few things in life are as satisfying as finding the perfect fit with your work. How you feel about your work affects your productivity. It also affects many other aspects of your life. People who are emotionally in tune with their work feel better about themselves, have better marital relationships, are happier, and tend to get more work done in less time.

Whether you find your calling easily or after a long search, you just seem to know when you're doing the right work. Your job feels a lot more like play than work. You don't even notice how many hours you put in. Time seems to fly. For many people, work is a chore. Their jobs feel very unpleasant, something they want to avoid. Minutes at work feel like hours.

Some people, from a very young age, seem to already know that they want to perform in front of others, build machines, or do something else that calls to them. Others may try a few jobs before realizing what their true calling is.

The following sections show you how to use your emotional knowledge to identify a career that's suited to your personality.

Testing interests, personality, and intelligence

Looking at your interests, your personality, your intelligence, and your aptitude and skills can help narrow the field of possibilities when you select a career path. You may rule out job areas that clearly aren't for you. The added dimension of emotional intelligence may help you in that search for the elusive career you've been seeking.

Most people who see a guidance counselor or career coach when they search for a career likely take some tests. The counselor may offer some or all of the testing described in the following sections.

Vocational interest tests

When you're looking for the right career, you most commonly take vocational interest tests. These tests are designed to help you navigate through a vast array of careers. Common examples include:

- ✔ **Strong Interest® Inventory** (`www.cpp.com`): This 291-item inventory takes about 25 minutes to complete. After being computer scored, your responses are compared to people successfully employed in specific occupations.

- ✔ **(CISS) Campbell™ Interest and Skill Survey** (`www.pearson assessments.com`): This inventory looks at your self-reported skills in specific areas as well as your interests when comparing you with people in various careers.

- ✔ **Self-Directed Search (SDS)** (`www.self-directed-search.com`): The SDS takes 20–30 minutes to complete. It produces a report that provides a list of occupations and fields of study that most closely match your interests.

- ✔ **Career Assessment Inventory™** (`www.pearsonassessments.com`): The Career Assessment Inventory assessment compares an individual's occupational interests to those of individuals in 111 specific careers that reflect a broad range of technical and professional positions in today's workforce. It takes about 40 minutes to complete.

Test developers generally create career-interest tests by testing people who work within a variety of career areas. These people can include teachers, nurses, physicists, carpenters, painters, chefs, navigators, pilots, and dozens of other occupational groups. The developers test these people and, based on the pattern of responses to the items (which tap different areas of interest), determine their interests.

For example, the tester may ask everyone whether they enjoy reading computer magazines, watching scary movies, or playing sports. When the test developers collect a large number of responses, patterns begin to develop. So, if your pattern of interests matches all the carpenters whom the testers tested, for example, the test might suggest that you explore carpentry.

Obviously relying on this kind of test result poses some problems. For example, you may have never tried any carpentry work before, you may have no aptitude for carpentry, or you may be looking for a higher-paying career that has more opportunities for advancement. No single test can ever reliably make these kinds of decisions for you.

Personality tests

Another group of tests frequently used when someone's trying to find the right career path are personality tests. These tests get at your personality type or personality factors, such as whether you're extroverted or introverted, sensing (people who prefer gathering facts) or intuitive (people who prefer abstract information), conscientious (folks who pay attention to details), and so on.

Some examples include the following:

- **Myers-Briggs Type Indicator® (MBTI®)** (www.cpp.com): This is a widely used personality type indicator that looks at your basic personality type preferences. Based on the theory of C. G. Jung, it looks at the degree to which you are extroverted/introverted, sensing/intuitive, judging/perceiving, and thinking/feeling.

- **NEO Personality Inventory-Revised (NEO-PI®)** (www.parinc.com): This personality test measures what's known as the Big Five, or the Five Factor Model of personality. These include Neuroticism, Extroversion, Openness, Agreeableness, and Conscientiousness.

Many career counselors believe that personality helps determine the type of work you may like to do. For example, extroverted people might make good salespeople. Personality tests can help you somewhat better understand your traits and how they may fit the type of work you choose to do, but you can always find exceptions to the rule. Some of the best salespeople are, in fact, introverts. They're great listeners and help their clients get what they need. This gains respect for the salesperson and helps the customer build a relationship with the salesperson's organization. Also, personality factors such as conscientiousness can probably improve performance in almost any job. People tend to respect others who come to work on time, work hard, show honesty, and follow rules. But knowing that you have that kind of personality really doesn't help you find a specific type of job.

Cognitive intelligence, or IQ (intelligence quotient)

Ability or cognitive intelligence tests are probably the most widely used type of test when it comes to hiring employees. Employers use these tests (not usually referred to as IQ tests in workplace settings) basically to determine whether the potential employee is smart (or cognitively intelligent) enough for the job.

Obviously, certain jobs require an intelligent person — someone who can remember facts, calculate, visualize spatial relations, or any number of tasks. Some organizational psychologists still debate whether people who have high intelligence actually perform better at some of these jobs. You may have the intelligence to be a waiter at a high-end restaurant — you can memorize the menu each day and know who ordered what at each table, but you may also see the job as a stepping stone to something else. In other words, you may not be motivated by or interested in the particular work at hand.

Aptitude or skills tests

Aptitude or skills assessment tests try to get at how well you're likely to perform the technical components of a job or career. Colleges widely use these kinds of tests as part of the admissions process for professional careers, such as medicine (Medical College Admission Test or MCAT), law (Law School Admission Test or LSAT), dentistry (Dental Admission Test or DAT), and business (Graduate Management Admission Test or GMAT).

You can also find tests for aptitude or ability in mechanical work, clerical work, electrical work, navigation, and many other specific areas. Some of these tests are written, and other tests include performance components. For example, for many years, the Dental Admission Test required applicants to carve a piece of chalk according to certain specifications. Now, students taking the DAT use a paper-and-pencil perceptual test that measures the same skills.

You may take one of these tests, and the results suggest that you're well suited in aptitude for medicine — but you hate the sight of blood. Or maybe your aptitude suggests dentistry, but you really prefer working outdoors. So, although aptitude tests may help you figure out one aspect of the puzzle, they don't give you the complete picture.

What EQ can add to the job equation

Emotional intelligence can add another dimension to the career search experience. Testing people's emotional intelligence by using tests such as the EQ-i or MSCEIT often provides additional insight to the career searcher (refer to Chapter 4 for more about those tests). Your EQ test results can help you look at strengths and weaknesses that you might not have considered before. Fortunately, many professional groups, colleges, and training programs now recognize the value of emotional intelligence. A number of medical schools, business schools, engineering programs, and others are now incorporating emotional intelligence into their selection criteria. Here are a few examples of how emotional intelligence can be relevant to your career choice:

✔ **Self-regard:** A person's ability to respect and accept his strengths and weaknesses. People who have high self-regard often work well at jobs that involve a great deal of rejections or obstacles. Cold-call salespeople who have high self-regard, for example, tend to be more successful in their job.

✔ **Emotional self-awareness:** A person's ability to be aware of and understand her thoughts and feelings and her impact on others. You'd find this ability useful in any job where you need to make a positive impression on others. Knowing how you feel helps you realize how you come across to others when you try to sell a product or an idea, for example.

✔ **Assertiveness:** Your ability to express your feelings, beliefs, and thoughts in a nondestructive way. Successful salespeople, managers, and leaders tend to have plenty of assertiveness.

✔ **Independence:** Your ability to self-direct and not feel emotionally dependent on others. At all levels in the workplace, employers want people to feel independent. In research carried out at Multi-Health Systems, we found that customer service and technical support people who are high in independence tend be rated as better performers than those low in this skill.

✔ **Self-actualization:** Involves your ability to set personal goals, realize your potential, and be passionate about your work. In research on hundreds of different jobs, carried out at Multi-Health Systems, self-actualization was one of the best predictors of success. People who are passionate about what they do are more in tune with their work and perform at optimal levels.

✔ **Empathy:** Your ability to be aware of, understand, and appreciate the feelings of others. Empathy is an important skill in many people-oriented jobs — such as sales, customer service, and leadership. People high in empathy seem to prefer working in jobs in which they meet and get to know other people.

✔ **Social responsibility:** Your ability to demonstrate yourself as a cooperative, contributing member of your social group. People high in social responsibility make good team players. Some of the Center for Creative Leadership's recent research shows that top leaders are high in this emotional skill.

✔ **Interpersonal relationships:** Your ability to establish and maintain mutually satisfying relationships with others. If you score high in this area, you're probably suited for a career in which you deal with other people and maintain relationships.

✔ **Stress tolerance:** Your ability to effectively withstand adverse events and constructively cope. Many of today's jobs involve dealing with stress. You really need high stress tolerance if you need to meet deadlines, deal with difficult people, and juggle many different tasks. People high in this skill can gauge the amount of stress on the job that they can comfortably tolerate. Some jobs are very predictable and involve very little in the way of stress. Other jobs may be quite stressful and include changing tasks, priorities, and deadlines that require that you have good stress-management skills.

✔ **Impulse control:** Your ability to resist or delay an impulse, drive, or temptation to act. Patience is a virtue in any job that requires attention to detail. Also, when you have to deal with difficult people, you need to be able to manage your impulses.

✔ **Reality testing:** Your ability to accurately assess the correspondence between what you experience and what objectively exists. For many jobs, reality testing can involve interpreting complicated information, such as accounting and engineering. People high in this skill don't let their emotions cloud their interpretation of reality.

✔ **Flexibility:** Your ability to adapt and adjust your feeling, thinking, and behavior to change. Flexibility involves whether you prefer fairly rigid, predictable work or flexible, changing jobs. Some people prefer routine work that has little change. More often than not, however, jobs today require a fair degree of flexibility.

✔ **Problem-solving:** Your ability to find solutions to problems of a personal and interpersonal nature. At work, employers highly value people who can solve problems. At my workplace, top leaders encourage people to come to their managers with solutions, not problems. By encouraging people to solve problems, managers give them more responsibility and room to grow. Also, having a workplace where everyone is encouraged to problem-solve creates a more efficient workplace. Not all problems have easy solutions, but by putting forth the effort and showing that you have the ability to problem-solve, you become a valuable employee.

✔ **Optimism:** An emotional skill that goes way beyond just thinking that the glass is half full. People high in optimism have the ability to be positive and look at the bright side of life, even during tough times. This set of skills enables you to rally the troops and get things done, regardless of the circumstances. At work, optimistic people look beyond the negatives and continue to be productive. You may find optimism very important in certain occupations that require overcoming obstacles, leading others, or delivering bad news. Your level of optimism can help point you towards certain career choices.

✔ **Happiness:** Happiness transcends the situations in your life. Happy people have the ability to feel satisfied with themselves, others, and life in general. Their happiness doesn't depend on their salary, which office they occupy, how many friends they have at work, or other circumstances. Happy people do well in dealing with customers, creating longer term relationships with their clients, and maintaining a positive culture at work.

Your general mood can help you narrow the options in your career search. You may find optimism, for example, very important in certain occupations which require overcoming obstacles, leading others, or delivering bad news. Your level of optimism can help point you towards certain career choices.

By going to a career counselor or coach, who can test you for emotional intelligence, you may discover a number of skills that can help you pinpoint the types of jobs that may be best suited to you. Feeling emotionally in tune with what you do professionally can go a long way in helping make your work enjoyable.

Assessing Your Work Life

Okay, so you already have a job. You're fairly happy with what you're doing, but you know that you could have a better career. You're not very excited about or happy with what you're doing for a living. When you wake up in the morning on a workday, you aren't excited about starting your day.

You may be thinking about changing your job. However, you might want to look at what you can change within yourself to make your job feel more comfortable for you. You can try three exercises that involve your thoughts and emotions if you want to change the way you feel about the work you're doing. I describe those three exercises in the following sections.

Understanding that you are what you feel

Think about how your feelings affect your work. Do you get more done when you're excited? Or are you more productive in a relaxed state of mind? Everyone has optimum emotions for getting work done. Sometimes, listening to the right kind of music can help get you in the mood to work.

If you feel bored with or disinterested in your work, that feeling affects your attitude and your performance. Feeling out of tune with your work can start raising questions about why you're doing what you're doing, whether you can find better opportunities, or whether you need to keep your current job just for the money. Being unsatisfied at work can really distract you, and your performance suffers as a result. Poor work performance can affect your feelings about yourself and your outlook on life, in general.

Also, different kinds of work may require different moods. You can often do careful, detail-oriented work more successfully when you're in a sad or depressed mood. You can be more productive in doing creative work when you're in a happy mood.

Think of some of the best work you've done. What mood were you in when you did that work? Getting to know your moods and how they affect your work can help you identify your most productive states and get the most enjoyment out of work.

Of course, you also need to examine the reverse process, too. What happens at work can affect your feelings. Getting into an argument with a co-worker might make you feel depressed and then unproductive for the rest of the day. Getting some bad news, such as a poor performance evaluation, from your boss can distract you from doing a good job or paying attention to the details of your work.

Knowing whether your job feels right

You probably have a good sense about how your current work feels for you. Does thinking about work get you all excited? Do you spend a lot of time when you're away from work talking about the good things that happen at work? When you wake up in the morning, are you excited about getting to work? Do you prefer Mondays or Fridays — or, as one of my colleagues put it, do you celebrate TGIM (Thank God Its Monday)?

On the other hand, you might dread going to work. You might be someone who wakes up with knots in your stomach, pressure around your head, or feeling just plain *ugh*. If so, then something's not going well for you in your current job position. You probably have a good sense whether the work you do is right for you.

Here are some signs that can help you know whether your work isn't working for you:

- ✔ I spend a lot of time at work doing non-work things (such as surfing the Web or reading magazines).
- ✔ When I'm at work, I look forward to quitting time all day.
- ✔ I talk a lot about things I'd rather be doing than my current job.
- ✔ I don't really like the people I work with.
- ✔ I wish I had more responsibility at work.
- ✔ I feel like I'm at a dead end with nowhere to go.
- ✔ I like figuring out new things at work, and that's not happening in my job.
- ✔ I'm not happy with my boss.
- ✔ I don't feel that my company has a bright future.

If you agree with any of the statements in the preceding list, then you need to start thinking about your options. You can go with the flow and continue on the path you're already on. You can decide to re-evaluate your situation, then start to change things at work and your feelings about them. Or you can re-evaluate your work situation, then decide to change jobs within the company or start looking elsewhere for work.

Getting a feel for what you do best

If you decide that you've reached the time to re-evaluate your work situation (I give some tips for finding out whether you're in that situation in the preceding section), you need to know where to start to make a change. Look at your current job — you must enjoy some aspects of your work. Maybe you like talking to customers on the phone, helping others with technical problems, problem-solving difficult situations, and so on.

Before you can make a change, you must know how you feel about your current situation. To help you assess your current situation, follow these steps:

1. **In your notebook, write down at least three activities, tasks, or responsibilities that you like about your job.**

   Or, at least, write down what attracted you to the job in the first place.

2. **Think of the activities, tasks, or responsibilities that you don't like at work and write three of them in your notebook.**

   You may not like some of the people you work with, the amount of paperwork, the lack of interpersonal interaction with others, or any number of things.

3. **Consider the activities, tasks, and responsibilities that you like about your job and ask yourself whether you can make changes relating to those activities, tasks, or responsibilities.**

   Can you

   - Increase the amount of time that you spend on the tasks you like.

   - Link the tasks you like to specific skills (such as dealing with people, solving problems, and working with technology).

   - Look at work in a general way — outside your specific job. Think of which aspects of work you really like doing (such as being with people, working on your own, and supervising others).

   - Think about other jobs at your place of work that incorporate these skills (such as customer service, technical support, and sales).

   - Think outside the box, considering other careers that use these skills.

   - Explore the careers or jobs that maximize these skills, either with friends, on the Internet, by checking job boards, by consulting your human resource person, or by talking with a career counselor.

4. **Consider how you might change the tasks or responsibilities that you don't like.**

   Figure out whether you can apply any of these suggestions:

   • Reduce the amount of time spent on the aspects that you don't like.

   • Delegate some of the tasks that you don't like.

   • Look for other jobs in the organization that avoid these tasks.

   • Look at other jobs elsewhere that avoid these tasks.

5. **Summarize what you like about your job, what you're good at, what you like about work in general, and changes you'd like to make regarding your career.**

   Focus on the tasks and responsibilities that you like most about your job. Use these activities as a springboard to get you where you want to go. Can you better develop your strengths in areas you enjoy through experiences, learning programs offered through your workplace, educational opportunities in outside institutions (colleges, skills training programs), or mentoring situations? Try to develop a game plan for your next steps.

6. **Visualize your future.**

   Think about where you see yourself five years from now. Try to fill in the gaps from your current strengths, where you want them to be, and your ideal career. You can then develop your action plan.

Knowing your strengths and weaknesses can give you a leg up when you're looking to make career changes. Too often, people apply for jobs in a hit-and-miss manner, just hoping for the best. But knowing more about yourself — what you like doing, what you're good at, and what you want to avoid — can really help you find a job that feels right for you. You may not be able to find the perfect job — doing only and exclusively what you want and like — but you can maximize the joy of work.

Testing can help you learn more about your strengths as well as your interests and skills. Start with a well thought-out list of likes and dislikes, which you can create by using the preceding steps. Testing your emotional intelligence can help confirm some of your strengths, identify some areas in which you can improve, and provide you with a clear roadmap ahead.

Improving Your Performance When Working with People

Most jobs today involve interaction with others. Not all interaction is face to face. You may interact with colleagues or customers on the phone, or virtually through e-mail, text messaging, or live video. Of course, depending on the job, the amount of time you spend with others varies.

Some jobs, including jobs in healthcare, service industries, manufacturing, financial services, information technology, and other areas, have a high degree of involvement with other people. Specific functions of these jobs may include sales, customer service, technical support, management of others, providing health services, or working in a team.

Here are some ways that you can gauge whether your job is people-oriented:

- ✔ You spend at least two hours of your day communicating with other people.
- ✔ You deal directly with customers (external or internal to the organization).
- ✔ You spend a lot of time on the phone at work.
- ✔ You supervise one or more people.
- ✔ You help people solve problems.

The preceding list gives you some examples of ways that you may spend your time at work with people. You may find it hard to think of many jobs in which you don't spend any of your time with others, but they're out there. For tips on working in a people-less environment, see the section "Improving Your Performance When Working Alone," later in this chapter.

Knowing whether you're a people person

After you establish how much of your job involves dealing with other people (as I discuss in the preceding section), you must determine whether you're a people person. Consider whether the responsibilities you like about work include other people or involve tasks that you basically perform alone.

This consideration gives you your first big clue about whether you're a people person. In addition, see how many of the following items apply to you:

- ✔ I spend most of my time at my desk, by myself, and not on the phone.
- ✔ I hate going to meetings.
- ✔ People chatting at work drive me crazy.
- ✔ I hate facing customers.
- ✔ I cringe when my boss comes to speak to me.
- ✔ I try to avoid a number of people at work.
- ✔ I'd be a lot more productive if people just left me alone.

If you agree with three or more of the items in the preceding list, you're very probably *not* a people person. If you don't agree with most of that list, you probably enjoy being around other people — and you're in the majority. For most people, one of the most important things about their work is the people they interact with.

If you're a people person, you can get more enjoyment out of work by balancing the amount of time you spend with others and working on your own. Some jobs require you to deal with people close to 100 percent of the time, basically requiring you to always be "on." Other jobs provide substantial down time, when you can catch up on paperwork or do other administrative tasks.

How do you rate your ideal time at work with others? Choose which of the following statements describe you best:

- ✔ I'm a people person — I want to be with people 100 percent of the time.
- ✔ I like being with people a lot — I'd be happy with 80 percent of my work time spent with people.
- ✔ I need some human contact, but I need my own space, too. I'd rather be with people 50 percent of the time.
- ✔ I prefer being on my own, but I need to connect with others occasionally — about 20 percent of the time.
- ✔ Leave me alone, I want no human contact 100 percent of the time.

Depending on the flexibility of your job, you may be able to structure your time alone and with others. If you can't work in the mix that suits you best, see what you can do to modify your time. If people distract you, speak to your supervisor about what accommodations your supervisor can make for you. If you need more time with others, see whether your workplace can accommodate it.

Dealing effectively with people at work

You may find yourself in a situation in which you have to deal with people more than you want to. Even worse, you may have to spend time with people you don't even like. You may want to know how to get the best out of the time you spend with others.

Here are some tips for dealing with people you don't enjoy spending time with on the job:

- **Know your work style.** Determine whether certain people bother you or whether you generally just want to work alone. If it's specific people, you can organize your day around those people.

- **Know your feelings.** Decide whether you prefer to work with some people (either employees or certain types of customers) and not others. You can organize your time as much as possible around the people you prefer to be with.

- **Pick a time of day.** See whether you're more open to dealing with others at a particular time of day.

- **Choose a place.** Decide whether you're more comfortable working with others in a particular place (for example, standing at his desk so that you can decide when to leave).

- **Plan ahead.** Plan your interactions (set a goal for them) in advance so that you can keep them structured and control the time.

- **Keep it short.** Set the amount of time for your interactions in advance and try to stick to it.

- **Be professional.** Be pleasant, even you if you don't like the person you have to deal with.

Don't be immature or unprofessional in your relationships with people at work. Be polite, matter-of-fact, and business-like. If you have difficulty approaching certain people at work, you may want to plan out the interaction in advance. Try practicing the scenario of what you want to happen in your mind before you approach the person. Rehearsing the interaction can make it easier to get through the actual encounter.

Improving Your Performance When Working Alone

You may spend most of your time at work alone or in front of a computer screen with minimal interaction. Some people prefer working on their own. They find it easier to focus and get things done without distractions such as the phone, e-mail, or people dropping by.

Nevertheless, in the real world of work, you do need to have some contact with others. The following sections show you how to manage those contacts that you must have while remaining productive.

Knowing whether you prefer to work alone

If you complete the activity in the section "Getting a feel for what you do best," earlier in this chapter, you have a good idea of whether you like working with people. Generally speaking, people who don't enjoy working with others gravitate to more technical jobs. So, you may be interested in more mechanical, mathematical, programming, or engineering kinds of activities. Or you may prefer writing, designing, composing, and other more artistic pursuits.

Of course, not all mechanics, artists, and the like work poorly with people. But, if given the choice, people doing this kind of work tend to prefer working alone rather than in teams or groups, for the most part.

Regardless of your preference to work alone, you do need to interact with others sometimes. For example, you may need to

✔ Get instructions on what you need to do.

✔ Get feedback on your work.

✔ Sell your ideas to others.

✔ Explain your work to others.

✔ Have new elements (tools or ideas, for example) of your work explained to you.

✔ Share your ideas.

✔ Deal with misconceptions about your work.

✔ Promote the quality of your work.

You need to have enough time to do your work without neglecting the need to communicate with others (for the reasons such as the ones in the preceding list). If you find yourself in this situation, you need the assets of time management and communication skills to come up with the optimal balance for you.

Getting better at working alone

Everyone can improve the work that they do. If you spend most of your time working alone, you need to be both a good communicator and a good time manager. You probably see the need for time management; any working person needs to be able to manage her time. But you may be wondering why someone working alone should be a good communicator.

Communicating well with others

In the preceding section, I outline a number of reasons that solo workers need to be able to communicate. You have to be a *good* communicator because you spend less time communicating with others. So, you have less of an opportunity to clarify or correct any miscommunications. You need to get your points across clearly and effectively. You also have to know whether the person you're talking to receives your communication. Too often, people pass along information without knowing whether the recipient correctly understood it.

Here are some suggestions for communicating well with others:

- ✔ **Know your message.** Know in advance what message(s) you want to deliver.

- ✔ **Be complete.** Write your message down in an item-by-item list so that you don't miss anything.

- ✔ **Visualize your delivery.** Imagine how you want to deliver your message.

- ✔ **Be pleasant.** Practice being pleasant (you probably don't get much opportunity for pleasantry if you work alone). For example, smile when you deliver your message. Even if you speak over the phone, the other person can hear your smile. Practice basic etiquette, such as acknowledging the other person, listening to both his verbal and non-verbal cues, and generally being polite. You can practice being nice to fellow workers and acquaintances by being nice to your family and friends.

- ✔ **Confirm that the person you're speaking to understands your message.** Figure out how you want to confirm that the other person properly received your message. Ask questions, such as, "Does that make sense to you? Do you need any more information?"

✔ **Relax.** If your emotions sometimes get in the way of delivering your message, practice relaxation methods such as deep breathing, distraction, and meditation (refer to Chapter 6).

Motivating yourself

When you work alone, you may find motivating yourself a difficult aspect of time management. Because you usually don't have many checks and balances on your time, you can easily get lost in distracting activities. You can overcome this obstacle by setting tight goals and deadlines.

Here are some suggestions for setting your goals:

✔ **Establish goals.** Make sure that you have goals for what you want to accomplish.

✔ **Establish milestones to meet those goals.** Break down these goals into small, measurable pieces, or *milestones.*

✔ **Create a timeline.** Tie each milestone to a specific timeline (for example, "Finish writing intro to report by 2 p.m. Tuesday").

✔ **Be realistic.** Don't be overambitious in setting your goals.

✔ **Reward yourself along the way.** Try to reward yourself for each of the milestones you reach. You can use small rewards (such as a piece of chocolate for small milestones) and bigger rewards (such as a walk around the block) for bigger ones.

✔ **Celebrate!** Celebrate the completion of each major goal or accomplishment (for example, go somewhere nice for dinner).

Influencing People at Work

Whatever you do, you probably need to influence other people at work. Most schools don't offer courses about sales, but everyone has something to sell. Even business schools today focus primarily on marketing. You may need to sell your ideas, point of view, strategies, tactics, techniques, and even yourself (think of the last time you tried to get a raise).

Influencing people at work is a lot like sales. The techniques of successful sales have changed a great deal over the years. Old-time salespeople, using the right tricks or manipulations, could sell anything to anyone. Today, people are much more skeptical — especially of people who *look* like they're trying to sell something. You can almost see the "what's his ulterior motive?" look come over people's faces.

In years gone by, sales was about benefits (not features). Salespeople used to list all the benefits of their product — saves time, makes you look younger, saves you money. Before that it was features — more bells and whistles such as greater horsepower, more colors to choose from, bigger trunk, extra radio speakers. Benefits are still important, but what's the most important word in sales today? Most people say it's listening. I say it's empathy.

The following sections cover the importance of empathy and assertiveness in the workplace.

Using empathy to make your sale

Influencing people at all levels involves knowing where they're coming from and being able to walk in their shoes. If you understand the other person, then you're better able to make your points. You don't waste your time trying to sell someone something that she's not interested in.

A large study that Multi-Health Systems did with the U.S. Air Force tried to determine what made Air Force recruiters successful. At the time that Multi-Health Systems became involved, recruiters had a high turnover rate. Recruiters, like salespeople, have to convince people that they can get many direct benefits by enlisting in the Air Force.

Traditionally, the Air Force selected recruiters largely based on their performance from various types of jobs. So, for example, a good mechanical person who wanted to change positions could be eligible to become a recruiter. The Air Force decided whether an applicant got the job based on a number of performance factors, but those factors usually had little to do with whether the person would be a good recruiter.

Together with the Air Force, Multi-Health Systems tested over 1,400 recruiters to determine their emotional intelligence, and then looked at how successfully those recruiters recruited. This information showed that a recruiter needed empathy to successfully influence others.

When the Air Force used the EQ-i as a major part of the selection process, focusing on empathy and four other EI factors, the Air Force increased the retention rate of Air Force recruiters by 92 percent, saving $2.7 million in the first year alone.

So, the next time you need to convince any of your co-workers, customers, or even your boss of something, remember empathy.

Here are some approaches you can take to help secure a sale:

✔ Try to put yourself in the other person's shoes and think about what he would want from your proposal, idea, or request.

✔ Put less emphasis on things that you find important and focus on what the other person is interested in.

✔ Put the other person's biggest wins up first. What's the biggest benefit that the other person can gain? Can you save her time, make her more relaxed, or help her earn more money?

✔ While you think of your presentation (or your sale), imagine how the other person will interpret everything that you say.

✔ Convince the other person that he wants the same thing you want.

By understanding and using empathy, you can be a lot more effective in influencing others around you.

Understanding assertiveness

Another important skill that increases your ability to influence others is assertiveness. A lot of people have a misconception about what assertiveness really means. Consider the following three ways of expressing yourself:

✔ **Passive:** You don't fully express how you feel and think about people and things.

✔ **Assertive:** You can express your thoughts, feelings, and beliefs without offending the other person. An assertive person can completely disagree with you on politics or religion, for example, and yet be your friend.

✔ **Aggressive:** You overly impose your views and feelings on others.

Here are some ways that you can become more assertive:

✔ Differentiate facts from opinions when you interact with someone.

If someone states opinion as fact, ask him how he knows the statement is true. Does he have evidence?

✔ Be aware of your own thoughts, feelings, and beliefs, and practice expressing them to people you are close to so you are at ease talking about these issues.

✔ Differentiate your own opinions and beliefs from facts when you interact with others.

✔ Be friendly and polite when you disagree with someone.

✔ Don't be afraid to state your preferences. You can do so without offending others by not getting personal — that is, without insults, put-downs, being derogatory, being overly inflammatory, overgeneralizing, or overstating your case.

✔ Get comfortable asking other people how they feel about things you're interested in.

Being assertive is a skill, and it takes some practice. However, becoming more assertive can certainly help you influence others more effectively.

Becoming a Better Team Player

In today's workplace, more often than not, people work in teams. These teams can be permanent, in which everyone in the team works together as a group, day in and day out. Or the teams can be temporary, getting together only sporadically to work toward specific, agreed-upon goals.

You're part of a team if you

✔ Work with at least one other person on a project.

✔ Work together with a group of people regularly.

✔ Share a common goal with people you interact with virtually (through e-mail, for example).

✔ Have a common goal or purpose with one or more co-workers.

✔ Depend on others to help you get your job done.

✔ Have others depend on you to get their jobs done.

The following sections show how you can be a more effective team player. Working well with your teammates has a number of benefits. People who work well together are much happier at work. Being part of a team gives you a feeling of belonging and a sense of being part of something bigger than yourself.

When teams work well, their members can find them very productive and rewarding. Of course, teams can also be dysfunctional. The first thing to consider when looking at your work team is how you feel about the other team members. Do you like the other people on your team, or do some team members have interpersonal difficulties? If you want a team to work, at a minimum, you all have to get along.

Understanding work teams

Being part of a work team means that you and the people you work with have a common set of goals that you're working toward. You also all pull together to reach those goals (hopefully!). High-functioning teams have great communication. When a problem arises, each member is comfortable expressing her thoughts, beliefs, and feelings about it. Individual petty politics don't belong in effective teams. The team critiques ideas, and team members don't take the criticisms personally.

Teams can work in face-to-face or virtual environments. Many of the rules are the same. For teams to work well, the members must respect each other. If a team has a member who fails to respect the rules or is inconsiderate to others, the members should talk about the issue and deal with it. When the other members think a person doesn't fully contribute to the team, you could face problems in morale that effect the performance of the team as a whole.

All team members should strive for the greater good of the team or the organization as a whole, and put aside their own personal issues. Emotional intelligence plays an important role in keeping a team flowing smoothly. The ability to manage your own emotions can help you keep a team on track. By managing your emotions, you keep your focus on the task at hand and the greater good of the group.

Fitting in on a team

Emotional intelligence helps teams function smoothly in a number of ways. The emotional skills of each of the team members play a role in making the team function smoothly. Select which of the following statements represents your attitude towards your team members:

- ✔ I really don't like my teammates — we just don't get along.

- ✔ I can take them or leave them. We really don't go out of our way to help each other.

- ✔ I like my teammates at work, but we really have nothing in common outside of work.

- ✔ I love my team — we're like a well-oiled machine. I know what my teammate is thinking before he even says it.

If people in your team just don't have any chemistry, you can't easily fix that problem. You might want to call in an outside consultant to work with your team, or you might just have it reconstituted altogether. However, if the team just isn't gelling, you can try a number of things to make it a better fit:

✔ Make sure your team has clear goals.

Make the goals measurable and time-limited (for example, "Have the exterior costs for the project completed by Wednesday at 2 p.m.").

✔ Clearly spell out everyone's responsibility regarding their roles in meeting the team's goals.

✔ Keep your discussions professional and avoid letting personal or petty conflicts interfere with reaching goals.

✔ Find time away from work to socialize with team members.

Helping your teammates

Sometimes, you may feel that other teammates just aren't pulling their weight. You work hard on a project, getting all your pieces of the puzzle together, only to discover that one of your teammates has let the others down. You naturally feel frustrated and angry.

However, being angry likely can't help the situation. You or one of your other teammates needs to confront the non-performer. Of course, I mean confront in an assertive — not aggressive — way.

Here are some tips to try if one of your teammates isn't performing:

✔ Ask the member directly whether she has a problem with the work or the team.

✔ If she does have a problem, try to problem-solve it together.

✔ See whether the teammate needs more resources.

✔ Ask whether the teammate has a perception of unfairness among the team members that the team leader needs to address.

✔ See whether the team member is the right fit for the team, both technically and emotionally.

✔ Give the member a timeline for any specific, agreed-upon adjustments that you want to take place.

You can't easily solve all team problems. Sometimes, you need to change the team to make it function healthily. See the sidebar "Changing the team," in this chapter, for an example of how you can handle this situation.

Changing the team

Sometimes, you need to change a team in order to retain a healthy work atmosphere and meet the set goals. In this example, Heather, a project coordinator, confronts Howard about missed deadlines and his overall commitment to the team.

The deadline's only a week away. Everyone has put in hundreds of hours getting their part ready for a major customer presentation. Everyone, that is, except Howard. Howard's unable, or unwilling, to get the costs worked out for his part of the project. The overall project, if the customer accepts it, could earn the company over $1 million.

"What do you mean, you couldn't get it done?" asks Heather.

"Well, I was kinda busy with other things," Howard sheepishly tells her.

"Howard, you know how important this information is to the team. The whole presentation depends on getting all the costs together," she firmly states.

"Sorry," he replies.

"Howard, this isn't the first time you've been late with your work. Are you having a problem being part of this team?" Heather asks.

"What do you mean?" asks Howard, a bit surprised.

"I just don't get the feeling that you're really a part of this team. I need to know right now whether you really want to be with this team or whether we should look at other arrangements. I really appreciate a lot of the work you've done, Howard, but I think it would we best for all of us if you decide where you really want to be," states Heather.

"I'm really sorry, Heather, but you're right. I have a lot of other projects I'm involved in right now. Maybe it's better if I retire from this team," Howard says.

Although someone leaving a team is never pleasant, it's much more productive than letting the entire team (and company) suffer because of one person's performance. Better to clear the air and come to a conclusion that lets everyone continue to focus on their work.

Of course, Howard could have decided that he wanted to stay with this team. In that case, Heather would work with him in setting and achieving clear goals that have measurable outcomes. She could negotiate and provide any additional support that Howard needed.

Chapter 11

Becoming an Emotionally Intelligent Leader

*W*hat does it mean to be a leader? People have written thousands of books about leadership. Who do you think of when you hear the word *leadership?* John Kennedy, Mohandas Gandhi, Martin Luther King Jr., Winston Churchill, Henry Ford, Bill Gates, Teddy Roosevelt, or Margaret Thatcher?

Everyone has his or her own image of who a leader is or what a leader should be. To complicate matters even further, leadership experts have developed hundreds of theories about leadership. You probably don't really see yourself as a leader or aspire to become president, prime minister, CEO, director, or some other kind of leader.

In reality, leadership is easily defined. *Leadership* involves any situation in which you want someone else to do something. You can't have leadership without followership. Think of all the situations in which you've tried to influence the behavior of others. In those situations, in fact, you acted as a leader. If you try to influence your spouse, children, friends, colleagues, neighbors, subordinates, service people, or anyone else in your life, then you're a leader.

This chapter shows you what it takes to be a successful leader and what you can do to get better at leading others. Not everyone, however, is suited to be a leader at work. I look at how being a leader at work can have some benefits, such as increased status or more money, but also some liabilities, such as the nature of the responsibilities and the amount of time required to supervise others.

Getting Others to Do Things at Work

Most people at work depend on others to help them get their jobs done. But you usually don't have authority over the people whose help you need. You may have noticed in your workplace how some people manage to get help from others all the time. Others, however, struggle when they try to pull in even a few favors from their colleagues.

Emotional intelligence plays a big part in your ability to get help from others. Your emotional skills play an important role in your capacity to be a leader, as well. Skills such as empathy, optimism, and the ability to develop effective interpersonal relationships can predict success in a leadership role (which I talk about in the section "Defining an effective workplace leader" later in this chapter).

Deciding whether you want to be a manager

Most working people dream about climbing the ladder of work success. Generally, people measure this success by a promotion to a management position. After a certain amount of time spent on the front lines at work — whether you work in sales, customer service, or technical support, or as an insurance adjuster or watch maker — you eventually expect that you'll receive a promotion. In fact, after a certain amount of time, you may suspect something is wrong if you don't get a promotion.

Of course, when the offer comes, you're extremely excited. Not only does the business that you work for recognize your good work, but you get increased responsibility, prospects for more interesting work, a chance to be the boss, and (not insignificantly) more money. What could be better than that?

Well, unfortunately, many people who get promoted from a staff position or line worker to manager don't work out all that well in the new job. After all, what does being a good plumber, doctor, or salesperson have to do with managing other plumbers, doctors, and salespeople?

Promoting someone who's good at one set of skills directly into a job that involves a completely different set of skills is a risky business. Here are some questions that you can ask yourself to help determine whether you're management material:

- Do you like supervising other people?
- Do you like administrative tasks and paperwork?

✔ Are you happy giving up the main (or hands-on) parts of your current job?

✔ Do you like doing performance reviews about other people?

✔ Do you like reporting on the performance of everyone in your group to your boss?

✔ Do you like setting goals for your group and ensuring that the group meets those goals?

✔ Are you good at keeping your cool when other people around you are stressing out?

✔ Are you good at keeping other people cool when they start stressing out?

✔ Do you like helping other people solve problems?

If some of these tasks sound exciting to you, you may be ready for a change to a management job; however, I strongly recommend that you prepare for a dramatic change in the type of work that you do.

You can take a management training program to prepare for this type of new challenge. Also, consider seeking a business coach or mentor to help prepare yourself to become a manager. Most importantly, enter your new challenge with both eyes open. Be sure to have a pretty clear list of your job functions, responsibilities, and objectives.

Getting someone to listen to you

If you want to be a leader, you must have at least one follower. If you want to lead others, you have to know how to get their attention, set clear objectives for what you expect of them, and monitor their performance.

Here's how you can know whether people are listening to you:

✔ People at work pay attention to what you say.

✔ Co-workers ask your opinion or advice on work issues.

✔ You can change other people's behavior.

✔ Other people see you as a source of new or interesting information.

✔ Other people at work find you trustworthy and see you as someone with whom they can confide.

You can improve your ability to get others to listen to you. They don't automatically respect you or obey your every command, but you can earn more positive attention from others.

A big part of being a leader involves being *credible,* or honest and trustworthy. Being credible helps you earn respect from others. Unfortunately, you can't use a quick fix to make yourself credible. You have to earn credibility over time, in part by keeping your word. When you make a promise or commitment, you need to follow through. If, for any reason, you can't follow through, you have to explain why as honestly as you can.

People also listen to someone who they feel has their best interests at heart. In emotional-intelligence terms, you can earn this trust by using empathy. If you're empathic, you're more likely to gain the cooperation of others because you show concern about their welfare. If you act in a self-serving or callous manner, people are more likely to avoid you.

Here are a few things you can do to become empathic at work:

- ✔ Pay attention to the people with whom you work.
- ✔ Find out about co-workers' interests.
- ✔ Reflect back your interpretation of what others tell you in order to make sure that you've captured the other person's concerns accurately.
- ✔ Check whether you accurately reflect the other person's feelings after he expresses them to you.
- ✔ Show others that you have an interest in them, their family, and their interests.
- ✔ Avoid trying to make yourself the center of attention.

If you have the courtesy and compassion to pay attention to others around you, you increase the likelihood that others will pay attention to you. By caring about others and demonstrating that you are not self-centered, you earn their trust.

Eliciting cooperative behavior from others

After you start to get other people's attention (as I discuss in the preceding section), you need to get others to cooperate with you.

Generally speaking, people tend to do what's in their best interests. If you want to convince someone to work with you or comply with your requests, make sure she knows that she can benefit. The benefit can be as simple as someone wanting to support you and feeling good when you feel good. Or you might need to establish a more complex interaction in which the other person receives some clear benefit, either immediately or sometime down the road.

You get the best type of cooperative behavior when people honestly want to help and support you. You usually have to earn this type of cooperation by helping and supporting others, having positive and likeable personality attributes, and winning people over.

You can work at being helpful to others. However, you may find changing personality attributes a bit difficult. Staying positive and outgoing in your relationships helps make changing personality attributes easier. But being likeable comes more naturally to some people than others.

As part of your strategy for getting people to change, try working toward winning them over. The components of the Bar-On model of emotional intelligence (covered in Chapter 4) that can help you include self-regard and optimism:

- **Self-regard:** Having high self-regard means that you have a good understanding of your strengths and weaknesses. Acting on this understanding requires that you have good self-knowledge and effectively strike a balance between being confident and being arrogant. People are more comfortable helping others who demonstrate the right amount of humility.

- **Optimism:** People find optimism and happiness attractive attributes. People are more likely to cooperate with someone who's optimistic. People who are optimistic have a way of letting you know that cooperation is in everyone's best interests. If you're going to go to bat for someone, you very probably help an optimist over a pessimist, someone self-assured over someone arrogant or uncertain, and someone who's happy over someone who's sad.

- **Happiness:** Happiness, like optimism, attracts people. When you're happy you are more pleasant to be around. Being happy adds to your "likability" factor. It can also be contagious. Everybody likes to be happy, and being around happy people contributes to one's own happiness.

Here are some tips that you can use to become an optimistic leader:

- Focus on the positive of situations and people, even when it's difficult.

- Look toward solutions, rather than problems.

- Tell people about their strengths.

- Focus on your successes, not your failures.

- Treat failures as lessons that you can use to increase your self-understanding and improve future performance.

Leading Other People

Business school professors, psychologists, and management experts have done a lot of formal research and writing about what makes a good leader. In most theories of leadership, emotional intelligence (as I define it in this book) plays a big role in those leadership definitions.

James Kouzes and Barry Posner have proposed one well-known theory of leadership, which they fully describe in their book *The Leadership Challenge* (Wiley). In their work, they surveyed thousands of people about what qualities of leadership had influenced them in their lives. Their results show that leaders of all types, regardless of industry, have a set of universal qualities. Although each leader had individual characteristics and styles of leadership, leaders shared patterns of leadership.

From these patterns, Kouzes and Posner identified five practices that describe the most effective leaders:

- ✔ **Model the way.** Set an example through both your words and deeds. Successful leaders say what they want to accomplish and then go out and get it done. The leader needs to walk the talk if he wants others to follow.

  In emotional intelligence terms, this practice involves assertiveness and independence. People who are assertive have no difficulty expressing their thoughts, feelings, and beliefs. Also, people who are independent listen to and take in the advice of others, but in the end, make their own informed decisions. Independence implies taking action in order to carry things out.

- ✔ **Inspire a shared vision.** Create a positive view of the future and share that vision with others. As a leader, you must convince others that you understand their needs and have their best interests at heart. Together, you can go out and build that vision of the future.

  Inspiring a shared vision requires a good deal of empathy and optimism. Your optimism gives your vision a positive and desirable flavor so that others want to share in it. You need to present your image so that people are attracted to the outcome and want to buy into it. Your empathy ensures that you hit the right chord in terms of what others want to see and hear from you.

- ✔ **Challenge the process.** Strive for change. Look for opportunities to improve and grow. Also, experiment and take risks. Not every new venture is successful, and you can find helpful information in your failures, as well as in your successes.

One of the key emotional intelligence skills that you need in order to challenge the status quo is flexibility. Flexible people are more likely to try new things, take risks, and face new challenges without fear. You also need empathy when challenging the process. You often get ideas about which direction to go when you listen carefully to others — customers, co-workers, researchers, management consultants, business coaches, business book authors, and the public at large.

✔ **Enable others to act.** Because success today usually requires a team (and because leaders, by definition, require followers), you need to enable others to act. Leaders can empower others in a variety of ways. You can test for a leader's success in this area by counting how often she uses *we,* rather than *I.*

Enable others by fostering collaboration and building trust. You must know how to engage other people in the work process. Do you, as a leader, share power? Can people get all the resources that they need to perform at their best? Successful leaders share power, delegate well, and do what's necessary to help others perform.

In terms of emotional intelligence, you need good self-regard and inter-personal skills to enable others to act. Good leaders know how to find people who complement them by making up for the leaders' areas of weakness. In order to build successful relationships, you need the skills to engage and relate to others in a meaningful way.

✔ **Encourage the heart.** The relationship of this practice to emotional intelligence is the most obvious. A key component of this practice involves recognizing the contributions of others. For example, send personal notes of appreciation to people who have helped you. Also, celebrate victories to enhance the group or community spirit. Rewarding people for their participation goes a long way in motivating them to be part of your team.

To encourage the heart, you need empathy, but you also need social responsibility. Leaders who encourage others not only need to know how those people feel but need to be capable of building relationships with them, as well. Socially responsible behaviors embody this ability to care about and contribute to others.

You need emotional intelligence to be a successful leader. Practically every modern theory of leadership includes significant elements that translate directly into the need for emotional skills. Although some theories of leadership are quite general — they encompass political, workplace, religious, and sports-team leadership — others have been developed specifically for narrower areas, such as leadership at work.

Defining an effective workplace leader

Although you can find many leadership theories out there, most of them seem to be directed at the workplace. One study that looked directly at emotional intelligence and workplace leadership was carried out by the Center for Creative Leadership (CCL) in Greensboro, North Carolina.

The CCL tested 302 leaders and senior managers by using the EQ-i (a test that measures emotional intelligence), along with a series of ratings of their on-the-job performance by superiors, colleagues, and subordinates. The pool of leaders included both highly competent and not so successful leaders. In general, the study found that emotional intelligence accounted for about 28 percent of leadership performance.

Their study also identified four pillars, or *competencies,* that successful leaders possessed, which I cover in the sections that follow:

✔ Being centered and grounded

✔ Having the ability to take action

✔ Using a participative management style

✔ Being tough-minded

Interestingly, all these competencies have emotional intelligence components.

Being centered and grounded

When successful leaders are centered and grounded, the people around them see them as having a stable mood, even when things get tough. Such leaders aren't erratic or extremely unpredictable in their behavior, and they tend to possess these traits:

✔ **Have high self-regard:** The good leaders have high self-regard. Leaders who claim to know it all tend to be poor leaders. Good leaders know their strengths — such as being a good speaker or networker — and capitalize on those strengths, as well as know their weaknesses — such as financial analysis — and fill the gaps with people who have strong skills in these areas.

✔ **Maintain balance in life:** Good leaders also seem to know how to balance their personal and work lives. They tend to avoid burning out by managing their time well. Traditionally, most leaders and aspiring leaders believed that in order to be a successful leader, you needed to be a workaholic. However, if you can manage your own life well — including stress, home life, fitness, and diet — then you have a better chance of managing the workplace well.

✔ **Are straightforward and self-aware:** People know where the good leaders stand on issues. Poor leaders tend to be wishy-washy. Also, good leaders know their own feelings and motivators. Because they know where they stand — their values and beliefs — they tend to be more consistent in their approach to issues.

✔ **Stay composed under pressure:** Good leaders don't flare up or lose control under difficult circumstances.

The following components of emotional intelligence relate to this competency:

✔ **Social responsibility:** By caring about others, you're less likely to put yourself in the center of attention.

✔ **Stress tolerance:** Managing stress involves staying focused on what's important and not getting overly taken up by your own reactions to stress or the reactions of others to the stress.

✔ **Impulse control:** People who manage their impulses well can avoid being distracted and losing control of the situation.

✔ **Optimism:** By looking for successful solutions to problems, you avoid putting yourself at the center of it all.

Having the ability to take action

Successful leaders make decisions and have a track record of making good decisions. As part of their decision-making process, they take into account the views of others. In the end, they make the best decision that they can with all available information.

Good leaders don't sit back after they make a decision. Instead, they execute. Also, as soon as they decide on a course of action, they tend not to give up easily. They know that follow-through is a critical part of the decision-making process. And they evaluate the effectiveness of the decision throughout the process so that they can constructively use both mistakes and successes.

The following measures of emotional intelligence relate to this competency:

✔ **Assertiveness:** Assertive people keep everyone in the loop by making their intentions known.

✔ **Independence:** Independent people take action. They evaluate the alternatives and take the initiative in executing the options.

✔ **Optimism:** Optimistic people have a target that they're aiming toward. These people are confident in their ability to carry out the required actions and meet the target.

Using a participative management style

Command and control leadership are no longer in style — even in the modern military, let alone in business environments. People resent being *told* what to do. Today's leaders need to win the hearts and minds of their constituents. The attitude of many people today is WIIFM ("What's in it for me?"). This type of leader needs to have a number of competencies:

- **Gets people involved:** Without getting support for their ideas, plans, and tactics, followers have little incentive to perform optimally. People want to feel involved in planning the interventions or tasks that they're assigned to carry out. They need to feel that they contribute in some way to the big picture. The more they feel that they have ownership in the initiative, the more likely they are to want to see that initiative succeed.

- **Has good listening and communication skills:** Although many leaders know how to present their ideas and directions to others, few know how to actively listen to their people to ensure those people are really onboard with the project, vision, or task at hand. Good leaders are sensitive to and can read even minor objections to ideas and requests. After good leaders recognize objections, they can easily deal with them, either by overcoming objections or by making slight adjustments to the plan. These leaders aim for what's best for the organization as a whole, not just for their own egos.

- **Puts people at ease:** Bad leaders scare people. People at ease are more likely to speak their minds, offering suggestions and ideas. Great leaders give people credit for their contributions and make them feel like an important part of the team. Even greater leaders take responsibility for bad decisions and mistakes made by their team or organization.

- **Gets everyone to support a decision.** Building consensus involves hearing everyone out. Successful leaders, after ensuring that they know everyone's position, pro and con, use their skills to get everyone on board with whatever decision the leader makes. Good leaders know that team members who feel they participated in the process are more likely to go with the prevailing consensus.

The following are the emotional intelligence skills most related to these competencies:

- **Empathy:** Being empathic enables leaders to really hear what others are saying and feeling.

- **Social responsibility:** Leaders who are *socially responsible* (who care about their community and people less fortunate, and respect society's rules) are more participatory in their leadership style.

✔ **Interpersonal relationships.** Interpersonal relationship skills help leaders cultivate the relations they need with others.

✔ **Impulse control:** Being patient helps you not interrupt others and allows you to hear out their views.

✔ **Happiness:** Happiness draws people in. People prefer working with leaders who are happy, but they tend to hide from those with less than friendly dispositions.

Being tough-minded

Successful leaders are resilient in dealing with obstacles and difficult situations. They manage to persevere in the face of obstacles, overcome challenges, and handle pressure well. These people have an air of confidence while they lead the way through difficult times.

The emotional skills related to this competency are

✔ **Self-regard:** People high in self-regard are self assured. They know their strengths and weaknesses. They use their confidence to weather difficult situations and times.

✔ **Stress tolerance:** Being good at stress tolerance means you know how to deal with difficulties when they arise. You can keep your focus and not get out of control because of the stress.

✔ **Impulse control:** Tough-minded people are patient. They don't make decisions impulsively and they don't change them willy-nilly. They can keep impulses at bay and be more focused in the long term.

Knowing your leadership skills

The skills required to lead at work are different from the skills required to do most other jobs. Review the preceding sections and think about your strengths in the areas discussed. Ask yourself how comfortable you feel about managing others. You may not want to be a leader at work, and that's okay.

In your notebook, write each of the areas below in which you feel strong. Below each one, write down a concrete example of a situation in which you demonstrated the skill. For example, you may be good at reading what others are feeling or really thinking. At a marketing meeting, you can tell that people are uncomfortable with Wendy's presentation, but no one speaks up. You're the one who nicely suggests that some of her assumptions might need checking, and if they're incorrect, she'd require a different approach.

Below are some competencies of leaders.

- ✔ Being direct with others about what you think
- ✔ Being concerned about the people you work with
- ✔ Keeping a long list of people whom you can count on when needed
- ✔ Not getting ruffled by stress
- ✔ Generally being in a good mood
- ✔ Acting in a purposeful way
- ✔ Effectively reading what others are feeling or really thinking
- ✔ Knowing what you're good at
- ✔ Being a self-starter
- ✔ Getting things done

The more of these skills you possess, the better your chances are of being a good leader. You also need some other skills, such as vision, cognitive intelligence, industry and market knowledge, technical skills, and financial/budgeting know-how. Clearly, the more skills you have, the better your chances are of being a successful leader. However, I've seen successful leaders who have good emotional and social skills, and just a few of the other skills. You simply need to use your strengths well.

Knowing your leadership weaknesses

Say that you have a number of the strengths described in the preceding sections. You're feeling good about being a manager, and you're ready to lead your workgroup. Sounds like you're on the way to being a successful leader. That's all great and good, but you need to be realistic about your weaknesses, too.

You should perform the following "self-check" before you dive into assuming a leadership role at work:

- ✔ **Confirm your feelings about your capabilities with someone else:** All too often, I find people overestimating their abilities in these areas. That's one of the reasons why I test people's emotional intelligence. When you take these tests, you can be compared to thousands of individuals of a similar age and the same gender.

- ✔ **Make sure that you have good interpersonal relationship skills.** A significant *derailer* (a reason that leaders fail) was leaders' lack of interpersonal relationship skills. Even if a leader was competent in many areas, such as technical skills, intelligence, and knowledge, she still might fail as a leader if she had poor interpersonal skills. So, if people find it hard to connect with you or you don't relate well to others, you should pay attention to this area. Meet with a coach or counselor and find out if she can help you improve in this area. With the right help, you should be able to improve your interpersonal skills.

Look for these signs regarding your interpersonal relationships:

- ✔ I find it easy to meet new people.
- ✔ I prefer socializing to being alone.
- ✔ People often come to me for advice.
- ✔ I know a lot about the people I work with.
- ✔ I'm very patient with people.
- ✔ I love showing new things to people.
- ✔ Nothing really gets me very upset.
- ✔ I'd rather ask someone for information than search through my computer.
- ✔ I have a very big contact list.
- ✔ I get more personal e-mails than junk e-mails.
- ✔ I love bouncing ideas off people.
- ✔ People love to check their solutions to problems with me.
- ✔ I rarely raise my voice or argue with people.
- ✔ I have a number of good friends with whom I disagree on issues such as politics or religion.

Be honest with yourself when you go through the preceding list. Put a check mark next to the statements that you think describe you. Put a circle around the statements that definitely don't describe you.

Knowing whether you're fit to be a workplace leader

After you honestly rate your strengths and perhaps weaknesses in skills important for workplace leadership (which you can find out about in the preceding sections), you can get a good idea what kind of leader you'd be.

You need to ask yourself a couple of questions:

✔ Do you have these leadership skills?

✔ If you don't have these skills, do you want to develop them?

The best leaders develop these skills before they take on a leadership position.

Some of the work Multi-Health Systems does with organizations involves testing young, high-performing people whom the organization has already selected for a leadership track. These people are highly intelligent and have excellent technical skills and industry knowledge. However, smart companies know that although a leader needs those traits to become a leader, those traits alone don't guarantee successful leadership.

By testing successful leaders in the organization, Multi-Health Systems can develop a star profile that outlines the emotional skills that are important for leaders in that organization. The star profile is developed through statistical formulas that identify and quantify the key emotional components that differentiate the best performing leaders from the rest in that organization. Using the top emotional skills of the star profile as a template, the organization then sets up leadership training programs or coaching opportunities for the employees who have the potential to be successful leaders. By reaching an agreed-upon standard or set of goals in each of the emotional intelligence components, potential leaders are better prepared for success after they're promoted.

If you're not yet a workplace leader or want to become an even better workplace leader, you can develop these skills. Or, on the other hand, you may decide that you really aren't interested in these skills — you prefer not to manage other people — and you want to continue using your current job skills. Don't feel discouraged if you choose not to be a workplace leader.

Rising to the occasion of good leadership

If you decide to become a workplace leader, you can use a number of your emotional skills to increase your chances of success. I assume that you already show the intelligence and technical skills that you need to be a leader. If you read through this chapter, you can get a clear idea of the social and emotional skills that you need to successfully lead others.

Keep these suggestions in mind if you're a leader at work:

✔ **Pay attention to the people you work with.** Get to know the people you're leading. Discover their likes and dislikes. Know what they think about their workplace and the work they do. Get their input on initiatives that you're considering. Although you can't do what everyone wants you to do, you can hear people out. Know both the pros and cons of various issues before you make your own decisions.

✔ **Be more socially responsible.** One of the surprises in the Centre for Creative Leadership's research involving leaders was that successful leaders show social responsibility. Nobody, to the best of my knowledge, has ever used social responsibility as a screening criteria for leaders. Nor has anyone before found evidence that socially responsible people make better leaders. In hindsight this may seem obvious, but you'll find very few organizations that have put this into practice. Think about what you can do to be more sociably responsible as a leader. How can you show the people you work with that you care, not only about them, but about the larger community in which you live? Try to develop ways in which you can personally contribute to people in need. Even better, look for ways that you, together with your team, can make a difference in your community.

✔ **Show integrity.** You can't command respect from others. You need to earn it. So, do what you say you'll do. Keeping your word, or having a good explanation when you can't, helps you earn people's trust. Trust and integrity have consistently been found by researchers to be important aspects of leadership. Take a good look at your behaviors. How consistent are your words with your deeds?

✔ **Be empathic.** Maintaining this skill in the workplace really involves good listening skills. You need to listen to everyone around you. At the same time, you don't need to do what others want — just hear them out. Also, let people know that you understand where they're coming from.

✔ **Be assertive.** Remember, being assertive doesn't mean being aggressive. By being assertive, you let people know where you stand on important issues. Leaders can't be successful if they're wishy-washy or indecisive.

Being assertive also means asking the right questions in the right way when you don't know the answer to a problem. Just be honest about it. Know what you need to find out in order to know the answer.

To be assertive, you need to be able to deliver both good news and bad news.

✔ **Be optimistic.** As a leader, if you want others to follow you, they need to know that you're taking them to a better place. After all, why should anyone follow you to a cold, dark place? Or to nowhere in particular? Optimists have a way of painting a picture of the future that others want to be part of. Even when times are difficult or the future appears dim, the optimistic leader knows how to rally the troops.

✔ **Find the best people.** If you don't know how to overcome certain obstacles that you're facing, enlist others to help you. Good leaders surround themselves with the best people they can find. You need to find people whose skills complement yours. Too many leaders surround themselves with people who are similar to them. Don't look at leadership as an opportunity to surround yourself with your friends — unless, of course, your friends are strong in skills that you're weak in.

By developing and working on your emotional and social skills, you can increase your chances of being a successful leader. Get a personal coach, if needed. Check out the International Coach Federation (www.coachfederation.org). Investing in developing these skills can pay off for you by making you a better leader. By developing these skills, you not only become a better leader at work, but you also become better at relating to your spouse and children at home.

Chapter 12

Creating an Emotionally Intelligent Workplace

CEOs frequently ask me, "How do I motivate my staff?" If only they could find the magic carrot that takes care of everything. Unfortunately, life isn't quite that easy.

Having an emotionally intelligent workplace takes a lot of thought, planning, and attention. It also requires constant monitoring and adjustment. Workplaces today are places of change. Emotionally intelligent organizations have an advantage when it comes to managing change.

One of the benefits of a winning organization is that it attracts the best people. I'm sometimes amazed when a CEO tells me how difficult he finds recruiting good people, whether in sales, marketing, programming, financial management, or operations. Then, another CEO in the same geographic region tells me that she can't believe how many great applicants she has to turn away — in sales, marketing, programming, financial management, and operations. These two companies aren't that far away from each other geographically — but they're hundreds of miles apart in organizational culture and effectiveness.

In this chapter, I define and describe what makes an emotionally intelligent organization. Regardless of whether you're in a position in your workplace to put these changes into effect, be aware of these approaches and champion the ones that you think can help your workplace.

Defining the Emotionally Intelligent Workplace

For some time now, I've been talking and writing about the emotionally intelligent workplace. Many people ask me, "How can a workplace be emotionally intelligent?" Well, people make up the workplace, and those people determine how emotionally intelligent the workplace is.

Together with my colleagues at Multi-Health Systems, we have identified and studied a number of characteristics related to emotional intelligence that can help create a productive work environment. I define the emotional intelligence of an organization as its ability to deal with change, reach its goals, and still care about the people that work there and interact with the organization, as well as the surrounding community and world.

In my book *Make Your Workplace Great: The 7 Keys to an Emotionally Intelligent Workplace* (Jossey-Bass), I go into great detail about the components of a high-functioning workplace.

Emotional intelligence is an important part of a person's ability to successfully contribute to an organization's success. Although you can find several different definitions of individual emotional intelligence, they all share themes that include awareness of your own emotions, the ability to express those emotions appropriately, the ability to recognize emotions in others, understanding emotions, and the ability to manage your own and others' emotions.

In the same way that a person's individual emotional intelligence affects individual performance, *organizational emotional intelligence* (the ways that employees feel about the organization) helps drive — or sabotage — organizational performance. In the case of organizational emotional intelligence, the whole is greater than the sum of its parts.

Just like bringing a whole bunch of smart (IQ) people together to work each day doesn't guarantee a successful workplace (and I've seen a number of workplaces with people that had sky-high IQs, but nobody talked to anyone else), bringing together a bunch of people with high EQ doesn't guarantee success. Although you have a much better chance of making a great workplace by filling it with high-EQ people, you must pay attention to a number of organizational issues, as well.

Using the benchmark of organizational intelligence

My colleagues at Multi-Health Systems and I have developed a *scientifically validated* (with norms, reliability data, and validation studies) tool, the Benchmark of Organizational Emotional Intelligence (BOEI), to measure the emotional intelligence of an organization. Through the development and refinement of this tool, my colleagues and I have discovered a lot about what makes some organizations successful.

The development of the BOEI began with a general theory about what constitutes organizational emotional intelligence (OEI). We developed a number of factors to encompass the major components of OEI based on these aspects of the factors:

✔ Emotional and motivational aspects of employees at work

✔ Variables that directly influence job performance

We then generated test items to measure each of the factors and circulated those items to experienced organizational and emotional intelligence practitioners for comments and suggestions before we completed the final version and collected large amounts of data to validate it.

Based on self-reports, the BOEI identifies blind spots around which organizational consultants or human resource specialists can formulate corrective development strategies. When deployed thoughtfully, the BOEI can help improve trust and interaction among individuals, teams, and departments by positively impacting team building, leadership development, and planning, among other functions. Personalized feedback enables individuals to compare their own scores against the organization as a whole and their workgroup. In this way, individuals can find out the degree to which they fit in the organization's culture and how their thoughts and feelings compare to others within the organization. That way individuals can make a more informed decision on whether to stay with or change their job. Both individuals and organizations benefit from improved performance when people are better aligned with their jobs.

Based on our testing of thousands of people in different types of organizations (which include for-profit businesses and nonprofit/government organizations), we identified seven key areas that drive organizational emotional intelligence:

✔ Job happiness

✔ Compensation

✔ Work/life stress management

✔ Organizational cohesiveness

✔ Supervisory leadership

✔ Diversity and anger management

✔ Organizational responsiveness

Looking at the typical workplace

At some of the workplaces I've visited, CEOs have told me about how people are the company's most important asset. But many of these places show few signs of organizational emotional intelligence. You can often tell just by walking through an office, warehouse, factory, plant, or showroom how people think of their workplace.

You can tell when people are bored:

- ✔ They don't see you when you pass by.
- ✔ They seem to move about slowly.
- ✔ No one chats or makes much noise of any sort.

I'm sure that productivity is much lower than it could be in these kinds of organizations. I dread few things more than having to go to a dreary, uninteresting, unrewarding place of work.

Consider Barb's predicament. Barb wakes up and gets herself ready for work. All morning, she can't stop thinking about all the things she'd rather be doing than going to work. She toys with the idea of calling in sick, but she's already used her limit of sick and personal days for the month.

The more her mind drifts back to work, the more she dreads going through the motions of the day. Not only does she find her work routine boring, she doesn't really looked forward to seeing anyone in particular there. She thinks about changing jobs, but that whole process seems like too much of an effort.

When Barb finally arrives at her workspace, she gets a cup of coffee and turns on her computer. She spends the next half-hour surfing the Web, checking out shoes and purses on eBay. When her boss comes by and asks whether Barb has prepared her report, Barb quickly switches gears and picks up working where she left off the day before.

Although not everyone in every job is as bored with their work as Barb, many places have very low levels of work motivation. Are jobs today just so boring that nobody's interested in their work anymore? I don't think so.

Some factors may be affecting Barb at work:

- ✔ **The work:** Barb should consider how happy she is with the work itself. She obviously doesn't feel very challenged or interested in what she has to do.
- ✔ **Compensation:** Barb would probably say that she's somewhat satisfied with her pay and benefits. However, she has no incentive built into her pay that relates to her performance, her co-workers' success, or the company's success as a whole. She has a list of benefits, but many of them aren't that relevant to her.

✔ **Stress:** When it comes to work and life stress, Barb doesn't have to deal with too many pressures. In fact, some people refer to her status as *presenteeism* — being there physically, but not all there mentally.

✔ **Co-workers:** Many people enjoy coming to work to see their fellow employees. They have a lot in common and plenty to talk about. In Barb's case, she seems to have little in common and even less to talk about with the people she works with.

✔ **Supervisor:** Barb's relationship with her boss is minimal. They talk about work assignments and little else. Barb gets no feedback on her performance, so at the end of each day, she really has no way of knowing whether she's accomplished anything.

✔ **Diversity:** Barb sees no women role models in her workplace. The organization is dominated by older white males, and the organization doesn't have any younger or culturally diverse people moving up the ranks. Although the ethnicity, culture, and gender of their customer base have been changing rapidly over the past few years, those changes don't seem to have caught anyone's attention — especially in senior management.

✔ **Management:** The people who run the company that Barb works in are very smart people. They all have degrees from top-tier universities. Barb would probably say that they make good decisions. But she probably couldn't say what any of those decisions were. She's rarely even seen the top managers. The CEO swept through her office once on the way to somewhere, but she didn't see enough of him to form any opinion.

Looking at an emotionally intelligent workplace

Janis works at a very different company than Barb's (described in the preceding section). When you walk into her workplace, it seems to have a buzz. People are talking, laughing, sharing, and moving about. You can find a lot of smiling faces and work activity going on. The place seems to have a purpose. Interestingly, Janis's and Barb's companies are in similar industries and in the same geographic region. Janis feels pretty excited when she wakes up on Monday morning because she knows that she's about to begin her work week. In fact, she has a case of TGIM (Thank God It's Monday).

She can't wait to get to the office and catch up with her friends at work. She's also pretty excited about completing the PowerPoint presentation she's been working on for a major client presentation. In fact, during the weekend, she spent some time thinking about how she might include some video clips of people using the client's products.

When Janis arrives at work, she stops by several cubicles to chat about the weekend. After getting her coffee and turning on her computer, she stops her boss in the hall to talk about her new idea for the presentation. He tells her that he thinks it sounds great and looks forward to seeing it. They agree to touch base again at the end of the day.

Janis loves her work. She found an employer that matches people's talents with the work that they actually do. She loves presenting to clients, creating marketing plans, meeting people, and being creative. She has opportunities to put all her skills to work. The following factors affect Janis at work:

- **The work:** In Janis's company, every employee has goals. Each person is part of a system that includes individual, team, and organizational goals.

- **Compensation:** Janis knows that when she helps bring in new business, she shares in the rewards. She feels directly responsible for how much she ends up earning.

- **Stress:** Because of the nature of the work, her hours aren't always straightforward. Some weeks, Janis works incredibly hard and puts in long hours. She knows that she needs to give her best effort so that she can give the best client presentation possible. She also knows that she can take time off when she needs to catch up on the basic necessities of life. She manages her own time. Although she probably puts in more hours than an average working person, she knows that she has a lot of choice in her hours.

- **Co-workers:** Janis loves her team. She has a great group of co-workers. They share similar values, and they all seem to work hard and play hard. They get great pleasure out of the work that they do and the recognition that they get for a job well done. Not only do they share work interests, but they share stories about family, hobbies, and sports.

- **Supervisor:** Her boss is more of a coach than a boss. Janis interacts several times a day with her supervisor. Much of the interaction relates to strategy, tactics, or problem-solving. After every interaction, Janis knows whether she's on the right track, and her boss always gives her clear instructions. Because of the trust between them, Janis's boss often gives her the goal for a particular job and then leaves her to carry out the tactics on her own. When she needs help, her supervisor provides her with assistance.

- **Diversity:** Janis can look up to a number of senior women in the company. She has a clear sense that she can get ahead in the organization. The company also seems to represent the diversity that exists in their customer base. They represent a number of nationalities and cultures, and they don't miss an opportunity to use their differences to their advantage. When they had to pitch to a Latino company, they included a number of their Hispanic staff in the presentation.

> ✔ **Management:** Janis has seen the leaders of her organization on a number of occasions. The chief executive officer (CEO) and chief operating officer (COO) hold regular town hall meetings where everyone, whether in person or on videoconference, participates. The senior staff visit the various departments on a regular basis. After Janis helped land a very large client, the CEO came to her office to personally congratulate her on her work.

At Janis's company, people feel that they're involved in what happens. Everyone shares successes, as well as failures. From the mail room, to the warehouse, to the C suite (CEO, COO, and so on), everyone knows how the company is performing. The leadership and the culture they created motivate everyone to make the company successful. People are *emotionally* invested in this workplace — like having family whom you care about.

Determining Whether Your Workplace Is Emotionally Intelligent

The place where you work may seem boring and lacking in challenge, or you may work at a pretty interesting organization. Have you ever wondered how your workplace compares to others? Could it be more interesting, and could you be more challenged? It might be worthwhile to consider how your workplace might compare to others.

How do you really feel about your workplace? Review this list of items:

> ✔ I really enjoy the work I'm doing.
>
> ✔ I clearly know how well I'm performing at work.
>
> ✔ I feel good about my workplace.
>
> ✔ I get a fair amount of pay for what I do.
>
> ✔ I have a generous benefit plan.
>
> ✔ I rarely feel that I put in too many hours at work.
>
> ✔ I'm generally not too stressed out at work.
>
> ✔ I like the people I work with.
>
> ✔ I feel like I'm part of a well-functioning team at work.
>
> ✔ I have a good relationship with my boss.
>
> ✔ I feel that my boss supports me at work.

✔ My workplace encourages diversity.

✔ My workplace is calm; people rarely get angry.

✔ I trust the leaders of my organization.

✔ My company takes bold moves when it needs to.

Decide which of the items in the preceding list you agree with and which ones you disagree with regarding your current work situation. You can come back to this list again as you continue reading this chapter. You may want to skip ahead and read the rest of the chapter before you carry out the rest of this exercise. To deal with the problem items you identified above, follow these steps:

1. **In your notebook, write down the first item in the preceding list that you disagree with.**

   For example, if you feel you get very little feedback on the quality of your work, you write, "I clearly know how well I'm performing at work."

2. **Below the item, write some ideas about how you could change your situation to make that statement true for you.**

   If you don't know how you're performing at work, you might write

   • Ask my boss

   • Have clearly established goals

   • Ask the people I work with

   • Check with the customers whom I deal with

3. **Repeat Steps 1 and 2 with each of the items that you don't think describe you or your workplace.**

4. **When you're done, identify which item you care about the most.**

5. **Try to figure out ways that you can start implementing changes at work for that item. Write your ideas in your notebook.**

The more items in this list that you agree with, the more likely your workplace is an emotionally intelligent one. Of course, no workplace is perfect, but this list gives you an idea of workplace factors to strive for if you want to work in an environment that offers you the most personal fulfillment.

Documenting your workplace strengths

Look at the items that you checked off the list in the preceding section. The statements that you agree with from that list can tell you the nature of your workplace strengths.

For example, do you seem to like the work itself or the people you work with best? Of the people, do you enjoy working with your team or your supervisor the most? What about the workplace itself? Do you see yourself as part of a winning organization? Are you getting what you need from your supervisor? Do you consider your organization a learning environment? Do you feel that you have room to grow, professionally?

Get to know what you see as the best aspects of your current situation at work. See whether you can capitalize on the strengths of your organization. You need to know what works well at your workplace. If and when you want to look at any change in your circumstances at work, you can find knowing the strengths helpful in your planning.

Cataloging areas for improvement

You probably aren't as happy with some areas of your workplace as you could be. Take note of the items in the section "Determining Whether Your Workplace Is Emotionally Intelligent," earlier in this chapter, that reflect areas you're unhappy with at work. You may want to also note any areas not covered in that section that concern you about your current workplace.

Experiencing problems with the work itself

If you're experiencing problems with the work itself, focus on the specific nature of the problem. You may not like what you're doing, and you took the job because you saw it as the best opportunity you had at the time. Take an honest look at yourself to discover what kind of work you really like. You might want to ask yourself some of the following questions:

- Do I like dealing with people as part of my work?
- Would I prefer to spend my time on the computer or doing things that don't involve people?
- Do I like selling to people?
- Do I like helping people solve problems?
- Do I enjoy explaining things or training people?
- Do I like solving problems?
- Do I have the resources that I need to do my job?
- Do I like my working conditions?
- Do I find my work challenging, or does it bore me?

If you have a problem with the work itself, you may need to find out what type of work you really want to do and whether you can find an opportunity to do it at your current workplace. Find out whether you need additional training or education to do the work you really want. Explore the opportunities you have to advance yourself.

Lacking resources to do the work

If you find that you don't have enough (or the right kinds of) resources to do your work, speak to your supervisor about those resource-related roadblocks. Ask yourself these questions:

✔ How sympathetic is your workplace to your needs?

✔ How realistic are your needs under the present circumstances?

You have to make some decisions about the working conditions that you're willing to accept. If you think that you may see light at the end of the tunnel, you may decide to wait it out. If you feel trapped in a no-win situation, consider alternative jobs, either within your current workplace or elsewhere.

Having problems with the people at work

You may be having problems with the people at your workplace. Maybe your team isn't getting along, or you just don't seem to fit in. You may want to think about why the team isn't working. Do the members have personality differences that clash, or can you resolve the temporary conflicts that your team faces? Do you feel that this team can, with some help, work for you? Perhaps your supervisor can call in an independent coach to facilitate the group. Of course, if you feel that the problems are overwhelming, or you don't want to spend the time and effort to correct the situation, consider asking for a change to a new team, or, if necessary, look for work elsewhere.

You may discover that the organization you're working for doesn't fit your own personal pace. You might feel that the upper management doesn't inspire you, the company isn't aggressive enough in the marketplace (or it's too aggressive), the environment doesn't promote learning, or you want to work for an organization that has more meaning for you.

Knowing whether your workplace is emotionally intelligent

You can figure out whether your workplace is emotionally intelligent by the way people who work for that company react to change. People in emotionally intelligent organizations embrace change as soon as they can see its advantages. Your workplace probably doesn't rate very high on the emotional-intelligence scale if, when you ask why the company does something in a certain way, you hear, "Well, that's the way we've always done it."

See whether any of these statements apply to your workplace:

- ✔ I find my workplace exciting.
- ✔ My company is seen as a leader in its industry.
- ✔ I'm always figuring out how to implement new processes.
- ✔ Change is part of the workplace culture.
- ✔ People in my workplace know the difference between healthy and unhealthy stress.
- ✔ My co-workers care about me.
- ✔ I have friends at my workplace.
- ✔ My workplace includes many different kinds of people.
- ✔ Nobody is afraid to make bold moves when needed, after reviewing all the options.
- ✔ People in my workplace support each other.
- ✔ My workplace is like a healthy family.
- ✔ I feel that I can talk to the most senior people in my organization.

Managing the Work-Life Balancing Act

While I travel around the world giving presentations to managers and working people throughout the United States, Canada, and Mexico, as well as in Europe, Asia, Australia, South Africa, and South America, the issue of work-life balance always comes up. Even in places where I least expect it, such as idyllic areas of Mexico and Thailand, working people are very concerned with balancing work life and home life. While globalization continues and the world gets smaller, people seem to need to work more, respond faster, and improve the quality of their work. As a result, they have less time for their family, friends, and recreational activities.

Whoever can master this balancing act has found one of the key secrets to success in business today. Everyone wants to do more with less, including getting more work done with fewer people. Of course, by reducing the number of working people, the few remaining workers have to work harder.

Although automation has made some workforce reduction possible, people are becoming more important to businesses as a competitive advantage. Computers and robots can do a lot of things well, but there are a lot of things they aren't very good at, too.

While I write this chapter, I've been on hold for over 30 minutes with a major airline. Although I'm sure that they have good reasons for cutting back their workforce, I can empathize with the remaining overwhelmed, stressed-out people who now have to handle all those phone calls.

In the following sections, I explore ways in which you can get a better handle on how to manage the time that you spend working, along with the time that you spend doing personal things. Although people usually use the term "balancing," the actual process probably feels a lot more like juggling.

Knowing your values

When you know your basic life values, you can measure your time against where you want it to go. Too often, people put together to-do lists and blindly run from one crisis to another. By starting with your values, you stake out where you think and feel you should place your priorities.

If your family ranks highest on your list, for example, you can look at how you can organize your life around your family. Do you give your most important area the time and attention that it needs? Continue to ask yourself this question for each of your priorities while you read through the list below.

What activities and people do you see as most important in your life? In your notebook, rank the following in order, from most to least important:

- ✔ Family
- ✔ Work
- ✔ Hobbies
- ✔ Sports
- ✔ Health and fitness
- ✔ Significant other
- ✔ Self
- ✔ Learning activities
- ✔ Recreation
- ✔ Social life and friends

Now, in your notebook, create a chart like the one shown in Figure 12-1. This chart represents the amount of time that you want to spend in each of your value areas. Review this chart every month to see if you are keeping your priorities or if they have changed.

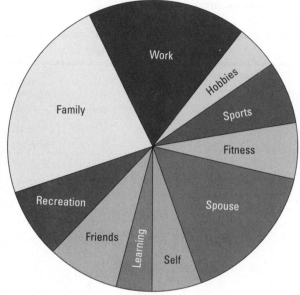

Figure 12-1:
Create
a values
chart, which
details how
you want
to spend
your time.

Looking at your work time

Say that work is one of your top-rated values. How do you feel about the amount of time that you currently spend, both at work and outside of work, on work-related issues? If you're satisfied with the time that you spend in this area, you can skip to the following section.

Few people report spending too little time at work. How much is too much? What do you see as an ideal amount of time to spend on work-related activities? Follow these steps to help you assess what works best for your needs:

1. **Decide how much of each weekday you want to spend working.**

   Select an amount of time that feels right for you:

   - 7 or fewer hours

   - 8 hours

- 9 hours
- 10 hours
- 11 or more hours

2. **In your notebook, plot out your ideal schedule on a chart.**

   Use Table 12-1 as an example.

Table 12-1			Ideal Schedule				
	Mon	**Tues**	**Wed**	**Thurs**	**Fri**	**Sat**	**Sun**
Before 8 a.m.	Breakfast	Breakfast	Breakfast	Breakfast	Breakfast	Sleep	Sleep
9 a.m.–noon	Work	Work	Work	Work	Work	Breakfast/shop	Breakfast
noon–1 p.m.	Lunch	Lunch	Lunch	Lunch	Lunch	Lunch	Lunch
1–5 p.m.	Work	Work	Work	Work	Work	Chores	Family
6–7 p.m.	Work	Fitness	Hobby	Fitness	Family/Dinner	Social	Family
7–8 p.m.	Family/Dinner	Family/Dinner	Family	Family	Family/Dinner	Social/Dinner	Family/Dinner
8 p.m.–midnight	TV	Rec	Social	Rec	Social	Social	TV

3. **Now, consider your actual weekly schedule. Put an X through the boxes that you want to change from your current schedule.**

   For example, if you want to do less work between 6 and 7 p.m. on Tuesday, put an X through that box.

4. **Write in what you'd rather be doing.**

   Socializing, exercising, reading, or whatever.

5. **List things that can get in the way of your schedule.**

   This list can include things such as a special assignment at work, a request from your spouse to do some extra errands, or your child needing help with schoolwork.

6. **Write down when disruptions would most likely arise.**

7. **Consider some alternatives and how you might shuffle your schedule around.**

   Suppose a concert or a play came up that you wanted to see. How would you change things around?

Don't spend too much time on the preceding exercise. Nobody can really predict the future. It can simply help you get your mindset ready for change if and when you need. Often, the biggest obstacle to change is in your mind. So, by figuring out how to be flexible, you help yourself prepare for life's unexpected events.

Looking at your life time

Think of your life priorities, or your life values. Think of these as the most important things to you — spending time with your children or your spouse, continuous learning, playing a sport, or enjoying a hobby. Instead of starting your time management program by managing all your to-do lists, begin with the big picture. If you establish your life priorities, then you can (with the help of your gut feelings) guide yourself toward doing the right things at the right times with the time you have available.

Here's an activity that can help you plan by using the big picture — your life priorities, or life values. Just follow these steps:

1. **Determine how much of the time in the chart you create in the preceding section is devoted to you.**

   Add up the things that you do in your life, other than work, for yourself. Record this in your notebook.

2. **Compare this figure with how much time you *want* to spend on yourself.**

   How far away are you from the time you want to spend on yourself?

3. **Tally the amount of time that you spend with your family, based on this chart.**

4. **Write down the amount of time, in an ideal world, that you want to spend with your family.**

5. **Figure out how much change you want in the amount of time you spend on your social life.**

6. **Compare the amount of work time that you currently spend to your ideal amount of time spent on work-related activities.**

Look at the differences between the time you actually spend and the time you'd like to spend in each of the areas. Start to think of adjustments you can make to get more in line with how you'd prefer to spend your time. Keep in mind that there are only 24 hours in a day, and you need your sleep time, so be realistic.

Managing your time requires you to make good decisions. By knowing your life priorities in advance, you can more easily make good decisions when you're confronted with various choices. Should you work a bit longer or go home and relax? Should you have dinner with your family this evening or work out at the fitness center?

These decisions are all, at some level, value judgments. Understanding your values can help you more effectively make these decisions and more easily plan your time. Also, time and life management includes a strong emotional component. People who lead a balanced life can do so because they're emotionally in tune with themselves. They make decisions based on their values and therefore feel good about these decisions.

How you can balance work and life

The chart that you can create in the preceding sections serves as a guide to help you balance your work life and personal life. You don't have to stick to this schedule in a robotic way, but it offers you a roadmap. You may not be able to find a perfect balance between your work life and the rest of your life, but you can definitely find different degrees of comfort. By planning your time within your degree of comfort, you can become better at many of the activities that you do. You can also affect your mood, becoming calmer and happier with your life.

When you use a values-based system to manage your time and priorities, you can make decisions in a more informed way in the future. When you're faced with the task of choosing between activities, you have an alternative way to look at your choices.

So, when you have to decide between going to the gym or going to dinner with a friend, instead of emotionally choosing the dinner — because it provides an easier, more short-term pleasure — you might want to consider how you rated staying in shape, looking after yourself, losing weight, and so on in your list of life priorities. Perhaps you can find a compromise — exercise, then go out to dinner or meet after dinner for coffee. Your values can play a role in negotiating how you spend your time.

Creating Emotionally Intelligent Teams

Today's workplace, for the most part, requires working in teams. Much of what businesses do today is too complex for one person alone to do. Somewhere along the line, you need to connect with others at work.

Consider Ted's story. Ted hates working with others. Part of the reason he became a programmer was so that he could work on his own with nobody bothering him. Staring at the computer screen, solving complex problems is Ted's version of heaven.

Unfortunately, when Ted starts working at a medium-sized software company, he becomes one piece of a rather large project. He writes computer software code that has to be integrated with the other programmers' code, technical support people always ask him questions about customer problems that need immediate answers, and the project manager needs information about milestones and deadlines.

"If only everyone would leave me alone to my programming," gasps Ted.

How do people like Ted adapt to today's workplace? Does he need a personality change to fit in? Should he stay away from corporate environments? Perhaps Ted has to find a way to successfully relate to others, even if it's something that he doesn't feel entirely comfortable with at this time.

Today's workplace faces the challenge of creating strong teams and ensuring that employees adapt well to working in teams. Some people are more suited to a team environment than others. However, everyone has to figure out how to adapt in some way.

Defining a work team

A *work team* generally consists of two or more people who have to communicate or work together in some way to complete a task or project.

The work team can have brief, online, or any other kind of interactions. But some form of communication or cooperation takes place, and the successful completion of the task, function, or project requires this interaction.

Here are some examples of work teams:

- Sales
- Research and development
- Marketing
- Executive (or C suite)
- Customer service
- Production
- Financial

- ✔ Investigative
- ✔ Quality control
- ✔ Technical support
- ✔ Warehouse control
- ✔ Cross functional
- ✔ Business development

The best-functioning work teams have goals that the team leader clearly articulates and all team members understand. The team leader makes these goals very specific, specifying timelines and dividing up responsibilities.

Understanding what makes teams work

A number of ingredients go into making successful work teams. One of these ingredients is a competent team leader. The team leader needs to function as a coach. His job involves ensuring that everyone on the team clearly understands what's expected of them and by when. Everyone needs to know

- ✔ Why they're part of the team (what special skills they may have)
- ✔ Their function on the team
- ✔ Their milestones or due dates for tasks or activities
- ✔ Whom they need to interact with and when
- ✔ When the team can consider itself successful

When everyone understands their roles and what the team has to achieve, you greatly increase your chances for success.

Teams are made up of people, and in order for a team to successfully work, people need to work well together. Teams that include people who have high emotional intelligence are usually very effective. Team members should be aware of their own, as well as their teammates', emotions. That way they can better manage themselves (not saying things that will upset others) and their teammates (being sensitive to their needs).

The following elements are critical to a team's success:

- ✔ **Expectations:** Everyone in a team must manage each other's expectations. If I'm dependent on you to get something done, I want to know that you're on schedule with your task. If you become delayed for some reason, I need to know that. In the worst scenario, you give me absolutely no information. If I know that you're going to be late, I can plan alternate activities in the interim.

✔ **Respect:** You don't have to be best friends with everyone on your team. You all do need to respect each other, however. Having mutual respect keeps the team operating at a professional level.

✔ **Trust:** You also need to develop trust among team members. You must trust that your co-workers are looking out for the best interests of the team and the organization as a whole, because if not, you will be distracted by trying to second-guess their motives. This can become demotivating for you and can reduce the team's effectiveness. If any member appears too self-serving, his attitude and behavior can begin to sabotage the team. Members should regularly compliment their peers and never take credit for someone else's work.

✔ **Support:** A successful team needs mutual support. Team members, without hesitation, support others on the team, when needed. In high-functioning teams, this support happens almost automatically. Supporting each other helps manage the negative stress that team members can feel when the team has to work under high pressure.

Increasing the emotional intelligence of your teams

What happens when some team members are more emotionally intelligent than others? If your team faces this situation, you need to recognize it because some members may be more supportive than others. Also, members lower in emotional intelligence may be more high maintenance, requiring more time and attention from the team leader. Understanding each member's ability in this area can help you better understand their behaviors. Understanding their behaviors allows you to be more tolerant and understanding, and hopefully, more productive.

You can discover and develop the emotional intelligence of team members by working with a coach. A coach who's specially trained in emotional-intelligence testing can help the team better understand and develop their EI. By having an objective and validated measure of EI, you can get baseline data and set goals for improvement.

Here are some examples of how you can improve the EI of team members:

✔ Enhance interpersonal skills so that teammates can relate more strongly to each other.

✔ Improve empathy so that members can better understand each other, which reduces misinterpretations.

✔ Manage stress better so that work doesn't get derailed.

✔ Increase emotional self-awareness so that emotions can be managed when things get tense.

✔ Get better impulse control because conflict often arises from someone saying something too negative without thinking.

✔ Increase optimism so that team efforts can focus on moving forward.

✔ Develop better problem-solving skills.

Making Your Workplace More Emotionally Intelligent

You may not feel that you're in a position to improve the emotional intelligence of your workplace. However, one individual can make important change in an organization.

As someone who knows a particular aspect of the workplace well, you can share your knowledge of what works and what doesn't with others you work with. Of course, you need to share this information in a constructive and helpful way, as opposed to complaining. By offering solutions to problems, or even offering to look for solutions, you become much more valuable to your organization.

Starting with you

Start with yourself and your own particular area of work. You're the expert in this area. You spend more time doing what you do than probably anyone else. What are some of the issues that you've noticed around your workplace? What changes could make you more efficient at getting your job done? How could you do a higher quality job?

Here are some things to consider about your role in the workplace:

✔ Can you make the work more efficient somehow?

✔ Could you make changes in the way that you approach your work to make it more exciting, challenging, and interesting?

✔ Do you have substandard or insufficient resources?

✔ Can training in any particular area make you more effective in your job?

✔ Are the people involved working together as well as they could be?

✔ Can your supervisor help you more by being a better coach?

✔ Could you be spending your time more productively?

Think of yourself as an efficiency expert. If you owned your division or workplace, what would you do differently? Compile a list of suggestions. Remember, you're looking for solutions, not problems.

Influencing your co-workers

After you come up with a list of things that you think could make your workplace more productive and a more exciting place to work (as I discuss in the preceding section), you may want to test your ideas with someone else. Here's one way to do so:

1. **Answer the following questions for each item on that list:**

    • Is this change practical?

    • What would my co-workers think about it?

    • What would my supervisor think about it?

    • Would the company support it?

    • How would it impact my work?

2. **Find the top three suggestions in your list, based on your evaluation of the questions in Step 1.**

    Choose which of your suggestions has the best chance of making an impact and being accepted by others.

3. **Think of someone at work whom you know fairly well and whose opinion you trust.**

4. **Arrange to meet with her over coffee to talk about some aspects of work.**

    Explain that you've been thinking about ways to be more effective and get more personal pleasure out of your job.

5. **Mention one of the problems or bottlenecks that you've encountered.**

6. **Present your colleague with your suggestions for change and ask for feedback.**

    Pay attention to both verbal and non-verbal cues. What does she tell you with her facial expression (refer to Chapter 7) and body language (refer to Chapter 5)? Are the signals positive? How enthusiastic or supportive does your colleague sound to you? And finally, what does she actually say?

Present all three of your suggestions and see how they go over. Your colleague may be able to add some idea that you haven't yet considered. Use this conversation as an opportunity to modify or shape your suggestions. Are any of your suggestions simply not workable? Don't be defensive about negative feedback. Finding out what flaws your suggestions have may lead you to sharpen your proposal or drop it altogether. Better to get it shot down at this stage, rather than after investing a lot of time, energy, and people in it.

Wait a day or so after your meeting and review the results. If you received enough positive feedback on one or more of your ideas, you might want to meet with one more colleague just to get an additional perspective. Of course, also take into account any constructive criticism that you received.

Managing your manager

After you come up with some great ideas and bounce them off your colleagues (as discussed in the preceding sections), you're ready to present those ideas to your supervisor. Carefully plan your approach in this potentially delicate situation. Of course, if you have a great supervisor and a good relationship, this conversation should go very smoothly. After all, he has your best interests at heart.

If your supervisor may be the type of person who can get a bit defensive or protective of his turf, be a bit creative in presenting your ideas. Here are some steps for presenting your ideas to your supervisor:

1. **Set up a time to meet during which you can discuss your performance.**

   You want to have a discussion with no distractions, so don't have this conversation while passing each other in the hallway.

2. **Begin the meeting by letting your supervisor know how you generally feel about your work and the workplace.**

   Always start on a positive note. Say something like, "You know John, I really like the work I'm doing and I really enjoy being a part of this team."

   You want to gain support, so you could continue with, "I've been thinking about ways in which I could be more productive and contribute more to our mission."

3. **You want to gauge interest. Is he giving you his undivided attention?**

   If you can't read his cues, you might want to be more specific, saying, "Is this something you're interested in?"

   At this point, you know whether he's receptive. If he is, you can state the problem: "I've noticed that we lose a number of customers because we can't always respond to all their questions when they first contact us."

If he's not receptive, you may want to say something like, "If this is a busy time for you, we can talk about this another time." He now has the option of either continuing or postponing this conversation. If he's not interested, you may have to consider whether you might be better off trying again or finding another supervisor.

4. **See whether your supervisor is aware of the problem.**

   If necessary, you might have to spell out the severity of the problem. How many customers? At what cost?

5. **Offer your solution.**

   You might say something along the lines of, "I was thinking, if I could have access to people in R&D and marketing when I'm dealing with a customer, I could deal with all their questions at the same time and not need to call back again and play phone tag for a week or two."

6. **Be ready for objections — your supervisor might raise some practical issues.**

   If you have really thought about the problem, considered alternate solutions, and considered the pros and cons of each, before the meeting, you're ready for these issues.

   For example, you might say, "Well, I've checked with Bill in R&D and Sharon in marketing, and they say that they can have someone on call whom I can contact to deal with customer issues in their areas."

7. **Gauge how supportive your supervisor really is.**

   For example, does he further the discussion in trying to solve the problem? Does he support your efforts? Or does he shut you down?

   By this point, you should have a good idea of how much support your current workplace — or, at least, your current supervisor — can provide for your efforts. If you succeed, you can appear as a contributor to your organization's success, which hopefully puts you on your way to further rewards down the road.

   If you're unsuccessful — and you find that you always make the effort, but it never works out — you may want to consider transferring to another part of the organization or to another company altogether.

Taking it to the top

You may have some ideas for improving your workplace that go beyond your own job or even your department. After you develop a track record for implementing improvements in your own area, you may want to be on the lookout for more general improvements that the leaders of the organization could implement at your workplace. Approach your supervisor to get his or her blessing to bring your idea to the attention of the human resource manager or any other senior managers.

Always keep your supervisor in the loop. After you have permission to speak to another manager, set up a convenient time to speak with her. In some cases you might want your supervisor to set it up and perhaps even join you in the meeting. Be prepared, have your suggestion and the reasons why you're suggesting it summarized and ready to present. Keep in mind the same steps you used when speaking with your supervisor (see the previous section).

If your suggestion is adopted, congratulations. You've had a good impact on the organization. If it isn't adopted, don't worry. You'll still be seen as someone in the organization who cares about the workplace and who makes an extra effort to improve it.

Chapter 13

Getting Through College with Emotional Intelligence

College is an exciting time for most people. It marks a transition between the adolescence of high school and the adult world of work. It's also an adventurous time during which you test responsibility and independence with newfound freedom, campus parties, and other diversions of college life.

Many college freshmen eagerly anticipate this new chapter in life and have many hopes and dreams. Others feel trepidation and concern about what this new stage might offer. Very little prepares high school students for what awaits them in college. Colleges have long assumed that if a student has the grades and the SAT score needed for admission, she must be ready.

When Martha arrives at her college, the first week is full of excitement. She's been anticipating all the changes that are to come — the chance to meet new people, many welcoming events, living on her own for the first time in her life, and no more curfews. It's the perfect start to what she believes will be a great experience.

Martha's the perfect candidate for college. She is an honor student, has high recommendations from her teachers, and is well-liked by her peers. No one ever had any doubt that she would attend a top-tier university. The only shock came when she failed to complete her first year of college.

Sadly, Martha's situation is far from unique. This chapter provides survival basics for college students who want to improve their emotional-intelligence skills in an effort to achieve success in school.

Why So Many Students Don't Make It Through the First Year of College

According to the U.S. Department of Education, over 30 percent of college students leave after the first year and almost 50 percent never graduate. For a number of these students, they leave (in part) because of a lack of money. According to the National Center for Public Policy and Higher Education, half of all entering freshmen borrow funds. One fifth of those who borrow drop out.

The dropout problem is worse for Hispanics and blacks than for white students. According to similar reports, after borrowing money and failing to graduate, many of these students may be worse off than if they never attended college at all. One report said 57 percent of white students finish their degree, compared with 44 percent of Hispanics and 39 percent of African-Americans.

To try to get a better grip on what's happening with first-year students, the Higher Education Research Institute (HERI) at UCLA and the Policy Center on the First Year of College at Brevard College have been conducting wide-scale surveys with first-year students (*Your First Year of College Survey*). Their surveys include over 38,000 students from across the United States.

Looking at school grades and SATs

When looking at the college-dropout problem, you might expect that the students who don't make it through the first year are those who don't have the grades or smarts to get through.

Most colleges require high school students to complete the SAT Reasoning Test (formerly known as the Scholastic Aptitude Test or just plain SAT). This test (or group of tests) supposedly measures the thinking skills that a student needs if she wants to experience college success. The test focuses on how well students analyze problems.

So, why use the standardized SAT scores along with grades? Well, grades vary — some schools grade students more easily than other schools. Most college admissions committees believe that by combining high school grades (a student's grade point average, or GPA) with the SAT score, you can more accurately measure a student's academic skills and thus predict how well that student will do in college. In fact, studies show that a student's SAT score combined with his GPA more accurately predicts freshman grades than GPA alone.

How well do these measures predict success? Taken together, the SAT and school grades account for somewhere around 52 percent of the variance of freshman grades. If you look at the percentages optimistically, these abilities account for about half the reasons students drop out.

In a series of studies by professor James Parker and his associates at Trent University in Canada, researchers tracked students throughout the United States and Canada over those students' first year of college. They were tested for emotional intelligence by taking the EQ-i (a test that measures emotional intelligence) at the beginning of their first year. Comparing high school GPA, academic progress during the first year of college, and EQ-i scores, Parker found that the EQ scores most accurately predicted dropouts. Students who persisted in their studies scored significantly higher on most EI dimensions than students who withdrew. (For a full description of the EQ-i, see Chapter 4.)

We're not in Kansas anymore: Welcome to college

In high school, when you got to your senior year, you were a big fish in a relatively small pond. Depending on the size of your school, you knew just about everyone in your graduating class, and they pretty well knew you. Your teachers all knew your name and how well (or poorly) you were doing.

High school is a pretty predictable place. For some students, it's comfortable, yet others find it tough — especially for students who belong to one of the "out" crowds or no crowd at all. Most things in high school are pretty familiar — where you hang out and where you find certain things or people.

For most people, high school life is simple: You pretty much come home to your family every night, and someone else takes care of your meals, laundry, and cleaning. Your main concerns center around your social life and where to spend your money — as in, which movie should I see?

Starting college is a pretty exciting time. Everything is new. You start off by meeting new people. You may know some students from your old neighborhood, but more likely, they're from all sorts of places.

If you go out of town to college, you live in a new place — perhaps a dorm room that you share with some stranger. Right away, you have to adjust yourself to someone else's habits. If you're lucky, your roommate has similar tastes to yours in music and wall art, and has similar habits (for example, being a night owl or an early riser).

At college, you attend lectures in large auditoriums led by professors (not teachers) who not only don't know who you are, but in many cases they don't even notice whether you're there. Suddenly, many students have to take the initiative in creating notes and keeping track of assignments and tests without reminders. Perhaps the biggest shock comes (especially if you were a good student in high school) when you get back your first test or assignment that has a grade considerably lower than your comfort zone.

Evenings and weekends are also new experiences — your time is pretty much your own. Do you have a beer with your classmates, or do you spend time working on an assignment? How much time should you spend preparing for tests, essays, and other assignments? What about chores such as getting food, doing laundry, and clearing off that desk? You may never have had to do some of this stuff before.

All in all, life in college is pretty different than life in high school. And you can't just sail through by using the same old ways. You need to adapt to changes in living, studying, coursework, lectures, and socializing.

Problems that first-year students encounter

The transition to college is a time of major change for students. Some of these changes are problem enough to cause students to drop out of college altogether.

You might think that student dissatisfaction with college might be a big reason for many students to drop out of college. The *Your First Year of College Survey* actually covered the area of dissatisfaction with college in its questions. In fact, close to three-fourths of students were "satisfied" or "very satisfied" with their college experience, according to this survey.

Most students were satisfied with the quality of instruction they received, the relevance of their coursework, the amount of contact with faculty, the campus, and the social activities available.

Interestingly, when asked about their academic experiences in their first year, although most students reported studying and discussing their courses with other students, many of those students reported being disengaged:

- Over half of the students surveyed reported arriving late to class.
- Almost half turned in course assignments that didn't reflect their best work.
- Almost half felt bored in class.
- One-third skipped class at least occasionally.

Here are some of the changes students reported at the end of their first year of college compared to the beginning of the year:

✔ Spending more time studying, partying, and socializing with friends

✔ Spending less time doing housework, exercising, doing volunteer work, attending religious services, and reading for pleasure

✔ Increased drinking of beer, wine, or other liquor

✔ Feeling more overwhelmed and depressed

✔ Feeling less worried about the cost of college

These findings remain fairly consistent with earlier surveys carried out by this group, indicating that these issues have not really been addressed:

✔ More than one-third of students reported feeling "frequently overwhelmed by all they had to do."

✔ More than one-third felt "frequently" or "occasionally"

- Lonely or homesick

- Worried about meeting new people

- A need to break away from their family in order to succeed, indicating family attachment issues

On a more positive note, these students also reported

✔ That "helping others who are in difficulty" and "integrating spirituality into my life" were "very important" or "essential personal goals"

✔ Undergoing significant improvement in their self-concept over the first year of college

According to Chip Anderson, a former UCLA administrator who has been involved in surveying and working with first-year students, "More students leave college because of disillusionment, discouragement, or reduced motivation than because of lack of ability or dismissal by school administration."

Preparing to deal with emotional and social issues

Building new relationships is one of the first challenges students face when they start college. Successfully building relationships can help buffer some of the other areas that challenge new college students. Good friends can act as a social support. Building interpersonal relationships is an important component of emotional intelligence.

Getting the jump on your study skills

Why not start adjusting your study-skill habits while you're still in high school? You can start practicing discipline. For example, plan ahead — develop a weekly schedule. Knowing when you have classes, sports, social time, and study time can help you more effectively manage your time. Practice sticking to your schedule — but make it flexible enough for change, as needed.

Make sure to schedule your study time when you're well rested and alert. Don't get into the habit of cramming late at night in the last few hours before a test. Also, make sure that you

have a quiet place set aside for studying. You can study in intervals (between 30 and 45 minutes each), taking a food break between each interval. The goal of managing your time and study habits, of course, is so that you can do well in school.

Finally, if you want to successfully adapt, both to college and adulthood, you need to live as a relatively independent adult through such activities as successfully managing money and time — which involve emotional-intelligence components such as independence and impulse control.

Going to college changes existing relationships with family and friends. This transition can often be a difficult one. Some students overly depend on their parents for decisions. Also, some students leave behind serious romantic relationships. This absence can sometimes result in additional challenges while the relationship gets tested like never before. If the relationship fails to survive, for whatever reason, additional turmoil gets thrown into the mix. Students need the emotional-intelligence component of independence (refer to Chapter 2) in these circumstances to overcome these challenges.

Figuring out how to become more independent during the last year in high school may have some benefits. Students can start taking responsibility for laundry, meal preparation, time management, and budgeting their finances.

Most students have developed their own study habits, or perhaps avoided any serious attempt at study habits, during their high school years. Those students need to adjust these habits to college, which offers far less supervision and accommodation, if they want to succeed. Students need to manage the emotional-intelligence component of impulse control to resist the temptation to engage in other activities that detract from schoolwork.

Warning Signs of College Derailment

How do you know whether you or your child is on the way to not making it through college? You can look for a number of signs:

- ✔ Change in mood (usually more depressed or angry than usual)
- ✔ Less communicative with others
- ✔ Poor grades on tests or assignments
- ✔ Sleeps through the mornings, maybe even into the afternoon
- ✔ Poor personal hygiene
- ✔ Lack of motivation
- ✔ Shows little or mostly negative emotions
- ✔ Excessively blames teachers for poor grades, boring lectures, and generally being unfair
- ✔ Negative attitude and statements about college
- ✔ Few or no friends
- ✔ Increased use of alcohol or drugs

Although none of these signs on their own mean college failure is imminent, look for a pattern of these behaviors. If you notice three or more of these signs, then you need to have a chat. If you're the student, speak to a college counselor. If you're a parent, speak with your child — in general and non-threatening terms — about how college is going.

Adjusting to the first year of college

The first year of college is a time of change — think of it as a testing ground. If someone drops out of college, he usually does it during the first year. So, if you make it through the first year, you have a much higher chance of making it the rest of the way through. Here are some changes you should prepare for:

- ✔ **Class structure:** In most colleges today, first-year students are exposed to classes in large lecture halls. Less opportunity exists for contact between students and professors.

- ✔ **Teaching style:** Also, the style of teaching is different from high school. Impersonal lectures are common in college, as opposed to high school, where teachers try to ensure that at least most of the class understands the lesson.

- ✔ **Guidance:** In high school, you receive several reminders for tests and assignments. Usually, the teachers make it pretty clear what information students are expected to master. At most colleges, you don't really know how much of a test comes from lectures, textbooks, or any other references that the instructor may have mentioned during a lecture.

You also experience big social changes during the first year of college. You leave behind old friends and your family support system:

- ✔ **Independence:** You usually have added responsibilities in looking after the basics — food, laundry, budgeting, and so on — when you go to college.

- ✔ **Social life:** Also, you need to develop a whole new support system of friends. You need people to socialize with, to help you with assignments or missed lectures, and to provide other areas of social support.

How to know when your first year isn't going well

Sometimes, you can get so lost in the day-to-day events of surviving your first year of college that you may not even realize things aren't going well. Slowly, you begin to show up late for certain classes or miss them altogether. You decide not to follow through on readings or other assignments from class. After all, the professor suggested them, but does he care enough to check whether you read them?

You might find socializing with friends easier than spending time working on assignments or preparing for tests. If you wing it a few times on assignments or tests, you may get grades lower than you expected. Your grades should give you some indication about how well you're coping with the new role of college student.

Also, pay attention to your mood. Do you find yourself feeling more irritable than usual? Do others find you difficult to be around? Stop and pay attention to how you've been feeling. Sometimes, you may be just too busy to realize how you're coming across to others.

Suggestions to Get Back On Track

If you find that you're not doing well or you're unhappy with how you're adjusting to college, first determine whether you're on the right career path. Sometimes, if you're disappointed by the course content, you might have second thoughts about the direction you're heading. First-year courses are often broad survey courses and may not get at the specific interest in a field that you were looking for. You need to have patience and perseverance to move forward so that you can get to the more interesting courses in your area of study.

Talk to your friends, both new and old. Compare their experiences at college with yours. Do you seem to be in tune with others? Find out what they like and dislike about their college experience. See how any of the concerns that you have compare with theirs. If you find that you're much more negative than others you talk to, consider making an appointment with the counseling professionals at your college.

Perhaps you're feeling overwhelmed balancing your assignments and managing your personal life. Most college counseling centers offer courses in study habits or time management. You might want to start one of these courses sooner rather than later. They can provide you with some great ideas about better managing your priorities. Some colleges now offer *First Year Experience* courses that directly relate to increasing emotional intelligence in students. Find out whether your college offers these experiences.

You may be having difficulty adjusting to the college lifestyle. You might miss your friends, parents, or even a special relationship you left behind. Are you making the best use of e-mail and phone calls? Do you plan visits that you can look forward to? You might want to formalize your next visit back home and mark it on your calendar.

Identifying possible problems

You first need to identify what might be going wrong in your college experience. If you're not satisfied with college, identify which of these areas you're unhappy about:

✔ Being away from home

✔ The college workload

✔ Struggling to get along with others

✔ Making new friends

✔ The professors

✔ Managing your time

✔ Just feeling lousy

✔ Dealing with meals, laundry, cleaning, and chores

✔ Having trouble understanding your courses

✔ General atmosphere at college

✔ Your courses (the content or how they're presented)

✔ Issues around your parents (missing them, interference from them, disagreements with them)

After you select the issues that relate most to you, rank them (based on amount of concern) in your notebook. Then, rate the seriousness of each issue on a scale from 1 (not at all serious) to 10 (extremely serious) and write that number next to the issue in your notebook.

For each of the top three issues, write down a few examples of why you're concerned about this issue. For example, if you wrote down "Making new friends," you could add this example: "I tried to make friends with a few people in my dorm, but they ignored me."

Then, write down more positive outcomes related to that issue, such as

✔ I easily made friends with others in my dorm or classes.

✔ I'm taking interesting courses.

✔ I could manage my time better.

✔ I understood my course material more quickly or more thoroughly than the classmates I talked to after class.

Taking stock of your resources

If you have a good sense of the issues that you find challenging and have some potential goals (which you can figure out in the preceding section), you can now really focus on your first challenging issue.

Harley's having a number of difficulties adjusting to college life. One of his biggest concerns is connecting with other people. He tries to make friends with some of the kids in his dorm, but nothing seems to click.

Harley's first goal is to make a couple of friends that he can socialize with when he's not studying. If those friends are in any of his classes, that's a bonus — they could compare notes and help each other out with assignments.

To develop the emotional skills you need to be more satisfied with your college experience, follow these steps:

1. **At the top of a blank page in your notebook, write down your first goal from the list you create in the preceding section.**

   For example, Harley's goal is to make new friends at college.

2. **Identify which emotional skills you need to work on to reach this goal.**

   Harley selects from this list of skills:

   • Being more emotionally self-aware

   • Increasing assertiveness

- Managing impulse control

- Improving stress tolerance

- Building interpersonal skills

- Improving empathy

- Being more socially responsible (thinking more of others)

- Being more optimistic

- Increasing happiness

- Setting and achieving goals

- Improving problem-solving skills

- Improving other skills

3. **After you've identified the skills that you need to meet your goal, write them down.**

   Harley writes

   - Increasing assertiveness

   - Building interpersonal skills

   - Improving empathy

4. **Create a plan to develop each skill.**

   For example, Harley plans for the first skill on his list, assertiveness, by following these steps:

   a. He writes down at least two situations from last week in which he could have met a new person.

   b. He makes a list of things that he could say to introduce himself to others.

   c. He makes it a point to talk to at least five students he doesn't know this week.

   d. He tracks his success in his notebook.

5. **Follow Steps 1 through 4 for each of your goals.**

   Take stock of the skills that you need to develop. Pay attention to both your successes and your challenges.

Getting into action mode

Figure out what you can do to develop the skills you need to help you better cope with the challenges that you're experiencing (see the preceding section). Now you're ready to implement your plan. Start with a commitment to move forward.

Depending on the severity of your challenge, determine whether you need help reaching your goal. If you rated your problem as a five or higher in the section "Identifying possible problems," earlier in this chapter, then you should seek help in reaching your goal.

Here are some people who may be able to provide that help:

- College counselor
- Career counselor
- Outside professional counselor or psychologist

If you rate your problem as less than five, you might want to use more informal methods of change. Some options include

- Talking to friends about how you can solve some of these problems
- Reading self-help books (such as this one)

Of course, you should always feel comfortable talking to a college counselor or advisor. Most colleges have a counseling or career department set up specifically to deal with these kinds of issues. They often offer both group and individual sessions.

Knowing Your Long-Term Objectives

Getting through college takes some discipline. So, step back and look at your long-term objectives. Why do you want to go to college? Here are some possibilities:

- To go on to a professional school such as law, medicine, veterinary, pharmacy, or dentistry
- For general education
- As a stepping stone before you enter the work world
- Because your friends are going
- As a great place to network
- To build certain skills
- To pursue your interests
- Because you love going to school
- A sports scholarship

People have different reasons for wanting to go to college. Be honest with yourself and try to understand why you really want to attend college. Understanding your motivations can help you plan your future.

Meaghan realizes that she's attending college because she enjoys going to school. At times, she feels guilty because many of her friends are in college to pursue a career. Meaghan writes her goal in her notebook:

I love going to school.

She often refers to that page as a reminder, especially when she feels down or lonely. Even if she does poorly on an assignment, this reminder of why she's at school keeps her going.

Cataloging strengths

Get to know your strengths. Knowing your strengths can help you through difficulties when times get tough.

Rate your strengths (from 1 to 10) in the following areas and record your top three strengths in your notebook:

- **Knowing yourself.** You're in tune with your own feelings and emotions. When you're in a bad mood, you know it and you know why. You don't get angry at others just because you're in a bad mood. You also can express how you feel to yourself and others. You need to know your emotions in order to manage your emotions. If you know how you feel when you approach certain situations or make decisions, you can make more informed decisions (knowing how big a part an emotion plays in the decision, for example). You can identify a bad feeling when you're faced with a certain choice, and you can use your knowledge of why you feel that way when making your decision.

  For example, friends ask you to go drinking the night before your final exam. You like the idea, but you get a bad feeling in your stomach when thinking about the choice. Although you really want to go, you realize (after paying attention to your gut) that the last time you avoided studying the night before a test, you did poorly on that test.

- **Managing others.** You're really good at getting other people to go along with things you want. You can read people well and know their likes and dislikes. You're good at making and keeping friends. You might even be the go-to person when someone has a problem or issue that they want to discuss.

  Say that you've had a hard time getting to know people in your dorm. It seems that a small group of people came from the same high school and generally hang out together. If you have good interpersonal skills, you can persevere and try to meet new people. You're confident in your ability and don't stop with a few unsuccessful experiences.

- ✔ **Dealing with stress.** You manage to keep your cool when everyone around you starts freaking out. When something unexpected happens, you can analyze what it really means and how you're going to deal with it. You're the go-to person when things seem to be getting out of control.

   For example, your prof just announced a test next week. You and your friends have been slacking, putting off the readings and assignments. Suddenly, it hits you — you have a lot of catching up to do in a week. But you know what you need to do. In fact, you organize your friends so that you can all study based on a system and meet at regular intervals.

- ✔ **Dealing with change.** You're pretty good at change. You may have gone away to summer camps and found that you fit in right away. You really like facing changes and then mastering the challenges they present. You figured out your way around campus pretty quickly. You know how to find everything you need, and you don't get disoriented. You manage events and tasks well.

   Say that you suddenly have a lot of tasks to keep up with. You need to organize your courses, shop for food, get laundry done, attend some club meetings, make sure you don't miss the good parties, and stay in touch with people back home. No worries. You're good at juggling things and dealing with commitments.

- ✔ **Managing your moods.** You always seem to be in a good mood. Even when things go wrong, you manage to look at the bright side. You persevere when the going gets tough. You're also good at putting other people in a better mood. You don't let yourself get down and certainly don't sweat small problems.

   For example, you've been a pretty good student all through elementary and high school. Your grades have always been around a B. You get your first test at college back, and it has a big D on it. It's quite a shock at first, but you adjust quickly. Rather than get depressed, you look at where you went wrong. Your mind is clear enough to make constructive changes based on your mistakes, move forward, and use better strategies the next time.

Identifying your strengths and weaknesses

After you establish a good sense of your strengths (as discussed in the preceding sections) and weaknesses (by reviewing the list for your biggest challenges), pay attention to your top three strengths and your bottom two weaknesses. Identify your three strengths and two weaknesses from this list (and record them in your notebook):

- ✔ Emotional self-awareness
- ✔ Assertiveness
- ✔ Independence
- ✔ Self-regard
- ✔ Finding your passion
- ✔ Setting and achieving goals
- ✔ Empathy
- ✔ Social responsibility
- ✔ Interpersonal relationships
- ✔ Problem-solving
- ✔ Dealing with the reality of events and situations (as opposed to denying what's going on around you)
- ✔ Flexibility
- ✔ Stress tolerance
- ✔ Impulse control
- ✔ Happiness
- ✔ Optimism

Set up a plan to deal with these areas. You can find many activities throughout this book for most of these areas.

Setting long-term goals

For the long term, select three goals for improvement. For example, you might want to improve your interpersonal skills, better manage your mood, and become more optimistic.

State your goals as aspects of yourself that you want to improve. Here are some examples of long-term goals:

- ✔ I want to be able to develop more acquaintances and closer friendships.
- ✔ I want to be more in control of my emotions.
- ✔ I want to manage stress more effectively.
- ✔ I want to look at events in a more positive way.
- ✔ I want to pay more attention to others.
- ✔ I want to help others in need.

Work out a long-term plan for each of your goals. Picture in your mind what you want to become. By setting your target, you have a concrete goal to work toward.

Achieving long-term goals

In order to achieve your goals, you have to set out a plan and put in the time needed to achieve the results that you want. The kind of change you're looking at may take time and require practice. You may want some help in reaching your goals. A career counselor or someone from your college counseling department can help you implement your plan. Basically, you want someone who can be your coach.

One of the most important things that you can do to reach your goals is to make a firm commitment to succeed. Your motivation acts as an important barometer measuring your success.

If you don't have access to a counselor or coach, you can use various self-help materials, such as this book. The resource *The EQ Edge: Emotional Intelligence and Your Success,* by Howard Book and myself (Jossey-Bass), may also help you by providing you with additional examples and exercises to help you make the changes you want.

Part IV
Using Emotional Intelligence at Home

The 5th Wave   By Rich Tennant

"Six of Jennifer's goldfish died today, and, well, I just don't think it's worth the three of us keeping our reservations at Takara's Sushi Restaurant tonight."

In this part . . .

Emotional intelligence can help you with your closest or most intimate relationships, including your relationship with your spouse, partner, or best friend. You confide in or bond with these people more intensely than with anyone else. Maintaining and nurturing these relationships often requires conscious effort. I provide you with steps and tools to build and enhance these relationships.

I also discuss the importance of being an emotionally intelligent parent. This part deals with ways that you can improve your self-control, even when your child or teenager seems to get out of hand. Additionally, I offer suggestions and examples that might help your child become more emotionally intelligent.

Chapter 14

Creating Emotionally Intelligent Relationships

So, how's your relationship? Are you intimately involved with someone? Do you feel a closeness in your relationship? Do you want to feel closer?

Mary and Jeremy had been together for three years. Their relationship started off like most romantic relationships do. For the first several weeks, they were infatuated with each other, always wondering what the other would think of one thing or another. Being together was exciting, and they were always on their best behavior. But now, they seem to have hit a rut. They take each other for granted. They're busy with their respective work responsibilities and pressures, and they have little time for each other.

What changes relationships in this way? These changes often happen over time. Any relationship can have difficulty maintaining the original romance. Partners gradually begin to take each other for granted. The communication changes. Emotional intelligence, especially the ability to be aware of and manage both your own and your partner's emotions, has a lot to do with keeping the flame alight in a relationship.

Of course, you can have many different kinds of relationships. You have intimate relationships with the people you relate to most closely and most frequently. Your most intimate relationship is with your spouse or significant other. Because of the nature of intimate relationships, you invest the most emotion in these relationships. In good relationships, you find strong bonds of love, whereas in poor relationships, you find anger and resentment.

Assessing Your Intimate Relationship

People who are high in emotional intelligence tend to be more satisfied with their relationships, including their intimate and social relationships. They're happier people, and happier people exchange more positive emotions with others. (I cover social relationships in the section "Building Emotionally Healthy Social Relationships," later in this chapter.)

Here are some signs that indicate your relationship is on the right track:

- ✔ Your significant other and you are good friends.
- ✔ You share interests and activities.
- ✔ You know how to end a disagreement.
- ✔ You respect each other.
- ✔ You manage conflicts well.
- ✔ You accept each other's shortcomings.
- ✔ You're satisfied with how often you have sexual relations.
- ✔ You care about each other.
- ✔ You agree about how you manage your children.
- ✔ You agree about how you manage your money.
- ✔ You enjoy meals together.

The preceding list shows just some of the areas in your relationship in which your level of emotional intelligence can make a difference. People higher in emotional intelligence are better able to manage each other's emotions, which results in a relationship of trust and respect and in the capability of resolving conflicts successfully.

Understanding why emotional intelligence matters in a relationship

Multi-Health Systems performed several studies on the role of emotional intelligence in marriage. When the researchers at Multi-Health Systems analyzed the results, I expected some emotional-intelligence factors — empathy, good interpersonal skills, and the ability to tolerate stress — to be highly related to marital bliss. Surprisingly, however, the most significant areas included the following:

✔ **Happiness:** The most significant EI factor that related to marital satisfaction — that is, the one with the highest correlation — was happiness. Happier people are more satisfied with their relationships. You might wonder whether they're happy because they're in a good relationship, or they're in a good relationship because they're happy. As I discuss in Chapter 3, happiness comes first, and the good relationship comes later.

People who are happy manage to deal with life's stresses better than those who are unhappy. Happy people also spread their positive emotions to others. Think of personal happiness as a form of resilience that you carry with you through thick and thin, good and bad.

Happy people make the best of situations. So, even when their marriages seem less than perfect, their ability to maintain their happy mood helps them get through the rough times.

✔ **Self-regard:** The second most important EI skill that contributes to satisfied marriages is self-regard. People high in self-regard tend to weather criticism better than people who are less self-assured because they are more secure in who they are. Because they're more confident in their strengths and weaknesses, they don't get flustered if and when negative comments or insults arise.

✔ **Self-actualization:** Third in MHS's analysis was self-actualization. People who like to continually develop themselves and try to be their best also tend to be happier in their relationships.

✔ **Realism:** Finally, reality testing was significantly related to marital success. You need to be realistic about your relationship. People who fantasize or have unrealistic expectations about their relationship are most likely to be disappointed.

So, not only does common sense tell you that emotional intelligence is a significant part of successful relationships, so does the research, which involved surveying thousands of people.

Rating your relationship

Jessica's concerned about her relationship with Mark. He seems distant and uncommunicative. At first, she blames herself and tries to pay more attention to him. Unfortunately, he sees this added attention as interfering and becomes annoyed with her each time she questions how he feels and what he's thinking.

On the one hand, Jessica feels that something's wrong. But Mark seems oblivious to their relationship. Sometimes, really knowing where your relationship stands can be difficult. Taking the temperature of your relationship can definitely have benefits. For one, you can be alerted to problems brewing before they start to escalate. Also, it gives you a good idea of how your partner views the relationship. You may see your relationship as troubled, but your partner may think that it's coasting along. This may help you understand why you aren't getting the cooperation or change that you've been asking for. Even if your partner won't measure your relationship right now, you might want to get the ball rolling. If you begin the dialogue on the right foot, you might find discussing your feelings with your partner easier than just bringing up the subject without preparation, or even worse, letting the problem fester.

Take out your notebook and follow these steps:

1. **Write down how you rate your feelings about your relationship, on a scale from 1 to 5.**

    A rating of 1 represents feeling very unhappy, and 5 represents feeling very happy.

2. **Record what you like best about your relationship.**

3. **Identify what you want most to change in your relationship.**

    Write that aspect of your relationship in your notebook.

4. **Write down how much you want to make changes in your relationship to make it happier, on a scale from 1 to 5.**

    Here's how the scale translates:

    - **1:** I'm not at all motivated.

    - **2:** I'm slightly motivated to make changes in my relationship.

    - **3:** I'm moderately motivated to make changes in my relationship.

    - **4:** I'm very motivated to make changes in my relationship.

    - **5:** I'm desperate and will try anything to make my relationship happier.

If you're moderately happy or above (3 or higher in Step 1 of the preceding steps), congratulations. At this point, you can decide whether you want to move your relationship from good to great. The rest of this chapter may help you make your relationship even happier than it is. If you rate your relationship lower than 3, you're clearly unhappy and may be looking for help. If you're somewhat unhappy, consider working your way through this chapter. The information and activities in this chapter can help make your relationship more satisfying.

If you're very unhappy, you might want to consider seeing a counselor to help you repair your relationship.

Also, consider the degree to which you want to see change in your relationship (Step 4 in the preceding steps). Whether your relationship is fine the way it is or whether you want to see some changes, you can still add to the satisfaction and intimacy of your relationship by continuing with this chapter. Again, if you're desperate about changing your relationship or if you no longer care, contact a counselor.

After Jessica considers how she feels about her relationship with Mark, she starts to think about how Mark might rate their relationship. She thinks about the conversations they've had in the past, as well as his behaviors toward her. Jessica believes that Mark would rate their relationship as just fine, thank you very much.

When she considers what he probably likes best about the relationship, she guesses he likes the fact that she prepares his meals and does a great job keeping the house in order. He probably wants her to stop what he refers to as her nagging. Finally, she assumes that he'd rate the relationship as not needing change.

Jessica decides to share how she guessed Mark would rate the relationship with him. She needs to approach this delicate step sensitively. Rather than interrupt Mark when he's watching TV, Jessica approaches him when no distractions can get in the way and asks whether they can spend a few minutes discussing how she feels. His immediate response is one of concern, asking whether she's sick.

"No, it's not that," she replies.

She then goes on to tell him that she's been thinking about their relationship. She describes the preceding activity in this section and asks whether he would complete it. At first, he's reluctant. But when she tells him she's guessed how he'd rate the relationship and will share her results with him afterward, he completes the exercise.

After Mark completes the exercise, Jessica agrees to share how she thought he would respond. They then compare their responses and discuss how they agree on some areas but disagree on others. Then Mark shares how he thought Jessica would respond and Jessica reveals her responses. They continue their discussion, focusing on both the similarities and differences they each perceive in the relationship. This leads them to the next stage of discussion, which deals with changes they're interested in making in the relationship.

Use the areas that you want to change as a springboard for talking about your relationship. See whether you can reach some agreement on making changes in the areas that either of you identify.

Understanding How Your Emotions Affect the Relationship

When you rate your overall relationship, you basically attach a feeling to all the components of that relationship combined. You mentally weigh all the pluses and minuses, and come up with your own complex formulation of the relationship.

Your relationship consists of the overall feelings that you have about each of the parts. You can feel good or bad about your partner. You might have felt good about having dinner together last night, bad about the argument over the kids in the morning, good about how he complimented you in the afternoon, and bad about how he left a messy kitchen the night before.

Your expectations can have a big effect on the relationship, as well. You might wake up in the morning expecting a great day. When things don't go so well at first, you might be predisposed to let it go. If you wake up in a bad mood or with low expectations, the slightest bad experience can confirm your feelings and make you feel even worse. Or you might be in such a negative mood that you don't notice how nice your significant other is behaving toward you.

The following sections explore the role of emotions in relationships — how they support growth and how they can drive you apart.

The benefits of emotional intelligence

A recent study looking at one aspect of emotional intelligence and intimacy was carried out by Professor Tim Spector, director of the Twin Research Department at King's College London and published in the *Journal of Sexual Medicine*. He and his colleagues studied 2,000 pairs of twins and found that women higher in emotional intelligence had more satisfactory sexual relations — specifically, they had more pleasurable sex and more orgasms than women lower in emotional intelligence. The explanation of these results was that women higher in emotional intelligence were better able to monitor their own and their partner's feelings, which was seen as a key to a more satisfying intimate relationship.

Emotions: The glue of relationships

Think of your emotions as the glue of your relationship. Your ability to manage both your and your partner's emotions can help determine the strength of your relationship. Successful relationships involve a lot of give and take. They also involve a strong willingness to work together. Check out Colin and Ursala's story.

Colin comes home one day in a bad mood.

"So what's for dinner?" he fumes.

Ursala looks up and answers, "Oh — hi, hun. And how was your day today?"

"Not so good, sorry. I had a bad day. What are we having for dinner?" he asks.

"Well, I didn't have much time, so I'm taking some of yesterday's leftover chicken and making pasta," she begins.

"Oh, no. Not those leftovers again," he snorts.

"I could order in if you really want. I just thought I'd try this new recipe. It's up to you," she responds chirpily.

"Well, okay," Colin concedes.

This situation could have set up a major explosion in some relationships. Ursala was doing her best to be pleasant and tolerate Colin's unpleasant behavior. She knows him well enough to realize that things must have gone very poorly at work and that his emotions and behavior would change soon enough.

By accepting Colin's negativity for a while, and not seeing it as a personal threat, Ursala could deal with Colin and his situation. She could have easily gotten defensive and told him to make his own dinner and stop complaining.

Give and take — it makes the relationship work. Ursala has to give a bit in this situation by being nice even though she's not exactly being treated with respect. But she knows that when she's ready to take out her negative emotions on Colin, he'll be like a duck repelling water. Even if they don't say it, they each know that their relationship is too important to be derailed by the inevitable unpleasant instances of life.

Because they generally feel good about each other, they're willing to make sacrifices for each other. Those sacrifices include handling the small unpleasantries that the other may bring to the table. The emotional bond in the relationship has to be strong enough to withstand these bumps along the road.

How emotions help you grow together

So, how can your emotions help your relationship grow? First of all, by being in control of your own emotions, you can be more focused on strengthening your relationship. Second, by managing your partner's emotions, your partner can also focus more on improving the relationship and not be distracted by other events in your busy lives.

Emotional self-management is an important part of successful relationships. Based on Multi-Health System's findings, the ability to maintain a sense of happiness maximizes your enjoyment and helps you maintain your resilience in tough times. Your happiness can help act as a buffer and prevent other, less helpful emotions from getting in the way.

Think of your relationship as a bank account. The more goodwill you deposit, the higher your balance. The more negativity you give each other, the more goodwill you withdraw. When you're happy, you have a lot to deposit so that you can build up your security. Oh, and your saved goodwill collects plenty of interest.

Managing your partner's emotions can take some work, but if you value your relationship, it's well worth the effort. No one has come up with a universal way to increase the bonding in your relationship, but marital researchers do have some clues about what makes relationships more successful. The amount of positive interaction between partners gives a good indication of how well the relationship is functioning.

Back in the late 1970s, I wrote my PhD thesis about improving marital relationships. In those days (not unlike today), marital therapists focused a lot on the importance of communication. Most marital therapists believed that having great communication between your partner and you could lead to a great relationship.

At the time, no one had collected any real evidence that this connection between communication and a good relationship was true. In fact, I suspected that in some very good relationships, one partner (usually the man) was relatively uncommunicative, yet the relationship remained pretty solid.

Another school of thought held that behaviors affected couple relationships more than what you say. In other words, acts of kindness between partners might be more important than flowery words. So, if I comfort my wife when she comes home from work by giving her a back massage, that act might make our relationship more satisfying than just telling her how much I love her.

For my research, I recruited couples who wanted to improve their relationships. My study compared two well-developed approaches (communications training versus behavioral contracting). I included a *wait list control period*, which involved evaluating couples at the beginning and at the end of the same period of time as the treatments took, but with no treatment taking place, so that I could see which approach gave the most benefit — above and beyond no treatment at all. The behavioral program primarily involved playing a board game in which each partner chose behaviors that they want changed (increased) in their partner and rewards that they'd appreciate from their partner in return.

At the beginning and end of the intervention and again six months afterwards, I had each person complete a comprehensive test battery assessing their relationship. I also videotaped couples discussing a problem in their relationship; the videotape was then independently rated by trained raters. Throughout the entire period I had each person monitor their actual behaviors each day. Basically, I found that the behavioral change led to more positive feelings and better relationships — even after the follow-up period — than just communicating feelings did. In fact, couples trained in communication skills gave fewer positive responses to each other following treatment and reported being less happy with their relationship.

Getting in the habit of doing good deeds for your partner is like putting money in the bank — the deposits of good deeds enhance your relationship and build long-term trust.

Why emotions sometimes grow apart

One of the most common issues that comes up in relationships is that one or both partners take the other for granted. The spark and excitement that you experienced at the beginning of the relationship seem to be gone.

How do you know whether your relationship has grown apart? Review the items below and determine which ones apply to your current relationship:

- ✔ You don't really greet each other when one of you comes home.
- ✔ You don't talk about how your days went anymore.
- ✔ You rarely ask how the other one feels, emotionally.
- ✔ You do fewer things together.
- ✔ You have less sex than you used to.
- ✔ You always seem tired when you're together.

If you agree with two or more of the statements in the preceding list, you might want to talk to your partner about whether she feels the same way as you do. If you're not sure how to approach the subject, let your partner know that you're reading this book. Tell her that you found a very interesting chapter on relationships that you think she might want to read. Share this chapter. Then, you can talk to each other about how you each see the relationship. You can also choose to each make a commitment to work on improving the relationship.

Maintaining a good relationship can take a lot of work for some people. Not everyone can easily be considerate of and in tune with the person he shares his life with. Of course, you (like everyone else) also tend to get distracted with your busy life and take the people who are closest to you for granted.

For some people — such as those who have a lot of emotional-intelligence skills such as happiness, self-regard, and self-actualization — maintaining a good relationship comes relatively easily. These emotional skills are a part of their natural (or learned) pattern of behavior.

Other people, if they don't work at these skills, likely see their relationship become stale. Over time, the nuts and bolts of relating can wear down all the excitement you knew when you first met your romantic partner. Some people feel taxed by going to work, dealing with stress, managing the children, balancing tight finances, maintaining a household, and making all the compromises required to keep a relationship going. The romantic luster can tarnish over time for these people.

Understanding and Managing Your Partner's Emotions

If you want to enhance your relationship, then figure out how you can better understand and enhance your partner's emotions. Skillfully managing your partner's emotions can lead to a number of advantages:

- **Learning to read your partner's emotions better:** By improving your ability to read your partner's emotions, you can know whether your partner finds you pleasing or annoying, for example.

- **Keeping your relationship steady.** By being able to manage your partner's emotions, you can create a relatively smooth relationship. Think of your relationship as a car driving along a dusty road that has numerous potholes. If you can steer around the potholes and keep the car driving smoothly and quickly, you'll get to your destination safely and efficiently. If you navigate your partner's emotions (sometimes by biting your tongue), you'll have a more satisfying relationship. There are times when you disagree with your partner, and you can choose between being right or being happy in your relationship.

Taking your partner's emotional temperature

When you want to manage your partner's emotions, you first need to recognize those emotions. How well can you detect whether your partner is frustrated, bored, embarrassed, angry, or suspicious? You can read some emotions more easily than others.

What can you do if you don't know what your significant other is feeling? Here are some ways that you can take your partner's emotional temperature:

- Listen to your partner's tone of voice.
- Look at your partner's facial expression.
- Pay attention to body language.
- Ask your partner how she's feeling.
- Communicate that you understand how your partner's feeling using empathetic language.
- Ask your partner whether you're correct about what you think she's feeling.

By confirming your partner's feelings, you're less likely to jump to conclusions. Also, confirming his feelings demonstrates to your partner that you care about his welfare. After you know where your partner is coming from, then you can move on to managing his emotions.

Knowing where to start managing your partner's emotions

Before you begin managing your partner's emotions, you need to be able to read them correctly. Being aware of your partner's emotions is like checking a road map while you're driving somewhere. You need to know where you are in order to plan the next turn.

Most often, your partner's mood falls into one of these categories:

- ✔ Glad
- ✔ Sad
- ✔ Mad
- ✔ Worried
- ✔ Calm

If your partner is experiencing positive emotions, such as gladness and calmness, you want to keep these emotions going — or, at least, not turn them into negative emotions. To keep your partner in a good mood, stick to topics that are *friendly* — topics that you both agree about.

You can steer the conversation away from *hot-button* (sensitive) topics. If you need to talk about an important or sensitive issue, arrange a time and place when you can both be prepared to talk about it. Your partner should be aware of the issue and you should both be prepared to calmly discuss it.

When you deal with your partner's negative emotions, keep these tips in mind:

- ✔ If you find yourself in an argument or the topic is too hot, call a time out and agree to discuss it when you're both calmer.
- ✔ Listen to your partner's concerns without getting defensive.
- ✔ Reflect back to your partner how she feels about the situation. (Refer to Chapter 7 for more about empathy.)
- ✔ Check with your partner that you correctly understand the situation and how she feels.
- ✔ Let your partner know that you take her concerns seriously.
- ✔ Find out what you can do to help your partner, either by just listening, by providing comfort (physically with a hug or emotionally), or by problem-solving.
- ✔ Don't respond to any personal criticisms or attacks — accept them and take them under consideration.
- ✔ Be understanding.
- ✔ Don't escalate the situation — don't argue, and bite your tongue if necessary.
- ✔ Don't suggest any solutions to the problem until your partner feels that you fully understand her.

You may feel that with some of these strategies you are simply avoiding the problem by not coming up with a solution. Women, especially, need to feel understood or heard before launching into solutions. Men tend to be more solution-focused. Men may be more satisfied with those strategies that lead more directly to a result.

Your goal is not to avoid conflict, but to deal with disagreements in a calm and respectful way. Pick a time and place that's convenient and neutral. Don't discuss contentious matters in the bedroom or kitchen. These are places where you spend a lot of your time and you want them to be nourishing, or at least neutral, locations. Dealing with contentious issues in these places gives them a negative stigma that will be hard to overcome.

Pushing the limit of managing your partner's emotions

Obviously, you can't completely manage your partner and his emotions. But you can do a lot to help keep your relationship satisfying. Everyone has issues that they feel strongly about — such as politics, religion, your mother-in-law, or other deep-seated matters.

You may have some fundamental disagreements with your partner on one or more of these issues. People in successful relationships sometimes simply steer clear of these issues. They manage to avoid discussing these topics with their significant other, which eliminates the friction that those topics can cause.

If you have a sense of humor and don't define yourself or others by your or their stand on these deep issues, you can treat those issues with humor. For example, in many couples, the wife is a Democrat and the husband a Republican, and they can respectfully disagree with each other. In some cases, they disagree humorously — but not by using the sarcastic, put-down type of humor.

You don't want to completely control your partner. Managing emotions can be like steering your car around potholes. You can control your car only so much — the size of the engine, the nature and quality of the tires, the state of the steering system and shock absorbers, and so on can affect your ability to successfully direct the car. Some people's emotions are easier to manage than others. By knowing the nature of your partner — how moody he is, what triggers emotional outbursts, what calms him down, what distracts him — you'll be better able to drive around his emotional potholes.

Aim to manage those emotional aspects of your significant other that can help lead to a more satisfying, mutually respectful, trusting, and loving relationship. Don't attempt a complete personality change — you don't have much chance of success. Your day-to-day interactions create the most benefit for your relationship.

Using Your Emotional Skills in Your Relationship

By getting a better handle on your emotional strengths and weaknesses, and by working to improve the most important areas (by practicing and improving your performance), your intimate relationships can become more satisfying. You and your partner can become closer, overcome obstacles more easily, and enjoy each other more. You can improve your emotional skills at work or at school. And you can transfer these skills from work or school to home.

Using your emotional skills in your relationship can provide you with a number of different action plans:

- Become more aware of your own emotions and how they can sometimes get in the way.

- Develop skills to manage those emotions. Those skills can be simple, such as knowing when to hold your tongue, or more complicated, such as getting a good feel for where your partner is coming from. Of course, one cardinal rule involves knowing which battles are worth fighting.

- Learn to differentiate real issues from minor annoyances in order to avoid unnecessary conflict in your relationship.

Taking your own emotional temperature

One of the toughest aspects of managing your relationship involves dealing with conflict. In intimate relationships, your emotions can really get out of control, and you're more likely to say things that you later regret saying.

Whenever disagreeing with your partner, you need to take your own emotional temperature. When you feel your anger rising, stop and take a break. Hold back from getting into a screaming match with your partner. Count to ten. Take a deep breath. You have to prevent yourself from losing control.

By paying more attention to your emotions — the feeling in your gut, your heart rate, your skin sensation, shortness of breath, and the thoughts racing in your mind — you can effectively recognize what you're feeling. By recognizing your feelings, you can more effectively control yourself.

When you start feeling out of control or overwhelmed by your emotions, you can appropriately intervene if you recognize those feelings. The sooner you recognize your feelings, the more easily you can change your direction.

Also, you can develop the ability to recognize, maintain, and increase positive feelings, such as happiness, love, surprise, wonder, relaxation, calmness, optimism, contentment, and others. Although life throws you nasty curves every now and then, you can become more resilient if you figure out how to recognize and cultivate these positive feelings. The more you experience positive feelings, the more easily you can draw on them, when needed.

Knowing what battles are worth fighting

All intimate partners have disagreements. Those disagreements can be over small things — which clothes to wear, where to go for dinner, what movie to see, what color looks better on you, and so on. Or they can be over the big things — I hate your parents, you're too lenient with the kids, you aren't interested in sex anymore, you're spending too much money, you're irresponsible, and so on.

Trying to change even one thing about another person is a big task. Trying to change a number of things about a person can be monumental. If you have disagreements with your partner, pick one that you want to tackle first. Here's how to select the battle that you want to focus on:

- ✔ Pick something doable. For example, don't try to change beliefs that she's had since childhood or convince him to lose 100 pounds on a diet.

- ✔ Pick something meaningful, not trivial.

- ✔ Select a behavior that your partner can change. Don't pick a fundamental personality characteristic.

- ✔ Define the change that you want as a behavior that you want your partner to increase.

- ✔ Set a goal for how frequently you want this behavior to occur.

- ✔ Be prepared to make a change in your own behavior, in return.

Put aside some of the small and relatively unimportant disagreements that you have with your significant other. Focus on one area in which you can make a difference. Set aside a time and a neutral place to discuss the issue. Have a calm discussion about what behavior you want to see your partner increase. Be prepared to state how that change can improve the relationship. Gauge your partner's willingness to change.

Now, here's an important part (as I found out in my research). In order to help motivate your partner, you need to offer some reward in return. Make this reward something that your partner values. Here are some examples:

- ✔ Giving a back massage
- ✔ Being intimate at certain times
- ✔ Eating dinner out at a restaurant of your partner's choice
- ✔ Preparing a specific meal for your partner
- ✔ Attending a certain cultural event (such as the opera or symphony) or sporting event (such as a baseball, basketball, or hockey game)
- ✔ Cleaning up a part of the house
- ✔ Giving your partner clothing or jewelry
- ✔ Not nagging for a week

Make the reward meaningful and proportionate to the change that you're asking for. Of course, be prepared to carry out the reward before you offer it. In your change-for-reward agreement, be as specific as possible. For example, you could say, "If you increase your behavior to four times over the next week, then I'll give you three rewards on Monday, Tuesday, and Wednesday evening before bed next week."

Knowing when to hold your tongue

If you want to maintain a good relationship, you need to know when to shut up. Don't try to win every argument, correct every wrong, or always be on top. Once in a while, you have to sit back and listen, even if you don't like what you're hearing.

After you take in an earful, then you can calmly think about what your partner said. Some of it might be wrong, vindictive, ugly, unfair, or demeaning. However, she may have presented a kernel of truth in the criticism. Okay, relax.

By keeping civil and not getting drawn into an argument, you're not admitting guilt. Often, people think that if they don't respond at least as noisily, they're accepting the blame. Keeping your cool is a virtue. Being a hothead doesn't win points in the long run. In fact, people who constantly lose their temper often aren't taken seriously by others. They tend to be regarded as immature. Many people learn to avoid them.

Using empathy to enhance your relationship

By being empathic, you chalk up credits in your marital bank account. You avoid debits — because you're not negative. You gain credits — because you're positive, caring, and working towards the good of the relationship.

Being empathic doesn't mean that you give in or admit that you're wrong. Instead, using empathy means that you're truly trying to understand the other person's point of view and validating your partner's feelings. Consider Martha and Herb.

"You're always making a mess and leaving it!" Martha yells at Herb. "When will you clean up after yourself?"

Herb's ready to blast back, "I was up late cleaning the dishes last night, I put things away you left out after dinner," and maybe three other examples that he feels justify his retaliative anger.

But he doesn't. He stops himself and lets Martha blast away. He waits until she gets it all out of her system.

Then, he calmly replies, "You're feeling pretty angry right now, aren't you Martha?"

"You're damn well right! I'm tired of having to deal with this again!"

"You're upset about me not cleaning the sink and leaving my stuff on the kitchen table," he replies.

"Yes, that's right," she says, a bit calmer.

"It really bothers you when I'm late or I forget to clean things up," he restates. "And you want me to be more thoughtful."

"Okay, now you understand," she replies, "What's your solution?"

Being empathic doesn't necessarily mean you're going to solve the problem. But it puts you in a more conciliatory state. It allows you to focus on the problem and not create another problem — yelling and shouting at each other — which often causes more harm to the relationship than the original problem. (I talk about empathy in greater detail in Chapter 7.)

Building Emotionally Healthy Social Relationships

Emotional intelligence helps you become more satisfied not only in your intimate relationships, but with your social relationships, as well. Sometimes, you can more easily practice emotional intelligence skills with your friends than with your significant other. Friendships don't tend to be as intense as more intimate relationships.

People generally like to be around others who have good emotional intelligence. Think of the people that you consider friends. How many of them tend to be moody, unhappy, poor communicators, pessimistic, or uncaring? These kinds of people just don't seem to attract many others.

Using your emotional skills in social relationships

The emotional skills that you can develop by using this book can help you enhance many of your interpersonal relationships. For example, friends look for empathy in their relationships.

Your skill in developing and building better interpersonal relationships also helps define your friendships. Developing your interpersonal skills allows you to

- Initiate relationships.
- Know what topics to talk about.
- Have interesting conversations.
- Draw people into the conversation.
- Share mutual interests.
- Laugh together.
- Give and get advise.

- ✔ Share stories.

- ✔ Enjoy sports and hobbies together.

- ✔ Celebrate events.

- ✔ Provide help and support in times of need (such as the loss of a loved one).

- ✔ Find out interesting things.

- ✔ Exercise together.

- ✔ Be politically involved.

- ✔ Participate in religious practices and ceremonies.

 Having better interpersonal skills can provide you with many benefits. You can increase your circle of friends, become closer with the friends you have, meet new people more easily, and have more enjoyable relationships. Being in tune with others, both emotionally and interpersonally (through good social skills), can enhance your relationships and your life experiences.

Finding the right balance of emotional and social skills

With some people, you want to have an emotional (intimate) relationship, but with others, you want to have a social (interpersonal) relationship. The closer you are with someone, the more emotional the attachment. With strangers, you're likely to have an interpersonal interaction.

Emotionally intelligent behavior involves knowing how to strike the right balance between social and emotional relationships. You can err in two ways:

- ✔ **You can be too aloof and not let people get close to you.** This situation sometimes happens in couples in which the male is more traditional or macho. Interestingly, I often see this aloofness or traditional behavior among men in certain professional groups, including engineers, math professors, surgeons, anesthetists, geologists, actuaries, and coal miners. It also occurs in certain cultures, especially where there are large disparities between the genders.

    You can find extreme examples of this emotional detachment or poor social skills in people who have Asperger's syndrome. This disorder is partly defined by a person's aloofness to other people — rarely making eye contact, lacking humor, rarely expressing emotions, and having almost robot-like interactions.

> ✔ **You can get too emotional — letting it all hang out — with someone you've just met.** You might disclose your entire life history to perfect strangers. Trying to get too close to someone you hardly know sends out mixed messages. For many people, it acts as a sort of danger sign — putting you on their people-to-avoid list.

Knowing how much to disclose to whom is a skill. For many people, it comes naturally. Others have to figure it out by watching how other people behave. You can identify some of these cues by watching the media. Movies and TV shows present the good and the bad of initiating and maintaining relationships. Generally, the more likeable characters are the ones who can share the right amount with the right person.

For many people, their life experiences help them figure out the rules of good relationships. For others, life seems to involve a pattern of initiating, then breaking off, relationships. Emotionally intelligent people can understand the rules of social relationships and apply those rules. Like most aspects of emotional intelligence, interpersonal skills have two parts:

> ✔ **Theoretical:** Knowing the rules and how they work. Being able to correctly predict how examples of human relationships will turn out. People with good theoretic knowledge of social relationships can look at samples of behaviors between two people and get a good idea on how that relationship is doing and whether it is likely to be a good or bad relationship.
>
> ✔ **Practical:** The ability to go out and successfully initiate, nurture, and maintain healthy relationships. The hands-on, day-to-day skill of communicating with and relating to people.

Some people may be good at the theoretical part of understanding relationships, but not so good at the practical side. Others may be good at both. Although you probably didn't get training in these skills in school, they can help you go a long way in the real world.

Chapter 15

Parenting with Emotional Intelligence

*Y*ou may have heard the old line that your child doesn't come with a manual (or a warranty). Maybe that's why you can find hundreds of books on parenting at your local bookstore.

In this chapter, I don't provide a complete course on how to raise your kids. But I do talk about some aspects of emotional intelligence that can help you with whatever parenting manual you choose to follow.

One of the most common problems in parenting involves the two principal players — the parents — not sharing the same child-rearing approach. Another widespread issue is the lack of consistency in applying whatever approaches you do use. This chapter explores some universal aspects of parenting that can help you with the monumental task of raising your kids.

How Intelligent People Become Emotionally Unintelligent Parents

I've often been asked why you don't have to take a test before you become a parent. Although the questioner is only half serious, he usually has in mind some kind of intelligence test, thinking that some people just aren't smart enough to know how to parent.

If intelligence was any guarantee of good parenting, this approach might make some sense. However, your IQ and your parenting effectiveness don't really relate to each other. In fact, Dr. Robert Goodman and his associates at the Department of Child and Adolescent Studies at the Institute of Psychiatry in London carried out an countrywide study looking at this issue in the U.K. They found that children of parents who had high IQs had more emotional problems, which both parental and teacher reports measured.

But wait, the picture gets even worse. According to a five-year study run by Indiana University's Kinsey Institute, having children significantly lowers the IQ of both male and female parents.

The researchers started out by testing the IQ of 200 married couples who planned to start a family within the next four years. All but 27 couples conceived within the time frame. All the parents took another IQ test six months after their children were born. In every one of the 173 cases, both parents scored at least 12 points lower on the second IQ test, with many scoring 20 points less.

According to Dr. Hosung Lee, the principal investigator, having children retards the brain's activity. Because this drop in IQ occurs for both parents, the researchers assume that this loss is psychological, as opposed to biological. Dr. Lee states that the parts of the brain dealing with logic and reality testing take the biggest hit.

The loss of logic and reality testing explains why every parent believes that her child is the cutest, smartest, best, and so on. It also explains why people who used to be open-minded now blame teachers and coaches when their children don't perform as well as they expect.

Not only do you become less objective when you become a parent, you also become less tolerant. You suddenly have expectations, and you measure your child against these expectations regularly. Although you can make your expectations more realistic by setting goals, you need to behave calmly and constructively when your child falls short of your expectations. Many parents may find it difficult to keep those hard-to-control impulses in check.

Losing impulse control is one of the ways that you may become less emotionally intelligent when you become a parent. Although intellectually (or objectively) you know that pushing your kids too hard and expecting too much can be demotivating, anxiety-producing, or anger-provoking, as a parent you tend to become impulsive and less tolerant of your child's unexpected or uncooperative behaviors.

What they didn't teach you about kids

Before having kids, you might have thought that you'd be able to manage them pretty easily. You had some good ideas about how nice and compliant they'd be and perhaps how they wouldn't do much to disrupt your active routine. For some parents, this situation might actually happen.

However, for the vast majority of parents, things don't seem to work out quite as expected. You seem to have less control than you thought you would over your child's sleeping, eating, and crying habits. In fact, you have to do a lot of adjusting of your own life to fit your child's. Many parents haven't quite prepared themselves for this scenario.

Although you probably know intellectually what to expect from your children, reality has a way of turning things around. You need to make an emotional adjustment to accepting your child's actual behaviors. Your ability to emotionally adjust to your children gives you a telltale sign of your success in emotional management.

If you have all the intellectual child-development knowledge that you want at your fingertips and have even memorized all the developmental milestones that your child will go through, you've really prepared yourself intellectually. But you need to figure out how to deal emotionally when your child wakes you up in the middle of the night, cries seemingly endlessly, or refuses to eat that wonderful concoction you put in his mouth.

In truth, you have more control over your own reactions to your child than over your child's behavior. The more self-control you have in managing your reactions, the more responsive your child will be to you — and the more easily you will be able to manage your child's behavior.

Managing your own emotions

You may find that changing the focus from managing your child's behavior to managing your own emotions will be a difficult transition to make.

Next time you find yourself not fully in control of your emotions in response to some behavior from your child, consider the following items:

- The behavior of your child (before you reacted)
- Your feelings about your child's behavior
- Your thoughts about your child's behavior
- What you did about your child's behavior

Here's an example:

- **The behavior of your child:** My child started crying and wouldn't stop.

- **Your feelings about your child's behavior:** At first, I was concerned. Then, I felt angry that she wouldn't stop. Then I felt guilty about feeling angry at my child.

- **Your thoughts about your child's behavior:** I thought she should stop this behavior now; she had no reason to be crying. I thought the noise would drive me crazy. I worried other people would hear her and think that I'm not a good parent. Then, I thought I shouldn't be thinking this way about my own child.

- **What you did about your child's behavior:** I held her, and then I gently rocked her. I tried to feed her, and I talked to her. Nothing seemed to work.

Look at the connection between your feelings and actions. Feeling concerned is only natural. Holding your child when you're concerned is a normal response.

What was the relationship between your thoughts and the anger you felt? In the preceding example, the thought that the child *should* stop crying might have triggered the anger. Commanding another person to change his behavior, especially a child or infant, likely doesn't get the results you want.

You understandably become frustrated when things get out of hand. But you need to recognize the difference between frustration and anger. Frustration is a manageable emotion. You can reason while you feel frustrated, asking yourself questions such as

- What are my options?

- Can I try some other approaches?

- What's causing this crying?

- Is my child uncomfortable in some way?

Being angry makes reasoning very difficult. When you're angry, your mind is too preoccupied with emotion for you to be able to make good decisions. So, pay attention to your feelings in these situations, and if you feel anger coming on, stop and take a time out. Just ask yourself, "Why am I upsetting myself over a child who's too young to manage himself?"

Understanding Where Your Partner Is Coming From

If you want to create a healthy child-rearing environment, you need to understand your partner's views on raising the children and make sure that your partner understands your views. If you're both on the same page, that's great. Otherwise, you want to find points of agreement and look for compromise in other areas. Coming to terms on child-rearing issues can reduce the disagreements in your relationship, increase your children's well-being, and enhance your own sanity.

Imagine that you're Ralph. He just came home from work.

"Hi, honey. I'm home."

"Oh, thank goodness," Leah says. "I've been waiting for you."

"What's the problem?" Ralph asks.

"It's the kids. I've had it up to here. I need you to deal with them. They haven't been listening to me all day. I've been warning them that you'll spank them as soon as you get home."

"You've what?" Ralph asks, surprised.

Ralph had no idea what he was coming home to. Spanking his children as soon as he came home from work was the last thing he was prepared for. Partners often have different ideas about child-rearing. For example, one parent may be the disciplinarian, and the other parent may be more easy-going.

You may find achieving balance in child-rearing a challenge, and you and your partner need to discuss your child-rearing practices. To start, each of you respond to these items by writing the answers in your notebook:

- ✔ Who's stricter with your children?
- ✔ Give an example of a situation in which you were strict.
- ✔ Give an example of a situation in which your partner was strict.
- ✔ Give an example in which you were lenient.
- ✔ Give an example in which your partner was lenient.
- ✔ Outline your basic philosophy about raising your kids.
- ✔ Outline how you see your partner's philosophy about raising kids.

After you and your partner have each independently responded to these items, arrange to have a discussion about your views. For each item, listen to your partner and then reflect back their point of view until you fully understand it. Have your partner reflect back your point of view until you agree your partner understands you. After you both know what the other believes, you're ready to move to the next section. The purpose of this part of the exercise is to get you to the point of understanding your partner's beliefs so that you can clearly discuss the key issues when coming to a solution. Very often disagreements escalate when the parties refuse to take the time to understand what they're even arguing about.

Working as a team

After you go through the activity in the preceding section, you and your partner should each take the time to summarize the other's views. Decide whether the following statements are true and record your answers in your notebook:

- ✔ My partner is more strict that I am in child-rearing.
- ✔ My partner understands my views about child-rearing.
- ✔ My partner is willing to adjust to accommodate my views.
- ✔ We're willing to work toward a compromise.

If you agree with the last item in the preceding list, you are likely to work out your differences in this aspect of child-rearing.

If you disagree with this last item, speak with an outside party about your issues. You can speak with a trusted friend or relative, if you can find one who wants to help. Or you can consult a professional counselor. You need to resolve this issue sooner rather than later for the sake of your child.

Your goal should be to work as a team. Find the areas that you both agree on. For example, if your child runs out on a busy street, you both likely agree that someone has to pull him off the street at any cost. Follow these steps to help you increase the number of areas of agreement:

1. **In your notebook, write down your areas of agreement.**

   Choose the areas from this list that you and your partner agree about:

   - Safety
   - Behavior in public
   - Manners

- Hygiene and health

- Food and eating

- Bedtime and sleep

- School

- Clothing and dress

- Type and nature of toys

- Time spent with your child

- Money spent on your child

- Chores

- Discipline

2. **Write down which areas in the preceding list you and your partner don't agree on.**

3. **Celebrate the areas of agreement.**

   Use these areas as examples for what you want to achieve. Talk to each other about some specific instances in which you agreed with each other in an area. Explore why you think you agree. See if you share other basic values. Are there some topic areas that are more important to one partner than to the other? Discover your shared values (where you both agree). By building on these shared values you can strengthen your relationship. Celebrate these agreements with compliments, hugs, or other ways of showing affection.

You want to be on the same page as your partner as much as possible when raising your children. Although you may never be able to get complete agreement on all issues, you need to develop strategies about how you want to deal with these differences of opinion.

Managing each other's emotions

When you establish a broad list of your partner's and your areas of agreement and disagreement in child-rearing (and maybe you even come closer to agreement on a number of issues), as I describe in the preceding section, you can better deal with your emotions and those of your partner when disagreements arise.

You probably know — and your partner probably knows — your one major area of disagreement concerning child-rearing. In this activity, you meet with your partner to discuss this area of disagreement. Follow these steps:

1. **Set a meeting time and place to discuss this area of concern with your partner.**

   Pick a quiet place where you likely won't get interrupted.

2. **State your partner's position.**

   For example, "Honey, let me see if I understand where you're coming from. You feel that I'm too tough on Bret when he misbehaves in public." Your partner should tell you whether you're correct.

3. **If you haven't stated your partner's position correctly, try restating it.**

   Repeat this step until you both agree that you've stated the position correctly.

4. **Ask your partner to state the behavior change that she wants you to make.**

   "Okay, honey, tell me how you want me to behave when Bret has a tantrum in the supermarket."

5. **Your partner should state how she'd prefer that you behave.**

   "I'd feel better if you were more laid back. Just let him blow off some steam."

6. **Don't argue with the suggestion, just state how you'd feel about applying that change**

   "Letting Bret act out in the supermarket would make me really anxious and embarrassed. I don't think I could stand back and watch him get out of control."

7. **Ask your partner to repeat how you'd feel in the situation.**

   "You said you'd feel really embarrassed if Bret was out of control in the supermarket and you did nothing."

8. **After your partner correctly explains your feeling, reverse the process so that this time your partner states your position, as you did in Step 2.**

Although you may not come to a complete agreement on how to handle these situations, this process gives you a better understanding of your partner's feelings about the issue. By understanding each other, you can likely come to a compromise position.

Keeping Your Cool with Your Child

One of the most common parenting problems is when you lose your temper because of your child's behavior. You can lose your cool for many reasons, but you need to manage your impulse control.

Any number of triggers can cause you to lose control when trying to manage your child. These triggers can range from the behavior itself to your own difficulty in accepting your child's behavior, or at least managing your emotional reaction to the behaviors. When you lose control of your emotions, you can end up yelling at or even hitting your child.

Here are some suggestions for keeping your cool:

- ✔ Start working on managing your impulsiveness at times when you're cool and collected.

- ✔ Understand that losing your temper isn't a good child-management technique.

- ✔ Recognize the kinds of situations that cause you to lose control (for example, when your child misbehaves, fails to listen, or has temper outbursts).

- ✔ Decide that you'll try to maintain calm during these situations.

- ✔ Count to ten when you feel yourself losing control.

- ✔ Plan in advance a distracter that you can use to attract your child's attention when you start losing control. For example,

  - Offer a reward to your child when he calms his behavior.

  - Draw your child's attention away with a toy she really likes.

  - Use a calming voice in a consistent way.

  - For very young children, use funny faces, high pitched sounds, or photos of familiar faces to draw your child away from temper tantrums.

Managing your temper takes time and practice. You need to start the process while you're in a calm mood. Think about how destructive losing your temper can be. If you convince yourself of the destructive nature of anger, you can really motivate yourself to change.

After you select a strategy that you think will work for you, try it out. Look at your child's next outburst as an opportunity to practice your new skills.

If impulse control is a serious problem for you (for example, you yell excessively or can become physically violent with your child), speak to a mental health professional about your situation.

Using Your Emotional Skills to Manage Your Child

You need self-management emotional skills to bring up your child in a constructive and nurturing way. Studies have found that excessively yelling at your child can do as much harm as — or even more harm than — spanking your child. The results of yelling at your child, name-calling, and putting her down last longer than a slap on the bum, for example.

The message you send to your child — the words and the emotion attached to those words — live on in your child's mind. That message can reinforce the idea that your child is a bad person. In addition, if you continue yelling, your child eventually becomes immune to the noise — she tunes it out and ignores it. She just thinks, "Oh, he's telling me how worthless I am again."

When you can manage your own emotional responses, you can become a better parent. Some of the most important emotional skills (which I discuss throughout this book) that apply to parenting include impulse control, empathy, and problem-solving. By working on your ability (and your partner's ability) in these areas, you can implement any number of parenting approaches. If you can't manage your own emotions, no parenting approaches can help you raise a happy, emotionally secure child.

The following sections can help you figure out how to focus on three emotional skills that are important in parenting. If you can manage your impulses, you're clear-headed in your approach to your child. By being more empathic, you can understand where your child's really coming from (maybe your child's goal in life isn't actually to drive you crazy). Finally, by improving your problem-solving ability, you can come up with better ways to deal with your child when she gets difficult.

Managing your impulse control

Losing control of your impulses can derail effective parenting. Getting a grip on your impulsive behavior can go a long way in making you a more stable, nurturing, influential, and supportive parent. Sometimes, you may not even realize that you're being negative and deflating to your child. Your voice gets louder, your temper gets shorter, you move quickly and impatiently, and you start making demanding statements (such as Do this! Get that! Bring it to me now!).

Imagine if you behaved that way toward a perfect stranger — how embarrassing! Or think of yourself in a job interview. Would you think about the questions that the interviewer asks you, or would you say, "That's a dumb question. Look, I'm too busy for this. Just finish your questions and let me outta here." Think you'd get the job? Try imagining that your child is thinking about hiring you as his parent.

You can use a number of long-term strategies to become more patient. Here are a few suggestions:

✔ Consider getting involved in meditation, mindfulness, or yoga. Chapter 6 covers these techniques in more detail.

✔ Over the next week, pay close attention to your anger or frustration when it begins to build — monitor your feelings and the things that you tell yourself while these feelings escalate. Try to dispute the thoughts that give rise to these feelings. At the end of each day, summarize your attempts to deal with your anger. See whether you can figure out how to better detect your anger when it just begins and it's easier to manage.

✔ If you consistently can't manage your impulses, you may want to meet with a professional counselor.

Using empathy as a guide

Empathy, which gives you the ability to read your child's emotions and understand where she's coming from, can help you manage her behavior.

Here are some ways that you can be more empathic with your child:

✔ When your child is upset, first try to understand what he may be experiencing.

✔ If your child is old enough to respond, ask what's wrong, or why she's feeling that way.

✔ Try reflecting back the emotion that your child is experiencing. (For example, you could say, "You seem to be very angry, Sarah.")

✔ Ask questions not specifically related to the feeling but about activities and events — what she was doing earlier today, what happened at lunch, what will she do this afternoon? Sometimes you can get clues to feeling issues through listening to what happened at recent events (for example, what did you do after Kevin said he didn't want to play with you?). Many kids have difficulty articulating feelings spontaneously.

If you attempt to understand your child, she responds with more useful information about what she's feeling, which she doesn't do if you try to control her behavior. Your child wants understanding and attention first — and solutions later.

Problem-solving your way through crises

After you manage your impulses and empathize with your child (which I discuss in the preceding sections), you're ready for some real problem-solving. Start considering what you can do to deal with your child's behavior.

You might want to pull out whatever resources you have. Use your parents, other relatives, or close friends for advice. How have they dealt with these behaviors?

Follow these basic steps when you're problem-solving:

1. **Make sure you have a good grasp of the problem.**

   Start by clearly and concisely describing the problem. (For example, Julia starts whining and complaining every time we go to Grandma's house.)

2. **Consider a number of alternative solutions.**

   Think your way through how each of your solutions might play out.

3. **Choose a solution that you can use, based on your trial-and-error thoughts.**

4. **Implement your solution.**

   Pay close attention to how well your solution works.

5. **Re-evaluate whether it was the best solution for you.**

   If it wasn't, try one of your alternatives.

   If your solution worked to your satisfaction, congratulate yourself on your success and remember this experience for the future.

When problem-solving in parenting, you usually have to go through some trial and error. Be optimistic. You can eventually find a solution that's right for you. But you also need to take away valuable information from your mistakes, as well as from your successes.

Getting a Grip When Dealing with Your Teenager

Dealing with teenagers leads to very complex situations. If you have a young child, you're one of the most important influences in his world. Teenagers, however, are more heavily influenced by their friends and the media. The media includes TV, movies, Web sites, and various online activities.

You need all your skills in impulse control, empathy, and problem-solving when dealing with a teenager, just like you do when dealing with small children (as discussed in the preceding sections). But another facet of emotional intelligence becomes important when dealing with adolescents — flexibility. Teenagers react badly if you remain rigid in your thinking and behavior toward them.

What you should know about flexibility

You may have grown up at a time when adults enforced strict discipline. Today's young people come from a different school of thought. They've grown up seriously questioning authority. They may decide *not* to do something simply because an authority figure told them to do it.

Young people today like options. And they don't respond well to rules or being told what to do. You can reason with them, but you have to be able to understand their needs (or, at least, where they're coming from) in order to make a persuasive case.

Parenting an adolescent today requires you to be flexible in helping your teen cope with various alternatives. Today's teen bases everything, from where and whom to socialize with to what kind of career path to take, on a broad array of choices.

Checking your own emotions and knowing how much you can trust your teenager are major challenges. Your teenager may choose a number of behaviors with which you're not happy or comfortable. You need to know where to pick your battles and give your teen some leeway in trying new things. Make your main concern your teen's personal safety.

Being flexible with your child can cause you a great deal of anxiety. So, while you become flexible with some of your teen's choices, you or your partner may start feeling more stress.

Where stress management comes in handy

Realize that your teenager will soon be an adult. As an adult, your child will be responsible for her own actions. Adolescence is a training ground for adulthood. If your teenager comes to you for advice, consider yourself lucky. You're probably good at the skills I present in the preceding sections — impulse control, empathy, problem-solving, and flexibility.

You may have found yourself in Sheila's position at some point or other. Sheila was checking the clock once again.

"Harold, it's nearly two o'clock in the morning. Something must have happened to Neil. He's not answering his phone."

"Sheila, I'm sure he's okay. He told us he'd be late. It's time to go to bed."

"I can't sleep until I hear something from him."

Teenagers sometimes stay out very late. Even though they now have cell phones, they don't always keep them on. Ideally, you want an agreement with your teen about how late he can stay out and how he can contact you if his plans change. But increasing your anxiety in these situations just makes it worse for you.

You can choose from two basic ways that you can better manage your stress:

- ✔ Coping with the stressful thoughts you're experiencing
- ✔ Distracting yourself

Stressful thoughts

Everyone experiences stressful thoughts. You can deal with these thoughts by refuting them, which means you must question those thoughts. Here's an example:

- ✔ **Stressful event:** Neil's out late, and I haven't heard from him.
- ✔ **Stressful thoughts:** Something must have happened to him. How could he be out so late without telling me? This is awful! He shouldn't be behaving this way!
- ✔ **Questions:** Do I have any sign that something happened to him? Has he been out this late before? Have I tried calling him and leaving a message? What's so awful about his behavior? Why shouldn't he behave the way he's behaving?

✔ **Possible answers:** I don't see any sign that something is wrong. He does have his phone, so if something was wrong, he'd call. I did leave him a message to call me. His behavior may be wrong, but it's not awful. He's chosen to behave the way he does, and I can talk to him about it tomorrow.

Distraction

Distracting yourself from a stressful situation is a short-term solution to your stress. You can distract yourself so that you can avoid the immediate effects of overreacting to a situation.

You can use two methods to distract yourself:

✔ **Physical:** Get involved in some activity, such as reading, watching TV, knitting, painting, searching the Web, organizing any room in the house, baking, or any other activity that calms you down.

✔ **Mental:** Meditate, listen to music or relaxing audio (such as cool jazz, classical music, classic pops, relaxation audios, podcasts, or old radio shows), practice yoga, do relaxation exercises, plan your vacation, focus on a work problem that needs solving, or do any other activity that refocuses your thinking.

Managing the Rollercoaster Teenage Years

Managing a teenager can take a lot out of you. The ups and downs in your teenager's life never seem to come when you might expect them. Some of the more common issues involve friendships, romantic relationships, school, drugs, smoking, alcohol, late-night parties, driving issues, too much multimedia (such as TV, Internet, and video games), and so on. People have written about the tumultuous adolescent years ever since humanity recorded histories.

Of course, you need to keep your own sanity and peace of mind. By not getting overly involved (by taking on the problem yourself) in your adolescent's issues, you can deal with them more objectively and calmly. You should be concerned about your child, but ultimately, she has to make her own way in the world.

The emotional-intelligence component that can help you when your adolescent starts to overload you with problems is your *self-regard* (your ability to know your strengths and weaknesses and to have confidence in your strengths). You can also help your child with interpersonal relationship skills and social responsibility if you have high skills in those areas yourself.

Keeping self-regard on an even keel

You can remain calm and in control of your own emotions most effectively by having good emotional self-regard. By being confident and knowing your strengths, you can more effectively use your emotional and social skills to be helpful to your teen. When you're low in self-regard, you tend to feel inadequate and give up more easily. Most parents can be good resources for their teenagers, but you have to be confident in your ability to strike the right note — often by knowing when to listen, when to console, and when to offer advice.

Using your strengths to guide your teenager can enhance your relationship with him. If your weaknesses get in the way, by causing you to overreact or react inappropriately, these destructive behaviors can hinder your relationship.

Here are some examples:

- **Your strength is impulse control.** You're patient, calm, and collected when dealing with your teen. Even when times are tough, you don't lose it. You think about the consequences of what you say, so you don't open your mouth and say anything that you might regret.

- **Your weakness is impulse control.** You're likely to react before you think, especially when your teen does something that upsets you. By not keeping your impulses in check, you risk overreacting, being too negative or critical, and therefore damaging your relationship.

- **Your strength is empathy.** You listen to your teen, and your teen feels that you understand her and her world. Because you gain your teen's trust, you're more likely to be part of her life.

- **Your weakness is empathy.** Your teen feels that you don't understand him and his world. Why bother even talking to you? You operate from your own values and fail to take into account where your teen is coming from.

Be aware of your strengths and play to them when dealing with your teenager. You want to build the parent-child relationship and keep the channels of communication open with your teenager. Don't expect your teenager to come to you first when she has issues that she wants to discuss. Friends play an important role at this age. But you need to be available if your teen does turn to you.

Gauging your teenager's interpersonal skills

Friendships and interpersonal skills play an important part in an adolescent's life. Many teens define themselves and judge how well their life is going through their friendships. Some teens, however, aren't very social. You need to determine whether your teen isn't social by choice.

If your teenager prefers isolated activities such as reading, watching TV, surfing the Web, or playing video games, you may have no reason to worry. Some adolescents are content with having just a few friends and carrying out solitary activities.

However, if your teen doesn't get along well with peers, he may have a problem. You can try discussing the situation with your teen, but he likely sees his social life as a sensitive topic. Generally, if your teen is having problems with his social life, he may show symptoms such as sadness, irritability, stubbornness, boredom, and general unpleasantness.

When you're dealing with adolescents, you may want to involve an outside party. See whether your teen will agree to meet with a professional counselor. A good counselor can help your child develop better interpersonal skills.

Showing your teenager social responsibility

One skill that people infrequently impart to kids today is *social responsibility* — that is, caring about others in the community and the world, especially those less fortunate. Of course, you can best introduce your child to social responsibility by modeling it yourself. If you demonstrate active behaviors of giving some of your time and resources to help others in need, and perhaps even involve your child, you can contribute to your own child's social responsibility and, by extension, emotional intelligence.

Social responsibility can go a long way in positively influencing your child. The earlier you give your child these skills, the better. By having a socially responsible child, you help prevent your child from becoming overindulgent and too fixated on material goods for success.

Here are some things that you can do to encourage social responsibility:

- Give generously to charities.
- Volunteer for worthy nonprofit organizations.

✔ Demonstrate environmentally friendly behaviors.

✔ Help those around you who are less fortunate.

✔ Be kind, generous, and forgiving in your interactions with people generally, regardless of how close they are to you.

✔ Get involved in your community.

Giving your child social responsibility can help make her a good team player. Social responsibility also provides a good antidote to a common problem among youth today — boredom. Getting kids involved in helping others adds an important dimension to those kids' lives by taking them away from their day-to-day exposure to materialism.

Chapter 16

Raising an Emotionally Intelligent Child

*E*veryone wants the best for their children. But you can easily get confused if you try to sort out all the things that experts tell you to do when raising your children. You don't find a shortage of experts in the parenting field.

You probably heard the advice that you should be strict and use discipline but also be lenient and not set too many rules. Get your child involved in as many activities as possible, but make sure that you don't make him a hurried child (one who is pushed into too many extra-curricular activities). And heaven help you if your child can't read or do algebra by age 3!

Seriously, at times, all the advice being thrown at you in newspapers and on TV, radio, Web sites, blogs, and social networks can make you dizzy. In this chapter, I deal with one aspect of child-rearing — helping your child become emotionally intelligent. New research demonstrates the benefits of helping your child develop emotional skills. Your child can better succeed in social situations at school, which can dramatically affect educational and future work success. Nurturing your child's EQ helps ensure that she'll have success as an adult in the workplace and more satisfaction in her intimate and social relationships.

Understanding Your Child

Understanding your child means finding out where he's coming from. You may find figuring him out to be difficult, but definitely put in the effort to try — otherwise, you can get into the bad habit of pushing your wants, desires, and prejudices on your child.

When my older daughter was growing up, gender issues were all the rage among young parents and the media. Parents were constantly warned by experts about the gender minefield. The child-rearing experts considered gender-stereotyping your child a no-no. I remember talking to a psychologist colleague of mine who specialized in gender disorders. We both bragged about the activities that we did with our daughters — baseball games, action movies, car shows, macho toys, and so on. After going through the list, we then both commiserated over how our daughters preferred Barbie dolls; dance lessons; shopping for clothes, purses, and shoes; and, well, you get the picture.

Also, if you have more than one child, you probably already know that they can be different in many ways. Even though you raised your children in the same home, you may wonder how they came out the way they did. Of my two daughters, one loves fashion, clothes, shopping, dance, and classic rock; and the other prefers reading, writing, drama, and alternative music.

Don't underestimate the importance of trying to understand your child. All too often, parents tend to jump to conclusions about either what their children want or what they think is best for their children. Getting to know your child by asking questions and listening to the answers can help you see where your child is coming from.

Modeling empathy early

You can begin to understand your child by gaining her trust. Let her know that you care about her. Unfortunately, in her normal day-to-day interaction with you as a parent, she may not often get that impression. Often, people are far too involved in their own worlds of work and other responsibilities.

You have to take the time, whether in the morning or after work, to communicate with your child. I don't mean that you need to communicate *to* your child (which parents often do), but communicate *with* your child. Spend part of the time that you communicate listening to what your child is saying.

If you demonstrate what it means to listen to and understand your child's feelings and thoughts, then your child listens to you and takes you seriously. In other words, if you walk the talk — and don't just say one thing and do another — you can gain credibility in your child's eyes. And if your child thinks that you're credible, he takes you seriously.

Here are some ways that you can show that you empathize with your child:

- Look at her when she speaks to you.

- When something's important to your child but you don't seem to understand her, try reflecting back what you think she said — attempt to put her feelings into your own words.

- Make sure that you know what she said before you tell her what you want her to do.

- Be patient with him.

- Give her attention.

- When you disagree with him on an issue, reasonably explain why you feel the way you do.

- Hear her out.

- Pay attention to how he's feeling, not just to what he's saying.

If you can consistently follow just some of the suggestions in the preceding list, you'll notice that you have a significantly more civil, responsible, gratifying, and closer relationship with your child.

Reading your child's moods

You have to listen beyond what your child tells you. By using your third ear and third eye (those extra senses that you may not have developed yet), you can pick up what's really going on with your child. Kids have a habit of expressing themselves in indirect ways. Consider the following example.

Jesse comes home from school, slams the door shut, and marches up to his room, barely acknowledging his mother, Joan.

"Jesse, how was school today?" she asks.

"Leave me alone, don't get on my back again!" he blasts.

Joan's ready to scold him for his rudeness. But she catches herself. Now isn't the time to start a fight with him.

Knowing when and how to engage your child is an important skill. Jesse's obviously not in a good mood, and trying to deal with him now about his rudeness or any other issue would likely lead to an unhealthy blowup.

Joan's wise enough to know that she should wait until Jesse has some time to calm down. She can distinguish the bad behavior from the bad mood. If she takes his behavior personally, and accepts the mouthing off as an insult or disrespect, she might escalate an argument that they would both regret later. She also would weaken whatever bond or trust they have in their relationship.

By being able to read your child's mood, you can guess when something is troubling him and just how serious the problem is. If you realize that he may be really upset about something that happened at school or with a friend, or some other incident, you can deal with the upset by knowing what to say without being overly invasive.

After Jesse cools down and comes back downstairs, Joan can try engaging with him.

"Jesse, you seem really upset. Can we talk about it?"

By asking his permission, Joan's checking whether he's cooled down enough, and she's also showing him some respect by giving him the option to respond. When he's ready to respond, Joan is more likely to get to the bottom of what has upset him.

Too often, family members react without thinking. You all have habits and patterns that protect you and keep others away. By being patient and trying to understand where the other person is coming from, you can hopefully build bonds and trust among family members.

Even when parents use these techniques, some children and teens don't share very much about their lives, for any of a number of reasons. In these cases, pay attention to whom your child does relate. Is it your partner, a sibling, or a friend? What about the other person's approach allows your child to open up? Does she see this other relationship as more accepting of her negative or unconventional behaviors? Pay attention and see what you can figure out from how your child responds in these other relationships. You may learn some new approaches from your child's confidents.

Helping Your Child Become More Aware of His Emotions

Children who are aware of their emotions have a head start in managing those emotions. These children also tend to manage the emotions of others in ways that can influence their behavior. A child who has good emotional awareness can describe whatever feels wrong to others. By communicating accurately, she can get her needs met.

Children are often unaware of their moods. Kids react to things when they happen. They usually don't interpret the situation or why someone behaves the way he does. They also don't analyze their own behavior.

The adults in the child's life need to help her understand herself and her world. Kids need tools to become emotionally self-aware because most children aren't naturally self-aware.

Using exercises in self-awareness

Maybe someday schools will focus on teaching skills of emotional intelligence. But until that happens, you as a parent can help develop these skills in your child in a number of ways:

- ✔ Focus on recognizing feelings. Show your child how you know when you're angry, rather than frustrated.

- ✔ Talk about the difference between positive and negative emotions, and explain why your child needs to recognize how he feels.

- ✔ Discuss how these feelings drive his behaviors and how he can manage his behaviors so that his feelings don't take over.

Here are some suggestions for conversation topics that can help explain self-awareness to your child:

- ✔ Ask your child how she feels about
  - School
  - Friends
  - Sports
  - Movies and TV shows
  - Local events
  - World events

  Focus on the feeling aspect, more than the actual content, of the discussion. When you child starts talking about other people's behaviors, stop and ask questions like, "How did you feel when he did that?" and "How could you have felt differently about that?"

- ✔ Find out what makes your child happy, sad, angry, and amused.

- ✔ Discuss what you figure out about your child's feelings with your child. Talk about how he seems to get happy when other people are doing poorly, or how he was sad about what happened to Jill, but not to Jake, or how difficult it seems for him to change his emotions.

✔ Talk to your child about the connection between how a person feels about certain things and how those feelings affect his behaviors. Use examples from

- Work

- Politics

- World events

✔ Tell your child how you deal with situations when you're

- Angry

- Sad

- Happy

- Surprised

- Frustrated

If you don't know how to recognize feelings and connect them to behaviors, then you should probably read through this book before having the discussions outlined in the preceding activity so that you can confidently teach these skills that your child can start to use right away.

Connecting emotions and consequences

Spending time with your child and helping her understand emotions can help teach her emotional self-awareness in a number of ways:

✔ **Communication:** You can help increase your child's vocabulary when he's feeling down or bad, so he can tell you whether he's feeling sadness, frustration, or anger. When you feel sad about something, you may deal with that feeling differently than when you feel frustrated about something.

✔ **Connecting feelings and consequences:** If your child understands her emotions, she can make the connection between feelings and consequences. The way you feel often drives the way you behave.

Use these exercises to help your child increase his understanding of the connection between feelings and consequences:

✔ When you feel happy, you likely want to

- Argue with someone

- Party

- Be by yourself

✔ When you feel angry, you likely

- Make new friends
- Are nice to people
- Yell at somebody

✔ When you feel surprised, you likely

- Don't know how to act
- Make a big decision
- Do your homework

✔ When you feel nervous, you likely

- Read a book
- Go to sleep
- Feel butterflies in your stomach

Ask your child to think of more situations in which her emotions or feelings have a direct effect on how she likely reacts. Many of the preceding situations are fairly obvious. You might also want to explore how emotions affect decisions or behaviors in more subtle or less obvious ways. For example, you may want to ask your child how emotions affect the way he

✔ Studies for an exam

✔ Performs in sports

✔ Takes a test in school

✔ Behaves at a party

✔ Gets to know someone he's romantically interested in

These topics can make for interesting conversations with your child — if you talk about age-appropriate topics, of course. Listen to your child's perspective about these issues. Knowing where your child is coming from, emotionally, can help you understand more about how positive and negative influences are handled by your child. This becomes more important as your child develops and becomes exposed to more undesirable risks in the community. And understanding your child helps build the emotional bond in your relationship. This bond is a strong protective factor should your child become exposed to irresponsible drinking, drugs, gambling, and other hazards in your community.

Managing Your Child's Withdrawn Behaviors

You may remember feeling surprise when you first realized that your child was her own unique being. Although you may have had many ideas or even expectations about how she'd be as an individual, she probably continues to surprise you.

Having a child who's shy can be one of those surprises. You may like to think of your kid as competent and social. Having friends is part of life, and you can feel disheartened if your child is socially isolated.

Kids who are excessively shy and won't socialize with others may have a social phobia. If your child seems to be having a severe problem in this area that involves chronic anxiety, which interferes with the socialization process, consult a child psychologist or psychiatrist who works with social phobia.

Why some children are shy

Research psychologists estimate that the number of people who have a *social phobia* (the severest form of shyness) is less than 1 percent of the population. But these same psychologists estimate that social anxiety affects about 7 percent of the general population. The general age of onset for social phobia is mid- to late teens, and it affects women more than men. In one survey, psychologists estimated that only 5 percent of the population report never having felt shy at any time during their lives.

A child may be shy for any number of reasons, including

- Personality trait or temperament
- Biological or brain functioning
- Poorly developed social skills
- Fear of failure, ridicule, or not being liked
- Preference for things (such as computers or video games) over people
- Victimization or being the target of bullying

You may not fully understand why your child is shy. If you feel your child's social avoidance is interfering with his life, you might want to consult a mental health professional to get a better understanding of your child's situation.

Bringing your child out of her shell

If your child has a mild form of shyness or social avoidance, you absolutely must talk to your child in a non-critical way. Try to find out more about your child's fears. Does she have a fear of evaluation, being teased, or making mistakes? If you can get more information about the problem, and about specific situations or people that contribute to the fear, you can more accurately plan social activities for your child.

Clinical social phobia requires treatment by a psychologist or psychiatrist. To find resources in your community, contact the local state or provincial psychology association. You may also find the following Web site useful: www. socialphobia.org.

Here are some ways that you can help your child develop more confidence socially:

✔ Include your child when you spend time with your friends in order to model good social interactions.

✔ Practice interacting with your child by discussing topics that don't make him feel anxious.

✔ Accompany your child to places she may want to go, but where she may become fearful (such as dance lessons or baseball practice).

✔ Help build your child's skills in an area that your child gravitates to (such as guitar lessons, karate, acting, or hockey).

✔ If your child agrees, facilitate any relationships that you can between your child and the children of your friends or any relatives who are around the same age as your child.

✔ Support your child with any hobbies that he likes (such as stamp collecting, music, or photography).

✔ Role-play difficult situations with your child in which you pretend to be a difficult person that she has to deal with.

✔ Coach your child on strategies that he might effectively use in a social situation, such as how to greet people, start a conversation, keep a conversation going, or use appropriate eye contact.

You need to support your child. As much as you want her to change her behavior, accept your child and encourage her when you can. Don't overemphasize the problem or talk to your child about it when he's uncomfortable doing so. For many shy children, one good adult relationship (with a parent, teacher, coach, or relative) can make a significant difference in increasing their self-confidence.

Managing Your Child's Overactive or Aggressive Behaviors

By far the most frequent problem behaviors that kids display are the overactive or acting-out kind, possibly because the shy, depressed, or anxious kids don't get noticed as much. Teachers, for example, far more often request help from other professionals for kids who are disruptive, as compared to kids who are mainly internally troubled.

Kids may display any of a wide range of overactive behaviors. Some kids get easily bored, but they carry on with their lives without much disruption or impairment. Others may get into serious difficulties by fighting, stealing, lying, or doing other anti-social behaviors.

If your child is involved in serious transgressions that interfere with her normal functioning, impairing her ability to participate without serious problems or restrictions at school, on sports teams, in extracurricular activities, or at home, then you should seek professional help for your child. These behaviors can include excessive lying, physical outbursts, fighting, stealing, or other forms of destructive behavior, as well as serious problems with attention and being overly active in ways that interfere with normal functioning.

You can manage relatively mild forms of overactive behaviors at home by being well informed and using consistent parenting skills. If you want your parenting skills to help your child manage her behavior and emotions effectively, you need to be calm, cool, and collected and have an even disposition in word and action. You need to be patient, accepting of your child, and consistent in your communication and your behavior.

The ADHD epidemic

If you read the frequent news reports about the increased use of stimulant medication for children, you might easily conclude that industrialized society is having an epidemic of attention deficit hyperactivity disorder (ADHD). In reality, although physicians probably have too many kids on stimulants who shouldn't be, physicians also have too many kids not on stimulants who should be.

Various estimates on the prevalence of ADHD in North America range from 3 to 5 percent. The estimates vary, in part, because of the different criteria used to identify kids who have ADHD in these studies. Clearly, the number of kids who are having problems with attention is rising.

The amount of research and mental health professionals' knowledge of childhood mental disorders has increased exponentially over the past 20 years, yet the frequency of children who have behavior problems (based on large-scale national surveys) has significantly increased. ADHD, which physicians and psychologists had given a number of other labels in the past (such as minimal brain dysfunction, hyperactivity, and hyper-motor dysfunction), is one of the leading child and adolescent mental-health disorders.

The most widely used criteria for diagnosing ADHD are based on the DSM–IV (Diagnostic and Statistical Manual – IV, from the American Psychiatric Association). The diagnostic criteria includes the presence of six or more symptoms of inattention, or six or more symptoms of hyperactivity-impulsivity, for at least six months.

Perhaps even more important than the number of symptoms, the child or adolescent must show serious impairments in more than one setting in the child's life — such as home, school, summer camp, dance class, or others. The most widely used and validated tools that can help assess ADHD in children and adolescents are the parent, teacher, and self versions of the Conners' Rating Scales – 3 (CRS-3). Dr. C. Keith Conners, professor of psychology (retired) from Duke University, developed these scales based on community norms of thousands of children and adolescents, and they serve as a benchmark against which you can compare your child.

Knowing whether your child has ADHD

In order to find out whether your child has ADHD (or, for that matter, whether you do — ADHD most likely has a genetic link), you need a professional consultation. Find a reputable child psychologist or psychiatrist who specializes in ADHD.

In order to make a proper diagnosis, the clinician needs to take a detailed family history; you and your child's teachers need to complete a standardized, *norm-referenced* (based on a stratified sample of the population matched to national census) checklist (such as the Conners' or CRS-3, discussed in the preceding section); and your child needs to perform a computerized attention task (such as the Conners' Continuous Performance Test, or CPT) and some additional testing, which might include abilities or intelligence tasks.

ADHD typically originates during childhood. The most prominent characteristics of ADHD are persistent patterns of impulsiveness and inattention, with or without a component of hyperactivity. However, one of the most essential components of making a diagnosis of ADHD is that it impairs or significantly disrupts the child in multiple areas (such as school, home and family, sports, social life, and friendships). So, the child can't function appropriately in school, at home, at summer camp, on sports teams, or at any number of places.

Why so many children behave aggressively

According to national surveys, children and adolescents are expressing aggressive behaviors at a significantly increased rate, as compared to the past. Over the past 20 years, the number of children under the age of 12 who have entered the criminal justice system because of violent behavior has greatly increased.

Various psychologists and researchers have proposed a number of theories that try to explain this increase in childhood aggression:

- Genetic inheritance
- Temperament
- Problems in infant-caretaker attachment
- Exposure to neurotoxins (such as parental alcohol, fetal cocaine, and prenatal and childhood lead)
- Academic underachievement and/or failure
- Body size and build
- Antisocial friends
- Social deprivation
- Poor family interaction and structure
- Parental psychopathology
- Community factors (such as neighborhood violence, gangs, and availability of firearms)
- Child abuse and neglect

Psychologists have also explored a number of factors that may help some children and adolescents avoid becoming antisocial or violent:

- Positive parenting skills
- Good parent-child relations
- High IQ

> ✔ Easy temperament
>
> ✔ High self-esteem
>
> ✔ Academic competence
>
> ✔ Social competence or good emotional intelligence
>
> ✔ Competence in activities (such as sports and music)
>
> ✔ Socially responsible or emotionally intelligent friendships
>
> ✔ Positive community role models (such as a teacher or coach)

I believe that aggressive behavior has significantly increased in young people in part because of desensitization. Over the past 20 years, humanity has become more accepting of violence in the media, for example. Movies and TV shows have increased the tolerance of what's acceptable. Scenes in TV shows today are more violent than what you could show in feature films 25 years ago.

Now, enter the Internet and video games. Violence has reached a new level. Rather than just the violence itself, the emotional and thought processes in how children react to the violence has become important. What today's youth experience online and in video games represents a whole new reaction to violence. You can very easily blast away your enemy, human or not. You can now find situations in which you don't have to feel remorse about killing a few individuals or a few million of your enemies.

When I was growing up, children spent more time than kids do today in the streets playing sports. Every so often, some kids might have a conflict, and they might fight it out to resolve the situation. Fighting is never the best solution to conflict, and should be avoided if possible. More often than not, the angry children would resolve the conflict by using words. Occasionally, fights would break out, but everyone else would intervene at that point.

In the end, the kids of yesteryear realized that fighting isn't a very good solution. As much as you may hurt your opponent, you take a few hits yourself. Most kids preferred alternatives to getting a bloody nose after the first few brawls.

So, all in all, when kids looked at the situation, they generally agreed that fighting wasn't worth the pain — emotional or physical. More and more, those kids figured out how to negotiate their way through situations.

The kids playing out on the street used those experiences to develop their emotional skills. They figured out how far they could go, what they should and shouldn't say, and other lessons of negotiation that you can pay thousands of dollars for today to find out at the Harvard Business School.

Unfortunately, kids practice emotional intelligence in this way less often today. Many kids, instead of figuring out how to deal with other kids, spend their time in front of screens (either TV or computer), where they discover how to destroy their enemy.

How to tell whether your child is too aggressive

You may believe that your child behaves too aggressively. Or other parents or a teacher may have suggested to you that your child is too aggressive to fit in with other children.

How can you tell whether your child is too aggressive? When you hear about or even suspect that your child has behaved aggressively, calmly ask your child about his behavior. Try to get some details about the situation:

- ✔ What aggressive action did your child take?
- ✔ How did the other child react to that action?
- ✔ What did your child do after the aggression?
- ✔ Did any adults see the interaction?
- ✔ What did the adults say to the children?
- ✔ How did your child and the other child end the interaction?

By having your child answer these questions, you should be able to get some sense of the severity of what happened. Was anyone injured? Did any of the children end up crying? Was anything broken?

If you start to see a pattern of aggression in your child's behavior, then your child likely has a problem that you need to deal with by speaking to his teacher (if at school), coach (if in sports), or any other responsible adult who supervises the activity or the place it occurs. If you feel overwhelmed by the problem, you should consult a child or adolescent psychologist who specializes in this area.

If teachers, coaches, or other adult supervisors give you frequent warnings about your child exhibiting aggressive behavior, take your child to a mental health professional. Find out whether you can access the school psychologist at your child's school. Otherwise, you might want to consult a private psychologist or psychiatrist who specializes in dealing with aggressive children and adolescents.

You need to deal with aggressive behavior firmly, but not through anger. When parents discover that their child is overly aggressive, sometimes those parents react with anger. Pay close attention to your own emotional intelligence (especially emotional self-management) when you have to deal with this type of behavior.

You can find some very good parent-management programs that focus on aggressive children, and any psychologist or psychiatrist who specializes in aggressive children and adolescents can refer you to those programs. You may also be able to locate some parent-management groups in your neighborhood.

The importance of callous and unemotional characteristics

Some very recent research points toward certain emotional characteristics of aggressive children — callous and unemotional responses toward their own aggression.

When your child commits any transgression, pay the most attention not to the actual transgression itself, but to your child's reaction to that transgression. Try to determine whether your child acts callous, unfeeling, or cold-hearted about someone else's misfortune. For example, your child may have a fight with another child and tell you that she doesn't really care about what happens to that other child. Or your child may hurt an animal and express no remorse — or may even find it funny or amusing.

Also, look out for unemotional responses in an aggressive child when the situation calls for sadness, sympathy, or perhaps empathy. A close friend of your child may experience some misfortune, such as a serious injury. Your child may show no emotion about it or seem not to even care about his friend.

 If you notice these signs, you don't need to panic. But you do want to monitor and perhaps discuss these signs with your child. Ask questions about the situation and about your child's feelings. Your child may just be confused or unsure about how she should express feelings.

 Callous and unemotional behavior in children who have been involved in anti-social behavior can be a warning sign of more serious conduct or criminal behaviors in the future. These children tend to persist in difficult behaviors, and they can get involved in more serious dysfunctional behaviors down the road. These children are at higher risk for involvement with illegal drugs, physically aggressive behaviors, stealing, and other antisocial behaviors.

Getting your child to be less oppositional and defiant

You may have a child who is oppositional and defiant. Of course, you can have degrees of oppositional behavior. Most kids challenge you somewhat when it comes to dealing with certain rules that they deem unfair. But some children and adolescents seem to argue a lot — especially with those adults who are closest to them (usually their parents). For some kids, life is an argument waiting to happen. Some psychologists have jokingly referred to this as the little lawyer syndrome.

Any family should strive to make cooperative behavior the norm. When disagreements occur, like they do in all families, you want to be able to turn down the heat, so to speak. In families that have oppositional children, every family member finds most family get-togethers rather unpleasant. Parents and siblings can find even meal time painful, if the family still bothers to eat together.

One of the problems in families that have oppositional children is that the patterns become relatively entrenched. You can almost predict what today's argument will be about, who'll yell the loudest, who'll leave the room steaming mad, and so on.

Oppositional, defiant behavior in children and adolescents can not only deteriorate the family relationships, but it can leave lasting emotional scars and bad relationships for many years to come if you leave it unchecked.

If your child's oppositional behavior is so serious that it interferes with family relationships or your ability to have a calm and relaxed home life, consult a licensed psychologist or psychiatrist who treats oppositional behavior in children and adolescents.

If your child's oppositional behavior tends to be of the mild variety, you can try a number of techniques to increase cooperation:

- Keep your cool and manage your own emotional intelligence.
- Don't take what your child says to you personally — think of it as a problem that your child is experiencing.
- Avoid arguing with your child.
- Try to listen to your child's insults and arguments without having an immediate reaction, no matter how difficult you find it.

✔ Reflect back what your child has said until he acknowledges that you got it right. For example

- "So what you're saying is that I'm an idiot, and I really don't know what I'm talking about?"

- "So because I don't want you to stay out late tonight, not only am I unfair, but I'm stupid?"

- "Let me get this right — you're not going to listen to me, and you're going to do whatever you want anyway?"

✔ Don't let your ego get in the way. Oppositional children can insult you to antagonize you, but don't take the bait.

✔ Pick the areas where you really need to disagree with your child; don't get into arguments over every little thing (also known as picking your battles).

✔ Be nice to your child. Your kindness may hit her as a surprise, but be complimentary when things are calm because it may get misinterpreted as sarcasm during an argument.

When you're nice to your child, you don't lose the battle or give in. You really do love your child, as difficult as he can be. Think of being nice as a strategy. In the long run, it can help rebuild trust between you and your child.

Making Your Teenager More Aware of Emotional Intelligence

Everyone wants their children to succeed, and everyone wants the best for their children. Sometimes, you, as a parent, can easily see that your child may be making poor decisions. At these times, you may be tempted to jump in and save her. You have to be judicious when rescuing your child from the friends she chooses, the clothes she wears, or the places she goes for entertainment. Of course your child's safety is always paramount. Trying to push your adolescent in a direction she may not be ready for can often cause a *push back,* meaning a reaction that's the opposite of what you intended her to do.

Wanting your child to excel in school, for example, is a good thing. Not all kids can do really well in an academic environment. But even if your child can do well, life isn't all about his IQ or cognitive intelligence.

Somewhere, out there in the real world, your teen has to prove herself. As book-smart as she may be, emotional skills can eventually make the difference in whether she succeeds. A lot of very smart people don't have any friends — no one likes them. Many of those smart people end up working for people who are less smart, but better liked.

Of course, emotional intelligence isn't about being liked. Managing your emotions may, in fact, lead you to be very tough in some situations. But people who have good emotional management tend to feel more self-fulfilled and generally happier in life than people lacking in emotional intelligence. And they often end up being better liked (and respected) than people lacking in emotional intelligence, as well.

The following sections can help you start the conversation with your teenager about important — and sometimes sensitive — issues.

Talking to your teen about emotions

You can find many opportunities to talk to your teen about emotions. You don't need to have this discussion in a lecturing way. For example, you can talk about emotional reactions in the context of TV or movie characters. By discussing another person, you make the emotions not personal to your child.

Take, for example, this exchange between Sarah and her father, Bill. Sarah's making loud noises while watching her favorite TV show. "Owww! How stupid!"

Bill, her dad, isn't quite sure what to make of the screeches coming from the other room, so he comes in to see what's going on. "Everything okay, Sarah?"

"Yeah, it's just this stupid Jennifer. She never really changes," she replies, eyes on the TV screen.

"Maybe you can tell me about it during the commercial," he replies.

After waiting respectfully for the commercial break, he begins, "So, what did Jennifer do?"

"Well, she went back to Guy. And it's so obvious that he's a loser."

"What makes Guy a loser?" he asks.

"Well, he just uses women, and then he gets into these ridiculous situations," Sarah says.

"How would Jennifer have known what he was like? And what could she have done?" Bill asks.

These kinds of conversations about third parties, done in a nonthreatening way, can help you find out about your teen's emotional knowledge. Knowing the right answers doesn't always mean your child will do the right thing. But having emotional knowledge can prepare your teen for figuring out emotional self-management.

After you gain the trust of your teenager, you can discuss situations that are a little closer to home. For example, you can talk about events and circumstances in which your teen's friends are involved. Again, third-person examples can be less personal and less emotionally loaded, and they can give your child the emotional distance to discuss them. These discussions give you some insight into your teen's friends and the level of emotional maturity that they have.

Of course, you ultimately want to discuss your teen's situations. Often, families don't have this kind of discussion because many teens do not feel at ease discussing personal and emotional issues with their parents, perhaps because the parents were critical of the teen in the past. However, you can get more involved in your teen's life if you remain calm and accepting. You don't have to agree with everything he says. But you do need to have good emotional management yourself.

Getting your teenager to read books such as this one

I've found, through my years as a psychologist, that encouraging teens to read well-written and relevant self-help material can help them better understand themselves and the behaviors of others around them. In many cases they have gone so far as to change the way they interact with others around them, and have showed a more mature style of behaving. The approach of self-help material has improved in many ways, when compared with the earlier generations of biblio-therapy.

I've received a number of calls and e-mails from parents (and some teenagers) who have read the book I wrote with Howard Book, *The EQ Edge: Emotional Intelligence and Your Success* (Jossey-Bass). In that book, we tried to make the material interesting, educational, and appealing to different age groups.

Now, you may not be able to get your teen to read self-help books very easily. Perhaps you could approach your child by saying that a book you read offered you ideas on how to cope with a problem similar to one he's currently facing. Suggest that the book has some good ideas, and that reading it, or at least parts of it, might help your relationship with each other be a bit smoother.

Now, if you're a teenager whose parents convinced you to read this book, here's a tip — this book contains a lot of information that can help you get your parents off your back. By managing your emotions — such as by keeping your cool — you can help others around you better manage their emotions, maybe by keeping their cool as well. You can get really good at telling your parents all that they need to know without feeling like you're giving up control.

Helping Your Teenager Become More Emotionally Intelligent

You can help your teenager become more emotionally intelligent in many ways:

- **Offer a good example.** You can help your child with her emotional intelligence by modeling emotionally intelligent behaviors yourself. If you're at ease with your own emotions and your ability to manage others, you can more easily have a healthy relationship with your teen than if you lose control and get into constant disagreements.

- **Spend quality time with your teenager.** Many teenagers today prefer more time away from their parents, so make the most of the time you spend together by doing things that you both enjoy. You'll gain his trust and you'll want to do more things together. When my daughter was interested in photography, an interest we shared, we'd go to photographic equipment shows together. The time is quality time when you can have relaxed and interesting discussions together. By both teaching and learning from my daughter, for example, we're building a better bond between us.

- **Keep the conversations positive.** Spend your time together discussing topics or issues that you agree on, instead of focusing on areas of disagreement. You may have to use some flexibility because you may not be as interested in, or accepting of, the topic, or even want to spend the time on some of the things that interest your child. But you'd probably rather have a good relationship with a teenager who isn't perfect than no relationship with a teenager in distress.

As a parent, you need to put in the time and effort required to build a good relationship with your teen. Your child can find your knowledge and guidance invaluable. Use it wisely.

Putting theory into practice

You can find a lot of theory floating around out there about parent-child relationships. But the important lesson here is to increase your ability to relate to your teen. Some parents can find relating to their teens very difficult and quite a stretch. Years of arguments and resentments have hardened the arteries of the negative relationship.

By making a concerted effort to manage your own emotions and behaviors, you put yourself in a better place to manage your relationship with your child. When you are in this position, you can have and enjoy discussions with your teen.

Letting them discover their own emotional intelligence

Fortunately, most teens want to do well in life. These days, life is more complicated for teenagers than in the past. Your teen has more choices, but that can lead to more confusion.

Although you can help guide your child, he has to find his own way in life. Providing deep and lengthy advice or tools — or even some gentle and helpful guidance — can go a long way when you do it in a constructive way.

Be calm and accepting of your teen's differences of opinion, and simply be there for your teen. Try not to be too opinionated, critical, or overbearing. Accept that you won't always agree with your child's choices. By maintaining a good relationship with your teen, you have a much better chance of positively influencing her. Whether or not your teen admits it, you're still a role model for her in many ways.

Here's some good news: The research carried out by Multi-Health Systems shows that while you age, your emotional intelligence increases (up until your late 50s or early 60s). With time and experience — and potentially some EI coaching — your child will develop his or her emotional skills as part of growing up.

Part V
The Part of Tens

The 5th Wave   By Rich Tennant

"As his friend, I'm thrilled that he's happy. As his manager, I don't think it was a great career move."

In this part . . .

This wouldn't be a *For Dummies* book without the Part of Tens. In this part, you can find quick lists that deal with improving your emotional intelligence, helping difficult people you know with their emotional intelligence, and making the world a more emotionally intelligent place.

Chapter 17

Ten Ways to Improve Your Emotional Intelligence

*Y*ou can improve your emotional intelligence. The best way to improve your emotional skills is through practice in the real world. Through practice and getting feedback on your performance, preferably by an experienced coach, you can adjust your behavior and become more effective in recognizing and managing your own emotions as well as the emotions of others.

Everyone has aspects of their lives that they can improve. Jill knows that she can become a more effective parent, but with so much turmoil in her family, she barely knows where to begin. Clinton wants to be more effective at work, both in terms of his productivity and relationships with others. Claudia feels out of balance — she has a job that pays well, but she's bored with her life.

In this chapter, I look at ways that you can work on your emotional intelligence so that you can begin to make a difference in your situation. Although each of the skills can help you in some way, you may find some skills more important than others, depending on your current needs.

Become More Self-Aware

One of the core areas of emotional intelligence is self-awareness. In many ways, this area is the cornerstone of all the other areas. In order to be aware of others' emotions, for example, you need to be aware of your own emotions.

You can become more aware of your emotions through various forms of meditation or mindfulness (refer to Chapter 6). By enrolling in a course, joining a group, or hiring an instructor, you can use these techniques to become more aware of your body, your feelings, and your thoughts.

You can also become more self-aware by using your notebook to record your feelings at various preset intervals. By increasing your emotional vocabulary (see Chapter 5) and using it to describe your full range of feelings throughout various parts of the day, you can figure out how to pay more attention to your emotions.

In addition to describing your emotions, pay attention to their intensity. Rate your emotions from 1 to 10. The better you gauge your emotions, the more easily you can monitor and change them.

Wilfred knows he's angry. In fact, he's so in tune with his emotions that he immediately knows he's a 9 in anger. Knowing he hit 9 triggers all sorts of cues for him. First, he knows that he has to take a time out. When he hits anything over 8, he knows he has to remove himself from the situation, both mentally and physically. Second, it reminds him of what he doesn't like about himself. He dislikes the thought of not being able to control his behavior. And finally, it reminds him of a time when he lost control of his anger and he hurt someone. That's a behavior he never wants to repeat again.

Express Your Thoughts, Feelings, and Beliefs

Knowing how to express your emotions can often help you in managing those emotions. You can, of course, bottle everything up and not share your real thoughts, feelings, or beliefs with anyone. But, not only is this approach hard to do, it makes for a very lonely life. Nobody really gets to know you, and you don't get to know others very well, either. All humans share the desire to have intimate relationships with a few trusted people.

On the other hand, you can choose to blather out your innermost thoughts, feelings, and beliefs to everyone. This approach can also be a mistake. First of all, some people don't really care about your thoughts and feelings. Second, others might be offended by your disclosures or find them rude.

Aim for a middle ground, which I like to call assertiveness. *Assertiveness* is the appropriate sharing of thoughts, feelings, and beliefs. Basically, you need to let the right people, at the right time, know where you stand.

Sheila has always thought Joe was rude. She doesn't have the heart to tell him. As a first cousin, she doesn't really have the option to completely avoid him. It often bothers her that she can't speak up about his behavior. She feels queasy whenever she knows that she has to spend family time with him. Finally, she discovers how to approach him.

"Joe, I know you like to think those racist jokes are funny. But I have to tell you, I think they're pretty offensive. And you make me feel pretty uncomfortable when you make them," Sheila says.

She feels relieved about finally being able to express herself in a way that isn't confrontational and that gets the point across. After all, she's entitled to let him know how she feels. Fortunately, that has the desired impact on Joe, and he stops making the offensive jokes in Sheila's presence.

Discover Your Inner Passions

Everyone tends to go about their work from day to day doing what they have to do. But how many people are really excited about the work that they do? I encounter many people who feel that they're stuck in a rut at their jobs. But someone didn't magically pluck them up and place them where they are. Usually, by following opportunities or money, people end up doing the kind of work that they do.

Few people strive to do the kind of work that really excites them. Most people have a passion for some kind of work, activity, or interest deep inside, but you can't always easily find it. You may know some starving artists who shun regular jobs in hopes of making their dreams come true. You may not be able to easily find work that you're passionate about, but with the right amount of planning, you can do it.

Ernie's an engineer by training, but he quickly worked his way into a management position at a large company. He's happy with the money he's earning, but he feels bored with his job. He's managing people and projects — and doing it well — but he has little interest in his work. As a teenager, Ernie played the trombone. He loves music and is involved in two community bands. His goal is to move out of his management job and find a more creative line of work that he does part-time, even if he makes less money. He wants to devote the rest of his time to his music.

Know Your Strengths and Weaknesses

Some people seem to think that they're good at everything. Others constantly underestimate their strengths. The ideal situation, of course, is to accurately know your strengths and weaknesses. Knowing yourself helps you make choices in life. For example, by focusing on your strengths you can get more of what you want out of life. Pursuing the things you're good at and have a passion for — such as science, music, art, writing, public speaking, woodworking, or gardening — enables you to live a richer and fuller life. By overfocusing on areas of weakness, unless they interfere with your life, you tend to hold yourself back from getting the most out of life.

When you have to make decisions, you may get messages that seem to come from your gut. Certain choices feel good, and others may give you a queasy feeling. You may think of these feelings as messages from your heart, as opposed to your head. People are often guided by their emotional knowledge, which they may not be fully aware of.

Samantha's a computer programmer. She's on her fourth programming job. She lasted less than a year at each of her previous jobs, quitting after she realized it was boring. You can probably predict that Samantha will soon be ready to give up on her fourth job.

Going through the effort of applying for a job, getting trained, and beginning a project is costly for both the applicant and the organization. Samantha chose programming as an occupation because it came easily to her. But she has no passion for the work. She's happiest when working with people. She's great at building relationships. Perhaps if she took into account her strength and passion for interacting with people, she'd choose more suitable work, such as sales or technical service.

Walk in the Other Person's Moccasins

Empathy is an extremely powerful emotion. Most successful politicians (such as Bill Clinton), philanthropists (such as Princess Diana), media personalities (such as Oprah), and leaders in the community and business are high in empathy.

Increasing your ability to empathize can help you get closer to others, win their support when you need it, and defuse potentially high-charged situations. By showing another person that you really understand where he's coming from, you gain a certain level of respect. You demonstrate, for example, that you're not self-centered.

Start being more empathic by paying more attention to other people. Listen carefully when communicating with someone. Listen to both what she tells you and what she wants you to hear. By getting better at picking up and paying attention to what people are really trying to say, you become more empathic.

"I don't really like this party," Bridgette says to Marcel.

"But you wanted to meet my friends," Marcel quickly answers.

"Yes, but I'm bored," she replies.

"Maybe you should have another drink," Marcel offers.

"No, I don't think so," responds Bridgette.

Poor Marcel. He's missing Bridgette's real intent. She really wants to say that she'd prefer to go somewhere where they can be alone. Marcel, not reading the cues very well, thinks that Bridgette doesn't like his friends. If he paid a bit more attention to what she said and how she was saying it, he could have suggested that they spend another half-hour socializing, then go back to her place. Alas, he had no idea of what he was missing.

Manage Another Person's Emotions

If you can manage the emotions of people around you, you have an impressive skill. You've probably seen leaders who can calm down or reassure an angry crowd. A good example of emotional management was how New York City Mayor Rudy Giuliani handled the aftermath of the 9/11 attacks in the United States. He was one of the few politicians who was constantly available, dealing with the media, attending funerals, and answering questions. He was able to manage people's anxiety, even though no one had any real answers or solutions to the horrible situation.

On the other hand, you've probably also seen how some people can mismanage the emotions of others. Think of the number of times a poorly prepared CEO of a company had to face the media in a time of crisis. By giving off the wrong body language, using the wrong tone of voice, or evading answers to questions, these leaders made people who were watching feel more annoyed or upset.

Managing other people's emotions is a two-step process. Just follow these steps:

1. **Increase your empathy.**

   You need to put yourself in the other person's shoes and feel his pain, joy, hopes, or fears (refer to Chapter 7). One way is by asking questions of people. Learn what you can by asking and observing. Does he like sports or exercise? What are his favorite teams and activities? What foods does she chose to eat? What makes her feel happy or sad?

   2. **Respond to him in the way that you would want someone to respond to you to relieve that pain.**

Managing someone else's emotions requires a certain amount of skill. First, you need to know where you want to lead the other person. Do you want to make someone happy, calm, vigilant, or aware, for example? After you decide how you want her to feel, then you have to know how to guide her there.

Think of the last time that you heard an inspirational speaker or saw a film that really moved you. Impactful experiences usually involve a build-up in which the speaker or movie director sets the stage for where he or she wants you to go emotionally. You can create this build-up yourself by setting a goal or letting the person know where you want to go.

Some examples are

   ✔ We have to look at this situation calmly.

   ✔ As a family we need to be aware of what's going on.

   ✔ Some bad things have happened, and we have to be on our toes.

Then, you can build your case through stories or examples. You need to convey to the other person that you're both on the same side — and it's in both of your best interests to be on the same page. By being consistent in your body posture, your voice, and your message, you can deliver a potent message that can move the other person's emotions closer to where you want them.

Be Socially Responsible

Social responsibility is one of the highest levels of emotional experience. It demonstrates that you really care about others, especially those less fortunate. Being socially responsible isn't about personal gain — it's about what you can contribute to help other people.

Social responsibility has several layers:

   ✔ At the most basic level, you can donate money to charity or a worthy cause. Although you want to make donations as a part of any socially responsible plan, donations are only a first step in the process.

✔ At the next level you might help a worthy organization collect money. You can solicit from friends, relatives, neighbors, or people you work with. You can get involved in events that raise money — charitable runs, car washes, danceathons, walkathons, pie bakes, or biking events.

✔ The most effective components of social responsibility involve you personally contributing to a worthwhile cause. Think of some ways that you can help others who may need it. You might want to start by identifying the causes that you see as most important to you. You may feel passionate about spousal abuse, homelessness, food shelters, elderly care, hospitalized people, specific diseases, specific causes, and so on.

After you identify a cause that you want to support, think of how you can best contribute. You can serve on a board, be a volunteer worker, or participate in any of a number of ways. Contact the agency or organization associated with that cause and ask how you can help.

Manage Your Own Impulses

Managing your own emotions, especially impulsiveness, provides another pillar of emotional intelligence (in addition to being aware of your emotions and managing other people's emotions). By becoming more emotionally self-aware (which you can read about in the section "Become More Self-Aware," earlier in this chapter), you better prepare yourself for emotional self-management. You can manage your impulses in three basic ways:

✔ **Distraction:** When you sense a problem in impulse control coming on, you can most quickly deal with it by distracting yourself. Shift your thinking by counting to ten or focusing on prepared distracting thoughts. You can train yourself to quickly change your thoughts, or the subject if in a conversation, to something such as the weather, what you ate for breakfast, where you plan to travel next, a project you're working on, or any other event.

✔ **Analytic:** An analytic approach involves stopping and analyzing your thoughts when you feel impulsive. You can ask yourself questions such as

• Why am I thinking about this stressful problem or event?

• How can thinking about this stressful problem or event help me?

• Could I be thinking about something else?

• What's a better alternative thought?

✔ **Coping:** A coping strategy involves a number of specific coping thoughts that you practice in advance. These thoughts include statements such as

- I know I can control my thoughts.

- I can just slow down a bit.

- Let me think this through.

- I don't have to rush with a response.

- I can think of alternatives.

Strategies such as the ones in the preceding list can help you successfully deal with stressful problems or events when you practice them in advance. You can't effectively try out these strategies on the fly. With planning and practice, you can go a long way in dealing with impulsive thoughts, words, and actions.

These techniques can work for normal levels of impulsiveness. If your impulsiveness is part of a problem with ADHD or ADD, then you need a more intense intervention. If you suspect you or someone close to you has a serious problem with attention, then you should consult a psychologist or psychiatrist who specializes in this area. To learn more about ADHD, visit the Web site of CHADD (Children and Adults with Attention Deficit/Hyperactivity Disorder), a nonprofit informational organization, at www.chadd.org.

Be More Flexible

Everyone has routines and set ways of doing things. For a society to run efficiently, it needs a certain amount of rules and regulations. However, you can experience problems when you get stuck in a rut and become inflexible to change. By being too rigid you miss out on opportunities, fall behind in learning new techniques and approaches, and tend to deal with personal and work problems in the same, sometimes unproductive, ways.

Being emotionally intelligent involves knowing when to stick to and when to switch your emotional attachments. When its time to move on, people high in emotional intelligence can make that adjustment.

If you find change difficult, look at the possible consequences. What might happen if you stay with the status quo? On the other hand, where might you be if you go with the flow? Change is part of growth. Throughout life, new experiences and new opportunities can provide you with personal and professional fulfillment, and you need to be open to these changes. Although you might find it uncomfortable to try new things, most people find the short-term pain worth the long-term gain. Part of growing as a person involves learning new skills and approaches and experiencing new relationships and places.

Pete has been at his job for a little over five years. He feels he can run his area by rote. He knows how efficient he can be and what his capacity is. One day, the company decides to update the equipment that Pete uses to a newer, more efficient model. Pete's quite resistant to any change. He likes things the way they are, and he doesn't want to compromise.

Unfortunately, Pete's attitude doesn't find much support in today's workplace. You'd have some trouble trying to find a workplace today in which things stay the same. Being an obstacle to change doesn't help your career advance through rewards or promotions, and it can, in some cases, lead to termination.

Be Happy

How happy are you? No, really, how happy are you, on a scale of 1 to 10? Are you a 5 or a 7? How about a 9?

People high in emotional intelligence are happy people. And they're not just happy because good things happen to them.

Happiness (real happiness, which feels like a warm, steady glow inside your body), comes from the inside out. A person who manages this emotion well wakes up happy in the morning. And when he encounters challenges throughout the day, he can maintain a certain level of his happiness. In fact, his happiness buoys his spirits when encountering the trials and tribulations of daily living, and it keeps his mind clear, preventing him from getting caught up in unproductive self-pity or other non-helpful emotions. Happy people come up with more solutions to problems than sad or depressed people do.

Although sad people generally pay more attention to details than happy people, happy people accomplish more than sad people. Of course, because happiness and sadness are emotions, they do fluctuate. So, you can control your mood to serve your own purpose. Being emotionally intelligent involves knowing when to be happy, sad, excited, anxious, or even vigilant.

People prefer being around other people who are happy. Happy leaders have followers who are very engaged. You can find many advantages to being happy. People will appreciate you more, you can get through tough times easier, you'll feel better, and you'll be more helpful to others. Research even shows that happy people live longer (or miserable people die sooner).

Gertie always seems to be in a good mood. Her life hasn't been easy. She's seen her share of tragedies. She lost her mother when she was young, and her brother had a handicap that required her to sacrifice activities and time with friends to help out. But Gertie treats every day like it's a new opportunity. She seems to just let go of bad feelings — they don't seem to stick with her for very long.

Gertie is one of those naturals, and negativity slides off her like she's made of Teflon. Somehow, she always manages to find the bright side of any cloud. As a result, people find her quite infectious. Others like being around her because she has a way of making them feel good, too.

Very few people really know how to manage their happiness. People all too often associate happiness with material goods or with getting things from others. The really happy people are the givers. The people who spread happiness tend to be happier themselves.

Hopefully, while you develop your emotional intelligence, you remember that it costs you nothing to spread happiness, and what you receive in return is priceless.

Chapter 18

Ten Ways to Help Difficult People with Their Emotional Intelligence

Do you know someone who needs to change the way he relates to others? Everyone knows somebody who could benefit from increasing her emotional intelligence. You might be very close to this person (a significant other or a child), you might see him regularly (a co-worker or fellow student), or you may have just encountered her (a stranger at the supermarket or another driver).

Is it your duty to get involved in changing someone else? What risks do you face when you try to change another person's behavior? When dealing with people who are close to you and whose relationship you cherish, you have a higher obligation to try to influence them, in the best interest of the relationship. When you change how someone interacts with you, you affect multiple relationships in which that person is involved. Convincing a husband to be more caring with his wife may also influence his relationship with his children.

When it comes to strangers, you might want to weigh the consequences. Although you may not personally benefit from correcting a stranger's rude behavior, you may think of it as your contribution to making the world a better place. Of course, there may be little opportunity to change a stranger's behavior in a short-term encounter.

Taking the Indirect Approach

You can influence the behavior of others in many ways. Some methods are direct and to the point, and others are subtle and indirect. Sometimes, being more indirect with people can give you an advantage. For one thing, it reduces their defensiveness. Most people don't like being told that they need to change. So, by being indirect, you may make them more open to your suggestions.

One way of indirectly communicating to someone is by telling him a story about someone else — making it less personal. Grace wants her husband, Cary, to help keep the house clean and tidy.

"Hi, Cary. I'm back. I was over at Lynda's place," Grace says when she returns home.

"Oh, what's going on over there?" Cary asks.

"It was fine. But their house is such a mess. I don't think Bob puts anything away, and Lynda doesn't seem to care," she reports.

"Oh," Cary says sheepishly.

"I can't understand how he can show so little respect for such a beautiful home," continues Grace. "What's the matter with him, anyway?"

"I don't really know. Maybe he's been too busy with some project at work. But I guess that's no excuse, right?"

Grace put Cary in the position of answering for Bob's mess. If she started to go after Cary directly for his messiness, he'd probably ignore her or they might get in an argument. Because Cary tries to explain Bob's bad behavior, he puts himself in a position in which he has to help keep his own house clean.

You can also make a point indirectly by discussing characters in movies or TV shows, people or issues in the news, or third parties that you both know. Recommending (or even giving) a book such as this one to someone can let her know indirectly that she may be able to better herself when it comes to listening to others, being more patient with the children, or being more supportive of her spouse, for example.

Having a Talk

Sometimes, someone's behavior is just too annoying or problematic for you to deal with it in a subtle way — you just can't beat around the bush. In that kind of situation, you need to take a more direct approach. Let the person know that you want to have a talk. Schedule a time and place for your discussion where you won't be interrupted.

If you're talking to a family member, try to avoid places such as the bedroom or the kitchen. You spend a lot of quality time with your spouse or other family members in these places and they should not be associated with dealing with difficult problems.

Plan out your talk in advance. Always start with positive comments. You can open the conversation by thanking the person for making the time available to talk with you. Also, you might want to comment on one or two positive things about the person or positive experiences that you've had with the person.

Then, move on to how you feel about some problematic behavior of the other person. Focus on your feeling about the behavior — its effect on you.

For example, you might say, "I feel really upset when you put me down in front of other people, like the way you did with Jan on Tuesday."

By doing this, you're not criticizing the person, but rather the effects of her behavior. You might want to practice saying it out loud by yourself a few times, or writing out point-form notes, so you can ensure that you can say the right thing in the right way before the time comes to actually deliver the message.

Knowing Whether You've Been Heard

After you deliver the message (which I talk about in the preceding section), you need to determine whether the person you're talking to heard that message. Often, these kinds of discussions can lead to increased emotions and failure to focus on the message. So, you might want to do a message check:

✔ "Do you understand what I'm saying?"

✔ "Do you know what I mean?"

Then, you might want to get the other person to repeat your concern. You want to know whether what you said is exactly what was heard.

This process ensures that the focus stays on your feelings — not on the other person being bad.

Gauging the Intention to Change

When you feel confident that the difficult person you're speaking to received your message (as discussed in the preceding section), you can see whether the other person has any intention of changing. Either the person gets it or he doesn't. If he justifies his behavior, or fails to acknowledge your feelings, then he probably doesn't have much intention to change. I talk more about messages not getting through in the section "Exploring the Effect of Poor Behavior" later in this chapter.

If, on the other hand, the person acknowledges your feelings and expresses some regrets, you may get some behavior change. At this point, you should be ready with some alternative behaviors that you want to see from the person, as I discuss in the section "Providing Strategies" later in this chapter.

Giving Feedback

Giving good, healthy feedback to the difficult person can help move the process along. The feedback that you give needs to include three aspects:

- Let the person know her positive and negative behaviors.
- Give suggestions about how she might improve the positive behaviors even more while containing or modifying the negative behaviors.
- Provide input about how well she's dealing with changing these behaviors once every couple weeks at first, then perhaps once a month, depending on how frequently you see each other.

Providing feedback effectively requires that you act like a good coach. You want to deliver delicate news, yet you also want to keep the person motivated to improve. The best feedback usually specifies a (positive) behavior that you want to see the person do more of. For example, you might say, "Maybe you could give me compliments once in a while?" This approach would probably be more effective than saying, "Stop insulting me!"

Providing Strategies

Some of the feedback that you provide may include strategies for change. By reading this book and other books that deal with changing difficult people's behavior, you may come up with various strategies for behavior change. By adapting these strategies to your specific situation and spelling them out for the other person, you can help start the change process.

Martha has a difficult time saying no to her boss. Her friend Claudia acts as a helpful coach in how to deal with the situation.

"Every time my boss dumps on me I just don't know what to do," Martha complains.

"Well, can't you stand up to him in some way?" Claudia asks.

"How can I do that? He's my boss," she replies.

"Yes, but that doesn't give him the right to dump on you or put you down. Maybe you could say something like, 'I appreciate your concern for having the work done a certain way, but I think it would be more helpful for both of us if you would give me constructive criticism. Tell me how you want it done. I believe we both want the same goal. The more helpful information you give me, the better I think I can do the job. Does that sound reasonable?'"

"I guess I could try something like that. I think I'd have to practice it a bit," Martha answers.

Claudia smiles, "Sure, I'll even help you practice. I know you can deal with this."

By providing concrete strategies and suggestions, you support the other person in his effort to change. Not all strategies work, and you may need to have some discussion — and even try a little trial and error — to come up with the best strategies.

Checking Progress

You can best find out whether a strategy for change is working by following up. Arrange for times to meet again with the difficult person so that you can discuss progress. Focus on examples of the person trying new behaviors. Try to determine which attempts achieved the desired results — and which didn't.

Consider these aspects of the person using new behaviors:

- ✔ The timing of the event (Did she try the strategy at an appropriate time?)
- ✔ Her preparedness for interaction
- ✔ How she carried out the interaction
- ✔ The response that she received
- ✔ How she felt implementing the action
- ✔ How successful she thought the interaction was

At these meetings, see whether the other person needs to make some changes to his strategy. Also, suggest some other opportunities to practice the new behavior.

Exploring the Effect of Poor Behavior

Sometimes, you may feel like your message just isn't getting through to the difficult person. You indicate how his difficult behavior makes you feel, but you seem to get no response.

You might want to consider some other consequences of the person's negative behavior. How does it affect other people, or even his own long-term interests? Bad behaviors usually have real-world negative consequences. See whether you can come up with some examples of areas in which the negative behavior might cost the person in personal or professional ways. He may lose out on friendships and social activities or opportunities at work, for example.

Your own emotional intelligence comes into play when you try to help someone change. Put yourself in the other person's shoes. What consequence would she really want to avoid? Or, even better, what reward would she really cherish if she made some changes to her behavior?

"Honey, I know you don't care how I feel about your rude behavior, but what about your friends? Don't you think Tony was insulted by the way you talked to him?"

"Ah, he knows I'm just kidding."

"He, does? Then why did he invite Mario and Neil to the baseball game, but not you? Doesn't he know that you love baseball?"

Sometimes, people are so caught up in themselves that they lose sight of their impact on others. Even worse, they don't realize the costs of alienating the people around them.

Explaining in Different Ways

When you make some people aware of their poor behavior, they may accept your advice, but they just don't know what it means to change or how to go about it. Just like when a kid tries to figure out long division, he has to go over it again and again until it sinks in.

You might have to explain the problem in different ways, several times. Use as many concrete examples as you can to get the point across. Point out actual behaviors that have gotten the person into trouble.

You might try using examples from TV or movies because they are once removed and not as personal or emotionally sensitive as real-life episodes. Some people get defensive when real-life examples are pointed out to them. You often find examples of people who act in self-defeating ways in TV sitcoms and Hollywood movies. Use these examples and ask the person to come up with alternative ways of behaving in similar situations. After you get the idea across, you can move into actual situations, getting the person to try out new behaviors herself.

Selling on Benefits

In the same way that salespeople sell cars and personal electronics, you need to focus on the benefits (as opposed to the features) of changing a behavior. In other words, telling someone to change so he will be a nicer person, will scream less at others, or will be in better physical shape focuses on the "features" of changing.

For many people, changing their behaviors just to become better people doesn't seem to wash. You need to provide an incentive or benefit. Benefits of change include getting the job of your dreams because you took the initiative to upgrade your skills or being invited to the big (hockey/baseball/basketball) game because your improved social skills resulted in some new friends.

Focus on the benefits of behavior change:

- ✔ Getting more of what you want in life
- ✔ Reducing hassles from others
- ✔ Feeling better about yourself
- ✔ Meeting and connecting with others
- ✔ Having better social relationships
- ✔ Getting support from others when you need it

By getting into the other person's shoes (using empathy, which is covered in Chapter 7) and finding out what matters to him, you can suggest the best incentive for change. Try not to select abstract, large, or unrealistic benefits. Think of benefits that the other person can see as within his grasp.

Chapter 19

Ten Ways to Make the World a More Emotionally Intelligent Place

In This Chapter

▶ Distinguishing between IQ and EQ

▶ Using your EI to improve your part of the world (and beyond!)

▶ Influencing others to improve the world

I wrote this book, in part, to introduce you to the benefits of being aware of emotional and social intelligence. When you know more about EI, you may experience direct changes in your thinking, feeling, and behavior. The personal benefits of these changes can improve your life, as well as the lives of people with whom you interact.

However, increasing your emotional intelligence can have benefits greater than the personal benefits you experience. When you become more emotionally intelligent, you begin to understand the important contribution that you can make to the world around you. Being truly emotionally intelligent means caring about others and making a positive impact in the world.

Caring for Others

Throughout this book, I talk about a number of differences between cognitive intelligence (IQ) and emotional intelligence (EQ). For example, someone who has a very high IQ might not contribute very much to society, or might even be cruel to others. You can find many examples throughout history of very intelligent people (intelligent in an IQ way) who contribute little to, or even act destructively against, their fellow human beings.

A few years ago, I was invited to take part in a national television documentary that focused on a Mensa convention. You've probably heard of Mensa. It's a society (created back in 1946) that offers limited membership to smart people. In fact, to become a member, you must have an IQ score in the top 2 percent of the population.

One component of this documentary looked at the accomplishments of all these smart people. You might expect to meet the best cancer researchers, nuclear physicists, world-peace negotiators, and political strategists. Well, they may have been there, but they weren't the most easily found.

One of the stated purposes of Mensa is to "identify and foster human intelligence for the benefit of humanity." Unfortunately, I didn't manage to find many examples of members providing disproportionate benefits to society. In fact, most of the people from Mensa whom I saw were either self-focused or concerned about abstract theories. One of the (self-proclaimed) brightest members of the group worked as a bouncer in a bar. He hadn't completed his college degree because he had been a day late in getting some administrative paperwork completed and was expelled (an area in which emotional intelligence could have probably helped). Another member spent much of his day, every day, in a coffee shop, completing the *New York Times* crossword puzzle. Yet another was a school bus driver.

My role on the show involved looking at the emotional intelligence of these people. Obviously, I couldn't see much EI in many of the members. In fact, some of the members, who were aware of emotional intelligence, seemed to dismiss it as relatively unimportant. The idea of emotional self-management, managing the emotions of others, or fostering social responsibility didn't resonate with these individuals. Abstract theories seemed to be much more important than making contributions that would benefit fellow human beings.

Possessing emotional intelligence means caring and contributing to your fellow human beings. So, although you may need a high IQ to successfully make your way through educational institutions or create complex theories, your IQ says very little about your capacity to care for and help your fellow human beings.

Focusing on Other People

Being emotionally intelligent involves making the world a better place. Because emotional intelligence includes concepts such as empathy, fostering healthy interpersonal relationships, and social responsibility, your focus moves away from yourself and toward other people. Emotionally intelligent people strive to make the world better. Because they can see things from other people's points of view, they have insight into the solutions to other people's problems.

People sometimes ask me whether you can fake emotional intelligence skills or whether bad people can use the skills to take advantage of others. Although some people can manipulate others by pretending to be interested in them or their families, that behavior doesn't fit into the major definitions of emotional intelligence (Mayer, Salovay, Caruso, or Bar-On).

Emotionally intelligent people are truly interested in others and the world around them. Narcissists, con artists, or Machiavellian people are primarily interested in themselves and what they can get out of other people. For an excellent discussion of this topic, read *Snakes in Suits,* by Robert Hare and Paul Babiuk (Collins Business), two experts who have studied psychopathy extensively.

Working on Yourself

Becoming more aware of your own emotions, which I discuss the importance of throughout this book, can start you on the path to increasing your emotional intelligence. It's not a goal in and of itself — think of it as a stepping stone. Getting a better handle on yourself and your own emotional functioning helps you understand others and their emotional functioning.

Not everyone needs to function the same way, emotionally. However, understanding where you're coming from helps you figure out both the state of mind and set of skills necessary to begin to understand others. So, build your own self-awareness, and view it as a step in the journey toward building a better world.

Helping Your Family

When you look beyond yourself, first consider your family. How can your emotional-intelligence skills benefit your family? If you live with a psychologically healthy family, you can more easily accomplish charitable and socially responsible activities directed to others in life. Psychologically healthy families have the energy and focus to act purposefully, whereas troubled families tend to get bogged down with their internal conflicts. Sharing these emotional skills with your family helps get them on the same page. Sharing values and increasing emotional skills leads to healthier relationships.

Fostering the values of emotional intelligence in the family helps promote caring, independence, problem-solving, and social responsibility. As a family, can you make a contribution to others? Do you participate in charity walks or runs together? Do you donate old clothes to charity clothes drives? Do you donate food to food drives? Or better yet, do you help staff soup kitchens or places where low-income or homeless people get the food they need?

As a family, you can make many contributions to help in the community. Take on at least one project that you can all do together that makes the community or world a better place.

Giving Back to Your Community

Someone who has emotional intelligence can contribute a lot to his community. Think of the needs around you. You may find a need that fits into one of these categories:

- **People-oriented:** Helping new immigrants adjust to the community, homeless people find food and shelter, low-income families get the resources they need, the elderly receive companionship and entertaining activities, or the blind get convenient transportation and up-to-date audio newspapers and magazines

- **Environmental:** Reducing your community's carbon footprint, picking up litter, or improving the aesthetics of your property and neighborhood

- **Animal-related:** Helping stray or homeless animals

Use your emotional intelligence to come up with ways to make your community a more hospitable place to live. Look for like-minded people in your neighborhood. Can you join existing groups? Can you connect with community leaders? Do a bit of research. Find out whether existing groups meet your community-improvement needs or whether you need to start a community action group.

Improving Your Workplace

How much does your workplace contribute to the good of the community? Does your workplace support any causes? If someone surveyed people at your workplace, would they get a clear idea about which charities or causes your organization supports? Would they know how much support your workplace provides?

Some organizations, such as Timberland and the Body Shop, clearly state what causes they support and how much they provide. Support goes beyond financial contributions and includes staff time, events, and direct-involvement activities. Do some research about these organizations and others that promote social responsibility at work.

Identify like-minded people at work. Speak to your manager and other higher-ups at work. Find out whether your organization has a corporate community-involvement plan. See who runs it. What kind of role can you play in it? Get involved!

Bringing Back Civility

The degree of civility people demonstrate toward others largely determines the impression they make on others. Here and in the many countries I visit, people used to be much nicer to each other. They opened doors, gave the right of way, smiled, and just all-around acknowledged others' existence.

I believe a number of factors — such as the media, the amount of stress in our lives, and our culture's increased focus on "me" rather than "we" — has changed our general day-to-day emotional demeanor. As a result, we pay less attention to how we come across to others.

By being calmer, looking outside of ourselves, and showing some common manners to others, we can help improve our world.

Reducing Hate

I'm often asked about the relationship between the violence we see in society today and our emotions. I perform research and give presentations that deal with the increase in terrorism we experience today. A number of researchers agree, after having examined the lives and histories of perpetrators of terrorist acts, that the most important issues are not poverty or lack of education but rather the spreading of hate.

While he was at Yale University, Dr. Robert Sternberg developed a duplex theory of hate that helped us get a better understanding of terrorism. Hate is an emotion that has not been studied nearly enough by psychologists. By teaching people to recognize hate and remove it from much of the political and some of the religious discourse we see today, we can help make our world safer. If we are to become a more peaceful society, we must be able to identify hate and teach others how spreading hate leads directly to violence.

While the Beatles said it well with "All You Need is Love," they left out the sad reality that we need to eliminate the hate first. By reducing the hate expressed in political and religious disagreements to emotions such as dislike and frustration, we can begin to more reasonably deal with our disagreements.

Taking Up a Cause for Your Country

Are you politically active? Do you participate in national, non-partisan organizations? Most people have strong feelings about events going on in their countries. What can you do to make a difference? If you're politically minded, you can join a political party and get involved at a grassroots level.

If you don't like politics, you can join a national organization that fights for change on specific issues. Take some time to think about the causes that interest you or that you want to get involved in.

Remember the famous words of former President John F. Kennedy, "Ask not what your country can do for you, but what you can do for your country."

Changing Your World

What can you do to change the world? You may find it hard to believe that one person can have much of an effect on the world around her. But, by your deeds, you can affect dozens and potentially hundreds of people directly. Through those people, you can indirectly affect hundreds and perhaps thousands more.

You can find examples of people who had good ideas that they spread around, helping others far beyond their own communities. Multi-Health Systems has been involved with a project that donates testing and mentoring to a Canadian program run by an organization called Youth in Motion. The program is called the Top 20 Under 20™ Awards Program.

This program celebrates and honors Canadian students who've demonstrated a significant level of innovation, leadership, and achievement before they reach the age of 20. Hundreds of applicants apply from all across Canada. These young people have accomplished so much that has led to the betterment of their school, community, or country.

For example, Stephanie Dotto, from Kirkland, Quebec, won this award when she was 18 years old. She'd heard a speaker at her school talking about how teens can make a difference in the lives of children around the world. Stephanie was inspired and decided to try to make a difference in the lives of African children by providing shoes, medicines, and educational opportunities.

Through Stephanie's leadership, her charitable organization, "It All Started With The Shoes," sent over 1,200 pairs of gently used shoes to children in Malawi, Africa; donated over 700 pounds of antibiotics, anti-malarial drugs, and vitamins to a local hospital in Malawi; raised over $35,000 to help build a school; and added a nutrition center named Stephanie's Kitchen to a local hospital, which shows mothers of malnourished babies how to add more nutrients to their cooking.

Stephanie now speaks to schools and at conferences in hopes of inspiring other teens to believe that they can make a difference. She was named West Islander of the Year by the *Chronicle,* a local newspaper.

If these under-20s can make contributions that have effects in far places of the world, you can probably come up with ways in which you can help make a difference. Emotionally intelligent people need to initiate these activities, and their emotional intelligence increases to new heights as a result of making a positive difference in the lives of others.

Resources for Emotional and Social Intelligence

• •

*E*motional and social intelligence are relatively recent and fast-growing fields of study. There is much more information on the subject than any single book can contain. This appendix points you toward some resources that you can turn to for more information on the emotional-intelligence topics that interest you.

Books

If this book whets your appetite for reading about this topic, I recommend the following books:

- ✔ *Descartes' Error: Emotion, Reason and the Human Brain,* by Antonio Damasio (Penguin)

- ✔ *Emotional Intelligence in Action: Training and Coaching Activities for Leaders and Managers,* by Marcia Hughes, L. Bonita Patterson, and James Terrell (Pfeiffer)

- ✔ *Emotional Intelligence: Why It Can Matter More Than IQ,* by Daniel Goleman (Bantam)

- ✔ *Emotions and Life: Perspectives from Psychology, Biology, and Evolution,* by Robert Plutchik (American Psychological Association)

- ✔ *EQ Leader Program,* by Dana Ackley (Multi-Health Systems, Inc.)

- ✔ *Make Your Workplace Great: The 7 Keys to an Emotionally Intelligent Organization,* by Steven J. Stein (Jossey-Bass)

- ✔ *The Emotional Brain: The Mysterious Underpinnings of Emotional Life,* by Joseph Ledoux (Simon & Shuster)

✔ *The Emotionally Intelligent Manager: How to Develop and Use the Four Key Emotional Skills of Leadership,* by David Caruso and Peter Salovey (Jossey-Bass)

✔ *The EQ Edge: Emotional Intelligence and Your Success,* by Steven J. Stein and Howard Book (Jossey-Bass/Wiley)

✔ *The Handbook of Emotional Intelligence: Theory, Development, Assessment, and Application at Home, School, and in the Workplace,* by Reuven Bar-On and James Parker (Jossey-Bass)

✔ *Working with Emotional Intelligence,* by Daniel Goleman (Bantam)

Web Sites and Other Resources

The World Wide Web can be a great resource, but not every site is reputable. The following sites have my seal of approval:

✔ **American Society for Training and Development (ASTD)** (www.astd.org): ASTD specializes in workplace learning and performance. As a proven predictor of performance in the workplace, EI skills figure prominently in their workplace testing and employee development program.

✔ **Collaborative for Academic, Social, and Emotional Learning (CASEL)** (www.casel.org): CASEL promotes social and emotional learning for families, schools, and communities.

✔ **EI Skills Group** (www.emotionaliq.com): EI Skills Group uses the ability model of emotional intelligence, proposed in 1990 by Peter Salovey and Jack Mayer, to help individuals, teams, managers, and organizations develop their emotional intelligence skills.

✔ **Emotional Intelligence Information** (www.unh.edu/emotional_intelligence): This site contains scientific information about emotional intelligence, including relevant aspects of emotions, cognition, and personality.

✔ **Human Capital Institute's Emotional Intelligence and Human Capital page** (www.humancapitalinstitute.org/hci/tracks_emotional_intelligence.guid): The Human Capital Institute is a membership organization, think tank, and educational resource for the professionals and executives in management, human resources and organizational development, and recruiting.

✔ **International Coach Federation (ICF)** (www.coachfederation.org): The International Coach Federation (ICF) sets high standards, provides independent certification, and is building a worldwide network of credentialed coaches. ICF currently has 17,000 professional, personal, and business coaches representing over 95 countries.

✔ **International Society for Performance Improvement (ISPI)** (www.ispi.org): ISPI ensures that its members are able to effectively use human-performance technology to help their organizations and clients meet their needs and goals.

✔ **Micro Expression Training Tool (METT)** (www.mettonline.com): The Paul Ekman Group trains people in the fields of facial expression, gesture, nonverbal behavior, emotion, and deception.

✔ **Multi-Health Systems** (www.mhs.com/ei): MHS has specialized in emotional-intelligence assessment for more than a decade. Coaches, consultants, and HR professionals in thousands of organizations around the world choose MHS's emotional-intelligence tests when seeking reliable, scientifically validated tools to predict and improve human performance.

✔ **Society for Human Resource Management (SHRM)** (www.shrm.org): SHRM assists human resource managers in becoming essential and effective partners who create and act on organizational strategies.

✔ **The Consortium for Research on Emotional Intelligence in Organizations** (www.eiconsortium.org): The EI Consortium advances the research and practice of emotional and social intelligence in various organizations.

✔ **The National Resource Center for The First-Year Experience (FYE) and Students in Transition** (http://sc.edu/fye): FYE is committed to supporting and advancing efforts to improve student learning and transitions into and through higher education.

Index

Notes

Notes

BUSINESS & PERSONAL FINANCE

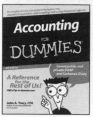

EDUCATION, HISTORY & REFERENCE

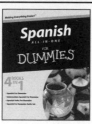
FOOD, HOME, GARDEN & MUSIC

GREEN/SUSTAINABLE

978-0-470-84098-6

978-0-470-59678-4

Also available:
- Alternative Energy For Dummies 978-0-470-43062-0
- Energy Efficient Homes For Dummies 978-0-470-37602-7
- Green Building & Remodeling For Dummies 978-0-470-17559-0

- Green Cleaning For Dummies 978-0-470-39106-8
- Green Your Home All-in-One For Dummies 978-0-470-40778-3
- Sustainable Landscaping For Dummies 978-0-470-41149-0

HEALTH & SELF-HELP

978-0-470-58589-4

978-0-470-445-39-6

Also available:
- Borderline Personality Disorder For Dummies 978-0-470-46653-7
- Breast Cancer For Dummies 978-0-7645-2482-0
- Cognitive Behavioural Therapy For Dummies 978-0-470-66541-1
- Depression For Dummies 978-0-7645-3900-8
- Diabetes For Dummies 978-0-470-27086-8

- Healthy Aging For Dummies 978-0-470-14975-1
- Improving Your Memory For Dummies 978-0-7645-5435-3
- Neuro-linguistic Programming For Dummies 978-0-7645-7028-5
- Understanding Autism For Dummies 978-0-7645-2547-6

HOBBIES & CRAFTS

978-0-470-28747-7

978-0-470-29112-2

Also available
- Crochet Patterns For Dummies 978-0-470-04555-8
- Digital Scrapbooking For Dummies 978-0-7645-8419-0
- Home Decorating For Dummies 978-0-7645-4156-8
- Knitting Patterns For Dummies 978-0-470-04556-5

- Oil Painting For Dummies 978-0-470-18230-7
- Quilting For Dummies 978-0-7645-9799-2
- Sewing For Dummies 978-0-470-62320-6
- Word Searches For Dummies 978-0-470-45366-7

HOME & BUSINESS COMPUTER BASICS

978-0-470-49743-2   978-0-470-11806-1

Also available:
- Excel 2007 For Dummies 978-0-470-03737-9
- Office 2007 All-in-One Desk Reference For Dummies 978-0-471-78279-7
- Pay Per Click Search Engine Marketing For Dummies 978-0-471-75494-7

- PCs For Dummies 978-0-470-46542-4
- Search Engine Marketing For Dummies 978-0-470-88104-0
- Web Analytics For Dummies 9780-470-09824-0

INTERNET & DIGITAL MEDIA

978-0-470-44417-7   978-0-470-87871-2

Also available:
- Blogging For Dummies 978-0-470-56556-8
- MySpace For Dummies 978-0-470-27555-9
- The Internet For Dummies 978-0-470-56095-2

- Twitter For Dummies 978-0-470-76879-2
- YouTube For Dummies 978-0-470-14925-6

MACINTOSH

978-0-470-87868-2   978-0-470-43541-0

Also available:
- iMac For Dummies 978-0-470-60737-4
- iPod Touch For Dummies 978-0-470-88001-2
- iPod & iTunes For Dummies 978-0-470-87871-2

- MacBook For Dummies 978-0-470-76918-8
- Macs For Seniors For Dummies 978-0-470-43779-7
- Switching to a Mac For Dummies 978-1-118-02446-1

PETS

978-0-470-60029-0

978-0-470-06805-2

Also available:
- Birds For Dummies 978-0-7645-5139-0
- Boxers For Dummies 978-0-7645-5285-4
- Cockatiels For Dummies 978-0-7645-5311-0

- Ferrets For Dummies 978-0-470-12723-0
- Golden Retrievers For Dummies 978-0-7645-5267-0
- Horses For Dummies 978-0-7645-9797-8
- Puppies For Dummies 978-0-470-03717-1

SPORTS & FITNESS

978-0-470-88279-5

978-0-470-15327-7

Also available:
- Exercise Balls For Dummies 978-0-7645-5623-4
- Coaching Hockey For Dummies 978-0-470-83685-9
- Coaching Volleyball For Dummies 978-0-470-46469-4
- Fitness For Dummies 978-0-470-76759-7
- Mixed Martial Arts For Dummies 978-0-470-39071-9

- Rugby For Dummies 978-0-470-15327-7
- Ten Minute Tone-Ups For Dummies 978-0-7645-7207-4
- Wilderness Survival For Dummies 978-0-470-45306-3
- Yoga with Weights For Dummies 978-0-471-74937-0